Independent CISA Exam Study Guide 2027–2028:

Certified Information Systems Auditor Prep with 750 Practice Questions and In-Depth Explanations

Caldwell Abiodun

Author Introduction

In an era defined by digital transformation, cybersecurity risk, and regulatory scrutiny, organizations depend on information systems auditors to safeguard data integrity and strengthen governance frameworks. The Certified Information Systems Auditor (CISA®) credential represents a globally recognized standard of expertise for professionals who assess, control, monitor, and evaluate information technology and business systems. This study guide has been developed by an experienced IT audit professional in collaboration with a team of cybersecurity specialists, governance experts, and certification educators dedicated to preparing candidates for CISA® success.

The lead author brings extensive experience in IT governance, risk management, internal controls assessment, and regulatory compliance across diverse industries. Information systems auditing demands both technical understanding and strategic insight. Professionals must evaluate system architecture, cybersecurity controls, data management practices, and business continuity planning while ensuring alignment with enterprise objectives. The CISA® examination tests this breadth of knowledge and the ability to apply sound audit judgment in real-world scenarios. This guide reflects those expectations by translating complex IT audit principles into structured, exam-focused preparation aligned with the domains established by the ISACA.

Working collaboratively, the contributing team conducted a comprehensive review of the CISA® exam content outline to ensure balanced coverage of its primary domains: Information Systems Auditing Process; Governance and Management of IT; Information Systems Acquisition, Development, and Implementation; Information Systems Operations and Business Resilience; and Protection of Information Assets. Each chapter integrates technical concepts with applied audit scenarios, reinforcing both analytical reasoning and professional judgment.

Recognizing that many CISA® candidates are working professionals balancing demanding audit or cybersecurity roles, this study guide is intentionally structured for clarity and efficiency. Complex topics—such as risk assessment methodologies, control frameworks, encryption fundamentals, and incident response protocols—are presented in accessible language without sacrificing depth. Practice questions, structured summaries, and exam strategies are incorporated to enhance retention and build confidence.

Above all, this resource reflects deep respect for the critical role information systems auditors play in protecting organizational assets and maintaining stakeholder trust. Earning the CISA® credential represents more than passing an examination—it signifies professional integrity, technical competence, and a commitment to strengthening IT governance and risk management practices worldwide.

Table of contents

Copyright

Readers are expected to adhere to the ISACA Code of Professional Ethics, emphasizing integrity, due care, objectivity, and confidentiality. These values form the ethical foundation of information systems auditing and are essential not only for exam success but also for professional conduct in assurance and risk management roles.

Disclaimer

Chapter 1: Information System Auditing Process

Purpose and Foundation

Information systems auditing is the structured evaluation of technological, procedural, and governance mechanisms that support enterprise operations. Within the CISA framework, the audit process confirms that information assets are safeguarded, integrity is maintained, and organizational objectives are achieved efficiently and in compliance with applicable standards. The practice is grounded in ISACA's IS Audit and Assurance Standards and is guided by professional ethics that demand objectivity, independence, and due professional care.

The purpose of this domain is to provide auditors with the ability to plan, execute, and report on audit engagements following a disciplined and repeatable methodology. The process embodies both strategic understanding and technical execution—bridging governance intentions with operational realities.

Audit Standards and Professional Conduct

Audit engagements begin with adherence to professional standards. ISACA's framework defines the expectations for planning, supervision, and documentation. Each engagement must align with organizational audit policies, internal charters, and external requirements such as regulatory mandates or contractual obligations. Independence is a central concept: auditors must be organizationally and mentally independent from the areas they review to ensure unbiased conclusions.

Professional ethics shape every phase of the audit. Integrity ensures truthful representation of findings; objectivity avoids personal bias; confidentiality preserves sensitive information; and competency ensures that audits are performed with appropriate expertise. These principles form the invisible scaffolding of every audit activity, protecting both the auditor's credibility and the organization's trust.

Planning the Audit Engagement

Planning is the foundation of audit effectiveness. During this stage, auditors assess business objectives, system architectures, control frameworks, and prior audit results to establish scope and priorities. A risk-based approach dominates modern planning, ensuring that limited resources are directed toward areas of greatest exposure or significance.

The auditor identifies relevant laws, regulations, and industry frameworks—such as COBIT's governance objectives, ISO 27001 security controls, or financial reporting standards—to set benchmarks for evaluation. The audit plan defines engagement objectives, the timing of fieldwork, the responsibilities of team members, and the expected deliverables.

A well-designed plan reflects both top-down and bottom-up perspectives: it translates enterprise-level risks into auditable components while considering technical realities at the system level. This dual lens allows auditors to maintain strategic alignment without losing operational depth.

Risk Assessment and Materiality

Central to the planning phase is the determination of risk and materiality. Audit risk represents the likelihood that a material misstatement or control failure will remain undetected. It comprises inherent risk, control risk, and detection risk. The auditor evaluates inherent risk by examining factors such as system complexity, transaction volume, and change frequency. Control risk is assessed through understanding the design and implementation of preventive and detective controls. Detection risk depends on the extent and quality of audit procedures performed.

Materiality sets the threshold for significance—what level of error or deviation would influence management decisions or stakeholder confidence. Determining materiality requires professional judgment, balancing quantitative measures with qualitative impacts such as reputational or regulatory consequences.

Risk assessment informs both audit scope and test design. It ensures proportional effort, focusing deeper testing on high-impact areas while maintaining efficiency in routine reviews.

Developing the Audit Program

Once risks are identified, the auditor translates them into an actionable audit program. This document details specific objectives, testing methods, sampling strategies, and evidence requirements. It also defines the linkage between each test and the associated control objective, ensuring traceability and logical consistency.

The program evolves as new insights emerge. For example, discovery of unanticipated systems or process changes may warrant additional procedures. Continuous alignment between the program and audit objectives preserves relevance throughout fieldwork.

Audit methodologies often integrate automated tools for evidence gathering and analysis. Computer-assisted audit techniques enable sampling from large datasets, identification of anomalies, and evaluation of transaction patterns. These methods improve both coverage and reliability of audit results.

Executing the Audit

Execution converts planning into evidence. The auditor performs control testing, interviews stakeholders, observes operations, and reviews documentation. Evidence is evaluated for sufficiency and appropriateness: sufficiency relates to the quantity of evidence, while appropriateness concerns its quality and relevance.

Fieldwork requires professional skepticism—an alert, questioning mind that seeks corroboration rather than acceptance. Auditors validate that controls operate as intended and that deviations are documented accurately. Testing can be compliance-oriented, confirming adherence to policies, or substantive, verifying data integrity and transaction accuracy.

Sampling methodology is integral to efficiency. Statistical and non-statistical sampling techniques provide a representative basis for conclusions while managing workload. Selection methods depend on risk, population size, and the auditor's confidence level.

Throughout execution, communication with management is continuous. Interim discussions clarify findings early, reducing surprises at reporting time. This transparency fosters cooperation while maintaining auditor independence.

Use of Data Analytics and Technology

Modern auditing relies on data analytics to handle volume, velocity, and variety of enterprise data. Continuous auditing platforms extract system logs, transactions, and exception reports for near real-time monitoring. Automated scripts identify patterns such as duplicate payments, unauthorized access, or abnormal resource utilization.

The integration of analytics transforms the audit role from retrospective evaluation to proactive assurance. It enables early detection of anomalies and provides a dynamic feedback loop to management. However, auditors must ensure data integrity within these tools—verifying source authenticity, completeness, and accuracy of extracted datasets.

Evidence Documentation

Audit documentation provides the foundation for conclusions. Workpapers record the procedures performed, evidence obtained, and rationale for findings. They support the auditor's opinion and facilitate peer or external review. Documentation must be clear, complete, and capable of standing alone as proof of professional diligence.

The principle of reproducibility applies: another qualified auditor should be able to reperform the work and reach the same conclusion based on the records maintained. Documentation also provides continuity across audit cycles, allowing future teams to trace historical issues and assess remediation progress.

Reporting and Communication

The culmination of the audit process is the communication of results. The audit report translates technical observations into business-oriented language, highlighting risk implications and recommended corrective actions. Reports should be concise, evidence-based, and prioritized by significance.

Effective reporting balances precision with clarity. Findings must specify condition, criteria, cause, effect, and recommendation, ensuring that management understands both the issue and its context. Tone is factual, avoiding exaggeration or understatement.

Follow-up procedures confirm whether corrective actions have been implemented. This iterative loop converts auditing from an isolated event into a cycle of continuous improvement, reinforcing the organization's control environment and governance maturity.

Quality Assurance and Continuous Improvement

A mature audit function incorporates its own quality assurance and improvement program. Periodic internal and external reviews evaluate adherence to standards, methodology consistency, and the adequacy of documentation. Lessons learned from completed audits feed back into training, template refinement, and methodology evolution.

Control self-assessment programs complement formal audits by empowering process owners to evaluate their controls proactively. When integrated into the audit universe, these programs extend assurance coverage without compromising independence.

Integration with Governance Frameworks

COBIT 2019 provides a structural reference for aligning audit findings with enterprise governance goals. The Evaluate-Direct-Monitor and Monitor-Evaluate-Assess domains define accountability and oversight mechanisms that resonate with audit reporting lines. Similarly, ITIL 4's continual improvement model reinforces the iterative nature of audit recommendations within operational management.

By contextualizing audits within these frameworks, organizations achieve coherence between governance objectives and control assurance. The auditor thus becomes not merely a verifier of compliance but a catalyst for strategic alignment and sustainable performance.

Understanding the Business Environment

Before an audit can be effectively conducted, auditors must develop a deep understanding of the business environment in which the system operates. This includes the organization's mission, objectives, structure, and the strategic role of technology in achieving those objectives. The context of an enterprise shapes the risk landscape; an auditor evaluating a financial institution, for example, will emphasize transaction integrity, segregation of duties, and regulatory compliance, whereas in a manufacturing organization, focus may rest on operational continuity, production data accuracy, and system availability.

Understanding the business environment requires engagement with management to identify key business processes and their dependencies on information systems. The auditor must assess the criticality of each system, the sensitivity of its data, and the consequences of failure or unauthorized access. Business impact analysis tools may be used to map information assets to business objectives, forming a foundation for prioritizing audit areas.

This contextual awareness transforms an audit from a checklist exercise into a strategic evaluation of control maturity and business alignment. It ensures that audit conclusions reflect the true significance of information systems within the enterprise.

Defining Audit Scope and Objectives

Defining the audit scope is one of the most critical planning activities. Scope specifies the boundaries of engagement—the systems, processes, or organizational units to be examined. Objectives, meanwhile, define what the audit seeks to achieve, whether verifying control effectiveness, ensuring compliance, or assessing efficiency.

The scope must align with both enterprise risk appetite and stakeholder expectations. Factors such as recent system changes, prior incidents, and new regulatory requirements often influence scope decisions. The auditor also considers resource availability, time constraints, and potential conflicts with other assurance activities. Coordination with internal control units or external auditors avoids duplication of effort and ensures comprehensive coverage.

Well-defined objectives drive meaningful outcomes. For example, an audit objective to "evaluate the adequacy of logical access controls" implies assessing identity management, privilege assignment, authentication mechanisms, and monitoring of access violations. The auditor must translate broad goals into specific and measurable tasks.

Establishing Audit Criteria

Audit criteria serve as the benchmark against which observations are measured. They can originate from internal policies, industry standards, legal requirements, or established frameworks such as COBIT, ISO 27001, or NIST SP 800-53. The auditor identifies which criteria are applicable based on system purpose and regulatory environment.

For instance, when auditing an information security program, COBIT's "Align, Plan, and Organize" objectives can be used to evaluate governance practices, while "Deliver, Service, and Support" objectives provide reference for operational controls. Selecting criteria ensures that conclusions are objective and comparable across audits.

Criteria must be relevant, measurable, and consistent. Overly broad or subjective criteria may lead to disputes with management or ambiguous findings. Documenting selected criteria in the audit plan enhances transparency and defends the auditor's rationale if challenged.

Coordination and Resource Management

Audit planning extends beyond technical design to include human and logistical management. The audit manager allocates resources based on complexity, risk, and auditor competency. Assignments should balance expertise—pairing technical specialists with process-oriented auditors—to ensure holistic evaluation.

Scheduling must minimize disruption to business operations while maintaining audit efficiency. Early communication with auditees establishes cooperation and clarifies expectations regarding data access, documentation, and interviews. Coordination also involves aligning timelines with organizational cycles, such as fiscal year-end or system migrations.

Audit resource management adheres to principles of confidentiality and independence. Team members must disclose conflicts of interest and avoid involvement in activities that could impair objectivity. Training and supervision throughout the engagement reinforce quality and compliance with audit standards.

Control Identification and Evaluation

The heart of information systems auditing lies in control evaluation. Controls represent the mechanisms—both manual and automated—that ensure systems function as intended. ISACA defines controls as measures that provide reasonable assurance that business objectives will be achieved and undesired events prevented or detected.

Auditors classify controls as preventive, detective, or corrective. Preventive controls deter errors or irregularities before they occur, such as access restrictions or segregation of duties. Detective controls identify incidents after occurrence, including log reviews or reconciliations. Corrective controls remediate issues and restore systems to desired states, such as incident response procedures or backup restoration.

Evaluation begins with understanding control design. The auditor determines whether the control, if properly implemented, would mitigate the identified risk. Next, operating effectiveness is tested through observation, re-performance, or data analysis. Weak design or inconsistent operation signals control deficiency.

Modern systems often embed controls within applications and infrastructure layers. Application controls ensure input accuracy, processing completeness, and output reliability. General controls, such as change management or physical access, support the integrity of all systems. The auditor must examine both layers to provide a complete assurance view.

Control Testing Methodologies

Testing methodologies depend on audit objectives and control types. Compliance testing confirms whether procedures are followed, while substantive testing verifies the accuracy of data and transactions. For example, compliance testing might involve reviewing user access approval forms, whereas substantive testing could involve verifying that recorded sales transactions match physical deliveries.

Sampling is used when populations are too large for exhaustive review. Statistical methods—such as attribute or variable sampling—enable extrapolation of findings to entire populations within defined confidence intervals. Non-statistical sampling relies on auditor judgment and is appropriate when population characteristics are not quantifiable.

Automated audit tools increase precision. Scripts may analyze system logs to detect unauthorized access or extract journal entries for fraud indicators. The auditor must validate the reliability of these tools and ensure proper documentation of sampling rationale and results.

Fraud Risk and Irregularities

An essential dimension of IS auditing is the consideration of fraud risk. While the primary role of auditors is not to detect fraud, they must maintain professional skepticism and be alert to conditions that indicate irregularities. Factors such as override of controls, unusual transactions near reporting periods, or unexplained adjustments may signal fraud.

Auditors evaluate anti-fraud controls, including segregation of duties, authorization procedures, and monitoring mechanisms. Interviews and data analytics assist in identifying potential red flags. When evidence suggests fraud, auditors must follow organizational protocols—typically reporting to audit management or legal counsel—to ensure proper handling and preservation of evidence.

The ethical obligation to act upon suspicion of fraud underscores the auditor's responsibility beyond compliance verification. Effective communication, discretion, and adherence to due process protect both the auditor's integrity and organizational reputation.

Audit Evidence and Reliability

Evidence forms the foundation of audit conclusions. It encompasses documents, observations, records, and corroborations supporting the auditor's findings. The reliability of evidence depends on its source, nature, and method of acquisition. Evidence obtained directly by the auditor, such as observing a control in operation, is generally more reliable than information provided indirectly.

Triangulation strengthens reliability. For instance, confirming an access control policy through document review, system configuration, and employee interviews provides stronger assurance than relying on one source alone. Electronic evidence must be safeguarded to prevent alteration or loss. Secure storage, access controls, and version management are critical.

Auditors must assess sufficiency—whether enough evidence exists to support a conclusion—and appropriateness—whether evidence is relevant and reliable. Excessive evidence can be as problematic as insufficient documentation if it obscures clarity or wastes resources. The goal is proportional, persuasive evidence that withstands independent scrutiny.

Audit Documentation and Review

Audit documentation is more than administrative recordkeeping; it is a demonstration of professional diligence. Each working paper must clearly state objectives, procedures, findings, and conclusions. Cross-referencing ensures traceability from testing steps to reported issues. Supervisory review verifies accuracy, completeness, and adherence to methodology.

Electronic working paper systems facilitate collaboration and version control. They also enable trend analysis across audits, revealing recurring control weaknesses or improvement patterns. Consistency in documentation structure enhances institutional memory and accelerates future engagements.

Review procedures provide an additional safeguard. Internal quality reviewers or senior auditors examine working papers to ensure logical consistency and compliance with ISACA's Audit and Assurance Standards. These reviews contribute to organizational learning and strengthen audit credibility.

Audit Reporting and Communication

The final audit report serves as the formal communication of results. It must be clear, balanced, and aligned with the engagement's objectives. The report typically contains an executive overview, detailed findings, and management responses. Although the CISA exam does not require knowledge of exact report formats, candidates must understand that communication clarity and objectivity are paramount.

Effective auditors tailor reports to their audience. Senior executives require concise summaries highlighting business impact and recommended actions, while technical teams need detailed descriptions of control deficiencies and remediation steps. The report's tone should remain factual, avoiding accusatory or speculative language.

In addition to the final report, interim communications during fieldwork keep management informed and allow early remediation of critical issues. Post-audit meetings reinforce accountability, providing a forum to clarify findings and ensure consensus on corrective actions.

Follow-Up and Remediation

Audit follow-up ensures that identified issues are addressed. The process involves tracking management's action plans, verifying implementation, and assessing whether controls now operate effectively. Follow-up may be scheduled at intervals based on risk severity—critical issues warrant immediate verification, while minor observations may be reviewed in subsequent audits.

The auditor must maintain independence during follow-up, confirming rather than managing corrective actions. Documentation of follow-up activities is essential, providing closure for the audit and contributing to the organization's assurance record.

Where issues remain unresolved, escalation to senior management or the audit committee ensures visibility. Persistent noncompliance may indicate deeper cultural or governance problems requiring broader intervention.

Audit Quality and Continuous Improvement

A professional audit function continuously evaluates its own performance. Internal quality assurance programs assess compliance with standards, methodology effectiveness, and staff competency. External peer reviews, conducted periodically, provide independent validation and identify opportunities for improvement.

Metrics such as audit cycle time, issue recurrence rate, and stakeholder satisfaction measure performance quantitatively. Lessons learned from past engagements feed into updated procedures, templates, and training materials. This culture of continuous improvement mirrors the continual service improvement principle in ITIL, ensuring that the audit function evolves alongside technological and organizational change.

Integrated Assurance and Risk Management

In contemporary enterprises, assurance is no longer isolated within audit departments. Integrated assurance combines the efforts of internal audit, risk management, compliance, and external auditors to provide a unified view of control health. The IS auditor contributes specialized expertise in evaluating technological risks and translating technical findings into business language.

Coordination avoids overlap and ensures coverage across governance layers. For example, an internal audit of access management may rely on risk assessments conducted by the information security team, while also validating the results independently. Unified reporting structures allow the board and audit committee to interpret assurance outcomes coherently.

This integration aligns with COBIT's governance components, where processes such as "Evaluate, Direct, and Monitor" depend on accurate information from multiple assurance sources. The IS auditor's role within this ecosystem reinforces governance transparency and decision-making confidence.

Ethical and Professional Responsibilities

Ethical conduct remains fundamental throughout the audit process. IS auditors must not only comply with the ISACA Code of Professional Ethics but embody it in their interactions. Independence is preserved through careful management of conflicts, disclosure of prior involvement, and refusal of inappropriate gifts or influence.

Confidentiality extends beyond the audit period; sensitive information learned during engagements must never be disclosed or used for personal gain. Auditors are custodians of trust, and breaches of confidentiality damage both individual and institutional credibility.

Professional competence is maintained through continuing education. Emerging technologies—cloud computing, artificial intelligence, and digital identity systems—introduce new risks and require continuous skill development. ISACA's Continuing Professional Education framework ensures that certified auditors remain current with evolving practices.

Evolving Technologies and the Audit Landscape

Technological evolution continually reshapes audit methodologies. Cloud services challenge traditional control ownership models, requiring auditors to assess both provider and customer responsibilities. Shared responsibility matrices and third-party assurance reports (such as SOC 2) become vital evidence sources.

Automation and artificial intelligence offer both opportunities and challenges. Automated audit bots can monitor configurations or transactions continuously, but auditors must validate their accuracy and interpret outputs critically. Ethical considerations arise when algorithms make audit decisions—accountability must remain with human professionals.

Blockchain, with its immutable ledgers, transforms transaction assurance. While it reduces certain risks, it introduces others, such as smart contract vulnerabilities. Auditors must adapt control testing approaches to new architectures while preserving foundational principles of evidence, independence, and professional skepticism.

Communication and Interpersonal Dynamics

Beyond technical skills, successful auditors rely on communication and interpersonal intelligence. Engaging constructively with auditees encourages transparency and reduces defensiveness. The auditor must listen actively, respect operational constraints, and convey findings in a manner that fosters cooperation rather than resistance.

Negotiation and diplomacy play key roles during exit meetings and report discussions. Auditors must defend findings with evidence yet remain open to management's perspectives. Balanced dialogue ensures fair conclusions and promotes a culture of mutual respect between audit and operational teams.

Strong communication skills also influence audit leadership. Clear delegation, constructive feedback, and mentoring of junior auditors contribute to overall quality. These soft skills, though intangible, are critical to audit effectiveness and organizational reputation.

Linking the Audit Process to Enterprise Value

Ultimately, the IS audit process contributes directly to enterprise value by ensuring that technology investments deliver expected outcomes and that risks are managed proactively. A well-executed audit improves decision-making, strengthens internal control, and builds stakeholder confidence. It provides assurance that systems operate reliably, securely, and in alignment with strategic goals.

This value perspective transcends compliance. Rather than viewing audits as reactive or punitive, mature organizations regard them as mechanisms for learning and optimization. Audit insights feed back into governance frameworks, guiding management in resource allocation and performance improvement.

COBIT reinforces this philosophy through its principle of value delivery, positioning governance and assurance as complementary forces. The auditor's findings, when integrated into enterprise governance, close the loop between evaluation, direction, and monitoring—ensuring that information and technology genuinely serve business objectives.

Download Audio file and flashcards

Chapter 2: Governance and Management of IT

Overview of IT Governance

IT governance represents the structure through which enterprises ensure that technology supports and extends business objectives. Within the CISA framework, this domain tests the auditor's ability to assess governance models, management processes, and strategic alignment between IT and enterprise goals. Governance defines accountability, while management ensures execution. The relationship between these two layers determines how effectively information and technology deliver value and mitigate risk.

The IS auditor must understand that governance is not a technical function but an executive responsibility. It involves establishing vision, defining direction, and monitoring performance. COBIT 2019 articulates this through its Evaluate–Direct–Monitor model, where governing bodies evaluate stakeholder needs, direct management activities, and monitor outcomes against objectives. This model provides auditors with a lens for evaluating how well enterprise governance mechanisms align IT strategies with organizational priorities.

Governance Frameworks and Principles

Several frameworks inform the practice of IT governance. COBIT remains the most widely referenced in the CISA exam. Its design principles—comprehensive coverage, stakeholder value creation, dynamic governance system, and alignment with enterprise goals—provide a structured method for integrating governance with management practices. COBIT's governance components include processes, organizational structures, principles, policies, information, culture, services, and people.

IS auditors assess whether these components function cohesively. For instance, a strong governance system ensures that policies are clear, performance metrics are defined, and accountability is traceable. The auditor evaluates whether IT decision-making follows established governance processes, such as steering committees or portfolio management frameworks, and whether roles are defined through a RACI (Responsible, Accountable, Consulted, Informed) matrix.

Beyond COBIT, auditors may encounter complementary models like ISO 38500 for IT governance or the ITIL 4 service value system for operational management. The key is to determine whether the chosen framework is applied consistently and adapted to the organization's context.

Strategic Alignment of IT and Business Objectives

Strategic alignment ensures that technology initiatives support the organization's mission and goals. Misalignment can lead to wasted resources, conflicting priorities, or missed opportunities for innovation. The IS auditor evaluates how IT strategies are derived from enterprise strategies, often through planning artifacts such

An effective IT strategic plan must mirror the organization's long-term direction and articulate how technology enables competitive advantage, operational efficiency, and regulatory compliance. The IS auditor reviews this plan for completeness, approval by executive leadership, and integration with enterprise planning cycles. Alignment is demonstrated when IT goals cascade naturally from business goals—measurable, actionable, and time-bound.

The COBIT 2019 framework formalizes this connection through its Goals Cascade, translating stakeholder needs into enterprise goals, then IT-related goals, and finally into enabler performance metrics. The auditor must evaluate whether this cascade is reflected in governance processes such as budgeting, project selection, and performance reporting. If, for example, a company's business goal is operational excellence, auditors would expect IT-related goals emphasizing service reliability, automation, and resource optimization.

Strategic alignment is not static. The auditor should confirm that governance structures provide mechanisms for periodic reassessment of alignment. This is especially critical when disruptive technologies—such as artificial intelligence or cloud computing—transform the organization's risk profile and opportunities.

Enterprise Risk Management Integration

Effective IT governance incorporates risk management at every decision level. Risk management identifies, assesses, and mitigates threats that could prevent the enterprise from achieving its objectives. The IS auditor evaluates whether the IT risk management process aligns with enterprise-wide risk frameworks, ensuring consistency in definitions, methodologies, and reporting.

Risk appetite and tolerance must be clearly defined by the board and communicated to management. These boundaries guide prioritization of mitigation activities and resource allocation. The auditor reviews documentation of risk assessments, treatment plans, and control ownership to ensure alignment with this appetite.

Mature organizations adopt a three-lines-of-defense model, where management owns risk, risk and compliance functions provide oversight, and internal audit delivers independent assurance. The IS auditor's role lies within the third line, validating that IT risk management operates effectively and that key risks—such as cybersecurity, data privacy, and continuity—are identified and addressed.

Tools like COBIT's "Manage Risk" objective (APO12) and ISO 31000 provide structure for evaluating risk processes. Auditors verify that risk registers are maintained, regularly updated, and integrated into governance reporting. They must also determine whether metrics such as Key Risk Indicators (KRIs) and Key Control Indicators (KCIs) are defined and monitored, providing management with actionable insight.

Resource Management and Optimization

Resource management ensures that people, infrastructure, applications, and data are deployed efficiently and effectively. The auditor assesses whether governance structures provide clear accountability for resource ownership and performance.

Human resource governance is evaluated by reviewing competency frameworks, training plans, and succession strategies. The auditor must confirm that staff skills align with technological complexity and that resource allocation follows business priorities rather than departmental influence. Performance evaluation mechanisms should reward outcomes that support strategic goals rather than isolated operational success.

From an infrastructure perspective, auditors examine asset management processes—whether hardware and software inventories are accurate, life cycles are tracked, and decommissioning follows security and compliance procedures. Under COBIT's "Manage Assets" objective, the auditor verifies that technology investments are justified through business cases and evaluated post-implementation for realized value.

Financial resource governance also falls under this domain. The auditor must ensure that IT budgets reflect strategic intent, expenditures are monitored, and deviations are explained. Chargeback and cost allocation models are reviewed for fairness and transparency. Auditors assess whether metrics like return on investment or total cost of ownership are applied consistently to evaluate IT initiatives.

Performance Measurement and Accountability

Governance effectiveness depends on measurable performance. The IS auditor reviews the use of Key Performance Indicators (KPIs) that reflect both efficiency and effectiveness. For governance to succeed, performance information must flow upward to the board and downward to operational units in a transparent manner.

COBIT's performance management model defines capability levels from zero (incomplete) to five (optimizing). Auditors use this model to assess the maturity of IT processes and identify areas for improvement. A capability level of three, for example, implies defined and established processes, whereas level five indicates continual improvement based on quantitative feedback.

Auditors verify whether management dashboards provide timely, accurate data for decision-making. They also evaluate whether accountability mechanisms exist for underperformance—such as documented remediation plans, follow-up reviews, or revisions to key objectives. Performance data must be linked to governance oversight; otherwise, reporting becomes ceremonial rather than actionable.

Information Governance and Data Management

Information is the enterprise's most valuable asset, and its governance ensures accuracy, availability, and security. The auditor assesses whether data management policies cover data classification, ownership, quality, and lifecycle controls.

Data governance frameworks establish accountability through defined roles such as data owners, custodians, and stewards. The auditor ensures these roles are understood and executed consistently. Proper governance ensures that data collection complies with privacy laws, that retention schedules align with business needs, and that disposal methods prevent unauthorized disclosure.

Information quality management is another focal area. Auditors examine whether data validation, reconciliation, and cleansing procedures exist to prevent errors from propagating across systems. They evaluate metadata management practices and confirm that system interfaces maintain integrity when transferring data between platforms.

The CISA candidate should understand that effective data governance links directly to compliance. Regulations such as GDPR or industry-specific mandates like HIPAA impose strict obligations on how organizations store and use information. The auditor's role is to confirm that governance mechanisms enforce compliance systematically rather than reactively.

Organizational Structures and Decision-Making

Governance relies on structures that define authority and accountability. The IS auditor evaluates whether committees, roles, and reporting lines are well defined. Examples include IT steering committees, architecture review boards, and risk management councils. Each must have documented charters specifying purpose, membership, and decision rights.

Auditors assess meeting frequency, attendance, and evidence of decision-making effectiveness. They review whether governance bodies receive accurate information from management and whether escalation mechanisms exist for unresolved issues. The goal is to ensure that governance structures do more than exist on paper—they must function as active channels of oversight and direction.

Organizational design should also reflect segregation of duties between governance and management. The board and executive committees direct strategy, while IT management executes plans. The auditor ensures that this separation prevents conflicts of interest, particularly in areas where control owners may otherwise audit themselves.

Policy, Standards, and Procedures

Governance translates strategy into action through policies, standards, and procedures. Policies set intent, standards define mandatory requirements, and procedures describe execution steps. The IS auditor evaluates whether policies are current, approved by the appropriate authority, and communicated to all stakeholders.

An effective governance system includes mechanisms for policy review and enforcement. Auditors assess how policy exceptions are managed—whether deviations are documented, approved, and monitored. They also confirm that standards align with recognized best practices, such as NIST frameworks for security or ITIL for service management.

The relationship between policies and operations is critical. Policies that are too rigid can stifle innovation, while those that are vague undermine control. The auditor must determine whether the organization strikes the right balance and whether policy noncompliance results in corrective action.

Information Security Governance

Security governance ensures that the enterprise's security objectives align with its business goals and risk appetite. The IS auditor examines whether security policies and programs are approved at the executive level, assigned to qualified leadership (such as a CISO), and integrated into enterprise governance structures.

The auditor evaluates the presence of a comprehensive information security strategy addressing confidentiality, integrity, and availability. This includes reviewing how risk assessments inform security investments and how security metrics are reported to the board. Governance requires that security is not merely an IT function but an organizational priority embedded in culture and process.

Auditors also review compliance with frameworks like ISO 27001 and regulatory obligations related to data protection. The presence of security awareness training, incident response governance, and oversight of third-party service providers are indicators of maturity. Security governance effectiveness is measured not by the absence of incidents but by the resilience and responsiveness demonstrated when they occur.

Vendor and Third-Party Management

Modern enterprises rely on extensive third-party relationships for cloud services, software development, and outsourcing. Governance must ensure that these external dependencies do not introduce uncontrolled risk.

The IS auditor examines the vendor management lifecycle—from due diligence and contract negotiation to performance monitoring and termination. Contracts should specify service levels, security obligations, and right-to-audit clauses. The auditor ensures that service-level performance is reviewed regularly and that deficiencies trigger formal remediation processes.

Third-party risk assessments must align with enterprise risk management. The auditor evaluates whether critical vendors undergo periodic reviews covering financial stability, data protection practices, and compliance with organizational policies. Reports such as SOC 2 Type II are used to verify control effectiveness, but auditors must also determine whether management evaluates those reports critically rather than accepting them blindly.

Business-IT Relationship and Stakeholder Engagement

Governance succeeds when business and IT leaders collaborate effectively. The IS auditor assesses the mechanisms that promote communication and shared accountability, such as joint planning sessions, balanced scorecards, and stakeholder feedback channels.

Resistance between business and IT often stems from misaligned incentives or unclear communication. Auditors must evaluate cultural factors influencing governance effectiveness—whether IT is viewed as a partner or a cost center, whether leadership promotes innovation, and whether governance decisions consider end-user impact.

Stakeholder engagement also extends to regulatory bodies, customers, and partners. Governance should ensure transparency, ethical conduct, and responsiveness to stakeholder needs. The auditor's role is to confirm that stakeholder interests are represented in decision-making and that reporting provides an accurate reflection of performance and compliance.

Change and Transformation Governance

Change is inherent to technology management, but governance ensures it occurs in a controlled, strategic manner. The IS auditor reviews governance over digital transformation initiatives, mergers, or large-scale system implementations. The focus is on whether governance structures anticipate risks, establish accountability, and measure benefits realization.

Transformation governance demands coordination between project management, architecture, and risk management functions. The auditor confirms that major changes undergo formal approval, risk assessment, and stakeholder communication. Post-implementation reviews should evaluate whether expected outcomes—cost savings, efficiency gains, or improved customer experience—were achieved.

Inadequate governance over transformation often results in cost overruns, scope creep, or unmitigated risk exposure. Auditors must ensure lessons learned from past initiatives are institutionalized into future projects, creating a feedback loop of continuous improvement.

Governance Culture and Ethics

Beyond structures and processes, governance relies on culture—the shared values and behaviors that shape decision-making. The IS auditor evaluates whether ethical principles, accountability, and transparency permeate the organization. This includes assessing leadership tone, employee awareness, and mechanisms for reporting unethical behavior.

COBIT identifies culture and behavior as core components of a governance system. Auditors should look for evidence of cultural alignment with governance objectives, such as ethical codes, reward systems, and open communication channels. A governance culture that values integrity and collaboration enables sustainable performance and compliance.

Ethics also influence technology decisions—how data is collected, how algorithms are designed, and how automation impacts employees and customers. The auditor's perspective must extend beyond compliance to consider fairness, bias, and societal implications of technology governance.

Governance Reporting and Board Oversight

The final responsibility of governance is to inform and guide the board of directors. The IS auditor assesses whether reporting mechanisms provide timely, accurate, and relevant information for oversight. Board-level reports should summarize key risks, project performance, compliance status, and strategic outcomes of IT investments.

Auditors examine whether the board engages in active challenge—asking probing questions, requesting clarification, and directing corrective actions. Passive receipt of reports indicates weak governance. The auditor may also evaluate the board's IT literacy and access to expert advice to ensure informed decision-making.

Effective oversight requires integration of IT reporting with overall enterprise performance dashboards. The auditor ensures that metrics used in governance reflect both technical and business perspectives, enabling balanced evaluation of IT's contribution to value creation.

Strong governance reporting transforms data into insight. An effective reporting framework connects operational performance to strategic objectives, enabling the board to identify emerging risks, evaluate investment outcomes, and guide resource allocation. The IS auditor reviews whether governance reports provide both historical analysis and predictive indicators. These reports should move beyond metrics of compliance to measure capability, resilience, and value delivery.

Board oversight requires transparency from executive management. The auditor must determine whether escalation procedures exist for significant control failures or risk events. Governance documentation should include board minutes that record discussions, decisions, and follow-up actions. The absence of such documentation may signal governance complacency.

The auditor evaluates the board's use of independent assurance sources, including internal and external audits. Ideally, the board integrates assurance findings into its performance reviews, ensuring accountability and learning. Governance oversight succeeds when the board not only approves policies but also actively monitors their outcomes and consequences.

Governance of Enterprise Architecture

Enterprise architecture serves as a blueprint for aligning IT infrastructure, applications, and data with business objectives. Governance of architecture ensures that systems are designed, implemented, and maintained in a manner that supports strategic goals while managing complexity and cost. The IS auditor evaluates whether architecture principles are defined, approved, and enforced across projects.

Architecture governance typically involves an architecture review board responsible for approving standards and evaluating deviations. The auditor confirms that these boards operate effectively, meeting regularly and documenting their decisions. Compliance with architecture principles—such as modularity, interoperability, and security—prevents fragmentation and redundancy.

Enterprise architecture frameworks such as TOGAF and COBIT's "Manage Enterprise Architecture" objective establish the principles and methodologies for ensuring coherence between IT assets and business processes. The IS auditor examines whether the organization maintains an up-to-date architecture repository documenting current systems, data flows, and integrations. The auditor evaluates how effectively architectural decisions control technological sprawl, reduce duplication, and support scalability.

Architecture governance ensures that every new project or system aligns with approved standards. The auditor reviews architecture compliance assessments, design approvals, and waiver documentation. When exceptions occur, governance mechanisms should justify them with risk assessments and compensating controls. Failure to enforce architecture governance often leads to fragmented systems, data silos, and escalating maintenance costs.

An effective enterprise architecture program also monitors technological obsolescence. The auditor determines whether lifecycle management plans exist to retire outdated technologies safely. This governance approach balances innovation with stability, ensuring that technological evolution supports the enterprise's long-term strategic direction.

Governance and Regulatory Compliance

In an era of complex global regulations, governance must integrate compliance into its foundation rather than treating it as an external obligation. The IS auditor verifies whether compliance responsibilities are formally assigned, whether policies reflect legal requirements, and whether continuous monitoring mechanisms exist to detect noncompliance.

Governance over compliance extends beyond information security. It encompasses data protection laws, industry-specific mandates, environmental standards, and financial reporting requirements. The auditor assesses whether compliance registers track applicable laws, whether controls are mapped to these laws, and whether evidence of compliance is maintained systematically.

Periodic compliance reviews should be incorporated into governance calendars. The IS auditor ensures that management reports compliance status to the board, that violations are investigated, and that corrective measures are documented. Mature governance systems treat compliance as a performance dimension linked to reputation and trust rather than as a constraint.

Governance of Innovation and Emerging Technologies

Governance must evolve as enterprises adopt new technologies such as artificial intelligence, cloud computing, and Internet of Things devices. The IS auditor examines whether governance frameworks anticipate risks and opportunities associated with these innovations.

Innovation governance balances experimentation with control. The auditor reviews whether pilot projects are authorized through formal channels, whether data privacy and security are considered during design, and whether ethical implications are addressed. Boards should have visibility into emerging technology portfolios and allocate resources for risk evaluation before deployment.

Cloud governance, for example, requires defining ownership, access, and accountability when services are hosted externally. The auditor verifies whether governance policies delineate shared responsibilities between provider and client. Artificial intelligence introduces governance challenges involving transparency, algorithmic bias, and accountability for automated decisions. The IS auditor ensures that the enterprise establishes principles for fairness, explainability, and human oversight in algorithmic processes.

Governance Maturity and Capability Assessment

Measuring governance maturity helps management understand strengths and weaknesses in its control environment. The IS auditor assesses maturity using structured models like COBIT's Process Capability Model or proprietary internal frameworks. Maturity levels typically range from ad hoc processes to optimized, continuously improving systems.

At the initial level, governance processes are informal and reactive. As maturity increases, roles become defined, policies standardized, and performance measured. At the highest level, governance integrates with culture and strategy, using analytics to predict and prevent issues before they materialize. The auditor collects evidence through interviews, documentation reviews, and performance metrics to assign maturity ratings.

The auditor's recommendations must reflect the organization's context—maturity goals should be realistic and aligned with resource capacity. A small enterprise may target defined processes, while a global entity may pursue predictive governance driven by data analytics.

Governance and Organizational Performance

IT governance contributes directly to organizational performance by ensuring technology investments deliver measurable value. The IS auditor analyzes performance frameworks that connect governance outcomes to business metrics such as customer satisfaction, operational efficiency, and innovation capacity.

Balanced scorecards are common governance tools, translating strategic objectives into measurable indicators across financial, customer, process, and learning perspectives. The auditor assesses whether scorecard metrics accurately reflect IT's contribution to enterprise goals. For example, system availability and incident resolution times support operational efficiency, while project success rates and technology adoption indicate innovation capability.

The auditor ensures that governance processes use these indicators for continuous improvement. Performance reporting should influence resource allocation, policy revisions, and leadership accountability. Governance loses effectiveness when performance data is collected but not acted upon.

Audit of IT Governance

When performing an audit of IT governance, the IS auditor follows a structured approach. The first step is understanding governance frameworks and their application within the enterprise. Next, the auditor evaluates governance design—whether policies, structures, and processes exist and are appropriate for the organization's objectives.

The auditor then tests governance operation by reviewing board minutes, examining performance reports, and interviewing executives to confirm oversight effectiveness. Evidence of decision-making, risk prioritization, and corrective actions demonstrates operational maturity.

The auditor's findings must articulate how governance weaknesses translate into business risks. For instance, inadequate oversight of IT investments can result in misaligned projects, wasted resources, or security vulnerabilities. The audit report should recommend improvements in structure, accountability, or measurement while acknowledging strengths.

Relationship Between Governance and Management

The distinction between governance and management is fundamental to this domain. Governance establishes direction and monitors outcomes, while management executes plans and reports performance. The IS auditor evaluates whether this relationship is balanced and clearly defined.

In practice, blurred boundaries often cause conflict. Overreliance on management reporting without independent oversight weakens governance, while excessive governance interference slows operational agility. The auditor determines whether policies delineate responsibilities appropriately and whether escalation protocols allow unresolved issues to reach governance bodies.

The COBIT framework formalizes this relationship through its governance and management objectives. Governance objectives reside under the Evaluate–Direct–Monitor domain, while management objectives span Plan–Build–Run–Monitor. Auditors must ensure these objectives operate in harmony and that communication flows seamlessly between layers.

Governance and Service Management Integration

Service management frameworks like ITIL 4 complement governance by defining operational processes that deliver value to stakeholders. The IS auditor reviews whether governance bodies use service management data—such as incident trends, capacity reports, and service-level compliance—to evaluate IT performance.

Integration between governance and service management ensures decisions are informed by real-world operational evidence. Governance committees rely on service reports to assess whether investments achieve expected service outcomes. The auditor examines whether governance feedback loops exist, where lessons from operations influence strategic direction.

Service improvement programs provide measurable evidence of governance effectiveness. When continual improvement initiatives align with strategic goals and receive governance oversight, the enterprise achieves coherence between policy and performance.

Human Factors and Leadership in Governance

Leadership behavior shapes governance success more than any policy. The IS auditor examines whether leaders demonstrate accountability, transparency, and commitment to ethical standards. A strong governance culture begins with visible support from top management—when executives champion governance practices, employees perceive them as integral rather than bureaucratic.

The auditor also evaluates succession planning for key governance roles. Leadership continuity ensures stability in governance execution. The presence of training programs and mentorship structures indicates maturity.

Governance depends on trust between levels of management. Auditors observe interpersonal dynamics, communication styles, and collaboration effectiveness. Dysfunctional relationships between business and IT leadership often manifest as inconsistent priorities or unimplemented policies. The auditor's insights into these dynamics, though qualitative, are vital to understanding governance health.

Crisis Governance and Resilience

Effective governance extends to crisis management and organizational resilience. The IS auditor assesses whether governance structures anticipate disruptive events and empower rapid, coordinated response.

Governance over crisis management ensures that decision rights, communication channels, and escalation paths are predefined and tested through simulation exercises.

Crisis governance integrates with business continuity and disaster recovery frameworks, which are addressed in greater detail in later domains. Here, the auditor focuses on the board's role in defining resilience objectives, approving continuity strategies, and receiving timely updates during disruptions.

Auditors evaluate how lessons from crises are institutionalized. Governance must ensure that post-incident reviews lead to policy adjustments, resource realignments, and culture shifts. A resilient governance system transforms crises into catalysts for improvement rather than sources of prolonged disruption.

Ethical Use of Technology in Governance

Modern governance faces growing responsibility to ensure technology is used ethically and responsibly. The IS auditor examines whether governance policies address fairness, transparency, and accountability in data-driven decision-making. Ethical technology governance extends to issues such as surveillance, data monetization, algorithmic bias, and environmental sustainability.

Boards must establish principles guiding technology use, supported by review committees or ethics boards. The auditor evaluates whether ethical considerations are documented in risk assessments and investment proposals. Ethical lapses—such as misuse of personal data or manipulation of digital platforms—can damage reputation and invite regulatory scrutiny.

The IS auditor ensures that ethics are embedded into governance metrics, not isolated as moral ideals. When organizations measure ethical outcomes, such as inclusivity or data stewardship, they demonstrate maturity and public accountability.

Governance Reporting Maturity and Continuous Improvement

Governance reporting evolves through maturity stages. Initially, reporting is reactive and focused on compliance. As maturity develops, reports become proactive, predictive, and aligned with strategic objectives. The IS auditor evaluates whether governance reporting includes root cause analysis, trend identification, and forward-looking insights.

Continuous improvement in governance reporting relies on feedback loops from both management and stakeholders. The auditor reviews whether report recipients provide feedback that leads to refinement of metrics and dashboards. Automation and data analytics enhance reporting timeliness and accuracy, but auditors must ensure governance retains interpretive oversight rather than delegating judgment to algorithms.

Governance improvement programs, including self-assessments and independent reviews, demonstrate accountability. The auditor verifies whether governance bodies set measurable improvement goals, track progress, and adjust practices accordingly.

Governance Metrics Evolution and Analytics in Oversight

Modern governance relies increasingly on analytics to drive performance evaluation and risk oversight. Traditional dashboards once centered on incident counts or project milestones; however, mature enterprises integrate predictive analytics to anticipate trends before they impact operations. The IS auditor examines whether governance committees leverage analytics derived from service management, project data, and security telemetry to inform decisions.

Metrics must represent both effectiveness and efficiency. Governance effectiveness is measured by how decisions achieve intended outcomes, while efficiency evaluates resource utilization in achieving those results. For example, a board that approves an enterprise cloud migration must later receive evidence showing that cost savings and scalability were realized without compromising security or compliance.

The auditor reviews whether metrics are continuously validated for relevance. Over time, indicators may lose significance as technology and strategies evolve. Governance frameworks should include procedures for reviewing and retiring outdated measures, ensuring reporting remains meaningful. Predictive indicators—such as trend lines of risk exposure, employee turnover in critical IT roles, or anomaly detection in financial systems—empower governance bodies to act preemptively rather than reactively.

Strategic Oversight Integration

Governance effectiveness depends on integrating oversight across strategy, operations, and assurance. The IS auditor evaluates whether the organization maintains alignment between long-term vision and day-to-day control execution. Strategic oversight ensures that initiatives funded at the governance level are tracked through performance reviews, project management offices, and operational reporting structures.

A mature governance ecosystem links three critical layers: the strategic (board and executive committees), the tactical (program and portfolio management), and the operational (service delivery and control). The auditor examines how information flows between these layers and whether escalation and feedback mechanisms are defined. The absence of vertical communication often results in governance decisions detached from operational realities.

The auditor also evaluates the role of assurance providers—internal audit, risk management, and compliance functions—in supporting strategic oversight. Assurance reporting should synthesize findings from multiple perspectives into a unified view of enterprise risk. Where silos exist, auditors recommend integrated assurance models that reduce duplication and enhance transparency.

Global Governance Trends and Digital Transformation

Globalization and digital transformation have expanded governance responsibilities beyond traditional boundaries. Enterprises now operate in complex ecosystems that span jurisdictions, regulations, and cultures. The IS auditor must assess whether governance structures are equipped to manage transnational risks and technology-driven disruption.

Digital transformation governance emphasizes agility and innovation while maintaining control. The auditor reviews whether boards balance experimentation with accountability. Governance charters should outline decision-making criteria for adopting emerging technologies, managing digital partnerships, and ensuring ethical standards in data use and artificial intelligence.

Cross-border operations introduce challenges such as data sovereignty, compliance fragmentation, and third-party dependencies. The IS auditor verifies whether governance frameworks provide mechanisms to reconcile regional legal requirements while maintaining consistent global standards. Boards must receive visibility into global IT operations and ensure that localized risks are aggregated into enterprise-level reporting.

Sustainability and corporate responsibility have also entered the governance agenda. Technology's environmental footprint—data center energy consumption, electronic waste, and supply chain ethics—forms part of governance evaluation. The auditor reviews whether environmental, social, and governance (ESG) metrics include technology dimensions, ensuring that IT contributes positively to corporate sustainability commitments.

Governance in Mergers, Acquisitions, and Divestitures

When enterprises undergo mergers or acquisitions, governance plays a critical role in integrating systems, data, and processes. The IS auditor assesses whether governance frameworks address due diligence, integration planning, and post-merger risk management.

Due diligence involves evaluating the target organization's control maturity, compliance posture, and technology architecture. The auditor examines whether governance bodies receive accurate information about inherited risks before the transaction. Integration governance ensures that technology convergence occurs systematically, preventing disruptions and maintaining data integrity.

Post-merger governance focuses on harmonizing policies, roles, and cultural norms. The auditor reviews how conflicting standards are reconciled and whether a unified governance structure emerges. Divestitures require similar oversight to ensure that separation of systems and data occurs securely and in compliance with regulatory obligations.

Governance and Cloud Ecosystem Management

Cloud computing has redefined ownership and accountability within IT governance. The IS auditor verifies whether governance structures define shared responsibility between the organization and its cloud providers. Governance documents should identify who manages security controls, incident response, and compliance validation in multi-cloud or hybrid environments.

Vendor governance frameworks must include periodic audits of service providers, review of SOC 2 and ISO 27017 certifications, and continuous monitoring of service-level compliance. The auditor evaluates whether governance committees receive reports detailing cloud performance, cost optimization, and data protection outcomes.

Effective cloud governance balances flexibility with control. Policies should allow innovation through on-demand resources while enforcing guardrails for security and cost management. The auditor ensures that governance integrates tagging, budgeting, and configuration management tools to maintain oversight of distributed environments.

Governance and Cybersecurity Oversight

Cybersecurity governance ensures that the enterprise's protection strategy aligns with its overall business objectives, risk appetite, and compliance obligations. The IS auditor evaluates whether cybersecurity is treated as a business issue rather than solely a technical function. Board-level oversight should include regular briefings on threat landscapes, incident trends, and resilience capabilities.

A mature cybersecurity governance structure assigns clear roles: the board defines expectations, executive management implements security programs, and auditors independently assess their effectiveness. The auditor verifies that the organization maintains an enterprise-wide security framework, such as ISO 27001, NIST Cybersecurity Framework, or COBIT's "Ensure Risk Optimization" objective. These frameworks guide the identification, protection, detection, response, and recovery processes critical to cyber resilience.

Governance bodies must also review incident response metrics—mean time to detect, mean time to respond, and recovery duration—to assess readiness. The IS auditor examines whether incident escalation protocols reach governance committees promptly and whether lessons learned are formally documented and tracked.

Cybersecurity oversight includes third-party assurance. Cloud providers, managed service partners, and vendors must comply with the same standards as internal operations. The auditor ensures that governance extends beyond organizational boundaries through contractual obligations, audits, and certifications.

Strategic cybersecurity governance also involves investment decisions. The auditor reviews whether funding allocations are risk-based and justified by quantifiable benefits, such as reduced incident frequency or improved compliance posture. Overspending without measurable improvement signals weak governance just as underfunding critical areas exposes the enterprise to unacceptable risk.

Information and Reporting Flow in Governance Systems

Information flow defines the nervous system of governance. It determines how data, analysis, and decisions circulate between operational management and the board. The IS auditor evaluates whether governance reports originate from reliable systems, whether data is aggregated correctly, and whether reporting timelines support timely decision-making.

Information distortion or overload can paralyze governance. Auditors must assess whether information presented to executives is filtered for relevance and clarity. Reports should integrate visual analytics and narrative context, helping decision-makers understand implications rather than simply displaying metrics.

Governance relies on both upward and downward information flows. Upward flows deliver performance, risk, and compliance updates; downward flows communicate directives, priorities, and policy changes. The auditor checks whether communication protocols ensure that governance decisions reach operational teams efficiently and whether feedback loops exist for operational concerns to influence governance revisions.

Documentation of these information flows—through governance charters, meeting records, and communication matrices—demonstrates maturity and accountability. Weak information flow is often a precursor to governance failure, as decisions may be made on incomplete or outdated data.

Governance of Change Management

Change management governance ensures that technology modifications support business objectives and minimize operational risk. The IS auditor assesses whether governance frameworks define approval hierarchies, segregation of duties, and rollback procedures for system changes.

At the governance level, change advisory boards or equivalent committees must oversee major transformations, ensuring alignment with strategic direction. The auditor examines whether these boards review risk assessments, test results, and implementation plans before authorization. Unauthorized or poorly controlled changes often indicate governance breakdown.

Post-implementation reviews form a key governance mechanism for learning. The auditor ensures these reviews assess whether intended benefits were achieved and whether unforeseen impacts occurred. Governance should mandate that lessons learned are fed back into project management methodologies and risk registers.

Change governance must extend beyond technical adjustments to encompass organizational and cultural changes. The auditor evaluates whether governance structures manage communication, stakeholder training, and adoption monitoring for large initiatives, as these factors determine transformation success.

Governance and Data Ethics

Data ethics governance ensures that information is collected, processed, and utilized responsibly. The IS auditor evaluates whether governance frameworks define principles for fairness, consent, transparency, and accountability in data handling. Ethical lapses in data governance—such as biased algorithms or unauthorized surveillance—can cause severe reputational damage and legal penalties.

Governance boards should establish data ethics committees responsible for reviewing projects involving artificial intelligence, analytics, or personal data. The auditor checks whether such committees include cross-functional representation from legal, compliance, technology, and business units. Ethical considerations must be documented as part of project approval, ensuring that innovation aligns with societal and organizational values.

Auditors assess whether the organization provides employees with training on data ethics and whether reporting channels exist for ethical concerns. Whistleblower protections, transparency reports, and public disclosures of data practices enhance trust and demonstrate governance accountability.

Performance and Value Delivery in Governance

The central objective of IT governance is to ensure that technology delivers measurable value. The IS auditor analyzes how governance frameworks define, measure, and communicate value realization. Value encompasses both tangible returns—such as cost reduction or productivity gains—and intangible outcomes like customer trust, innovation capacity, or regulatory compliance.

The auditor examines project portfolios to determine whether investment decisions align with value criteria approved by governance bodies. Benefits realization tracking ensures accountability: each initiative must demonstrate alignment with business goals and report actual results against expected benefits.

Chapter 3: Information Systems Acquisition, Development, and Implementation

Introduction

The third domain of the CISA framework examines how organizations acquire, develop, and implement information systems in alignment with business objectives. The IS auditor's role is to assess whether systems are planned, designed, tested, and deployed under controlled, secure, and auditable conditions. Failures in this phase often introduce systemic risks that persist throughout the system's operational life. Effective governance and rigorous project management are essential to ensure systems meet quality, security, and compliance requirements while delivering expected value.

Information systems acquisition encompasses both internal development and procurement from third parties. Auditors must understand methodologies such as traditional Waterfall and iterative Agile frameworks, system development life cycle (SDLC) controls, and post-implementation evaluations. Their objective is to confirm that each stage—initiation, design, development, testing, implementation, and maintenance—is governed by policies, documented standards, and measurable quality criteria.

System Development Life Cycle Governance

The SDLC provides a structured approach for system creation and modification. The IS auditor evaluates whether the organization follows an approved methodology that includes planning, requirements definition, design, coding, testing, deployment, and maintenance. Each phase must have documented deliverables, approval checkpoints, and defined responsibilities.

In the planning phase, the auditor reviews feasibility studies, business cases, and cost-benefit analyses to confirm that the proposed system aligns with strategic and operational goals. Projects initiated without a sound business justification pose inherent risk to return on investment and resource utilization. The feasibility assessment must consider technical capabilities, operational readiness, and compliance constraints.

During requirements definition, auditors examine whether functional and nonfunctional requirements are captured comprehensively. These include performance, security, privacy, and usability parameters. Requirements should be reviewed and approved by relevant stakeholders to prevent scope ambiguity. Traceability matrices linking requirements to design and testing artifacts ensure accountability.

Design governance translates requirements into system architecture. The auditor ensures that design specifications incorporate security principles such as least privilege, segregation of duties, and data classification. Documentation should identify interfaces, dependencies, and data flows. The presence of design review boards or architecture committees demonstrates governance maturity.

Development governance ensures adherence to coding standards, version control, and secure development practices. The auditor verifies that source code management systems enforce access control, track changes, and maintain audit logs. Secure coding practices—input validation, error handling, and encryption—must be integrated into development processes rather than applied retroactively.

Testing governance validates that the system meets defined requirements. The auditor reviews test plans, cases, and results to determine coverage completeness. Independent quality assurance teams should verify both functional accuracy and nonfunctional attributes such as performance and resilience. Defects must be documented, prioritized, and resolved before system acceptance.

Project Management and Governance Structures

Effective project management provides the control environment within which systems are developed. The IS auditor assesses whether projects adhere to recognized frameworks such as PMBOK, PRINCE2, or Agile methodologies, depending on organizational culture and risk appetite. Governance mechanisms must define roles, responsibilities, and escalation paths.

Auditors review project charters to confirm approval from authorized governance bodies. Steering committees should oversee progress, budget adherence, and risk mitigation. The auditor evaluates whether these committees receive accurate, timely updates and whether corrective actions are documented and implemented.

Change management within projects is critical. The auditor ensures that scope changes are approved formally and evaluated for impact on time, cost, and quality. Informal or undocumented changes frequently lead to cost overruns or compromised system integrity.

Risk management integration within project governance is a strong indicator of maturity. The auditor confirms that risk registers identify technical, operational, and strategic risks, along with mitigation owners and monitoring frequencies. High-risk items should receive visibility at the steering committee level.

Feasibility and Cost-Benefit Analysis

A well-governed acquisition begins with a feasibility study that evaluates whether the proposed system is practical and beneficial. The IS auditor reviews these studies to ensure they address financial, operational, and technical aspects. Feasibility analysis should include alternative solutions, projected costs, expected benefits, and risk evaluations.

Cost-benefit analysis quantifies both tangible and intangible factors. The auditor checks that cost estimates consider not only acquisition but also lifecycle expenses such as maintenance, licensing, and training. Benefits should be expressed in measurable terms—revenue enhancement, efficiency gains, or risk reduction.

The auditor verifies whether assumptions underlying cost-benefit projections are documented and periodically reviewed. Unrealistic or outdated assumptions can lead to governance failures. Post-implementation evaluations should compare actual outcomes with projections, allowing lessons learned to refine future feasibility assessments.

Vendor Selection and Procurement Controls

When systems are acquired externally, procurement governance ensures fairness, transparency, and value for money. The IS auditor examines whether vendor selection follows approved procedures including request for proposal (RFP) issuance, bid evaluation, and contract negotiation.

Procurement governance must define evaluation criteria—technical capability, security posture, cost, support quality, and compliance history. The auditor verifies that evaluations are evidence-based and that scoring documentation is retained. Conflict of interest declarations must be obtained from all participants in the selection process to safeguard integrity.

Contract governance is another focus. The auditor reviews whether contracts include performance metrics, penalties for noncompliance, service-level agreements, and right-to-audit clauses. Provisions for confidentiality, intellectual property, and data protection must align with organizational and legal requirements.

Post-award governance requires ongoing monitoring. The auditor evaluates vendor performance reports, issue logs, and escalation records to ensure continuous accountability. Failure to monitor vendor compliance may result in undetected deficiencies or financial loss.

System Design and Security Integration

System design determines the foundation for reliability, maintainability, and security. The IS auditor assesses whether design processes incorporate security by design principles—embedding controls within architecture rather than applying them as afterthoughts.

Key aspects include segregation of environments (development, testing, production), secure configuration standards, and defense-in-depth architecture. The auditor ensures that data flows are documented and that sensitive data paths incorporate encryption and access restrictions.

Auditors also verify alignment with enterprise architecture standards. Design deviations must be justified, approved, and documented. Failure to adhere to standards increases complexity, cost, and risk exposure.

Security governance requires threat modeling and risk analysis during design. The auditor checks whether potential attack vectors—such as input injection or privilege escalation—are identified and mitigated. Controls should address authentication, authorization, logging, and monitoring.

System Development and Quality Assurance

During the development phase, governance ensures consistency and quality. The IS auditor examines whether project teams use formal coding guidelines and peer review mechanisms. Code review not only detects defects but also verifies adherence to security and performance standards.

Version control systems, such as Git or Subversion, must enforce traceability between code changes and approved requirements. The auditor ensures that only authorized developers have commit rights and that emergency changes follow documented approval.

Quality assurance extends beyond testing. The auditor assesses whether metrics such as defect density, test coverage, and rework rates are tracked. High defect recurrence may indicate inadequate requirements or weak design validation. Independent testing teams or external quality audits strengthen governance assurance.

Testing and Acceptance Controls

Testing validates that systems meet intended functionality and quality standards. The IS auditor evaluates the comprehensiveness of testing strategies, which should include unit, integration, system, user acceptance, and regression testing. Each level serves a distinct purpose. Unit testing ensures individual components operate as designed. Integration testing verifies that modules interact seamlessly, maintaining data integrity and performance efficiency. System testing evaluates end-to-end processes, confirming that functional and nonfunctional requirements—such as scalability, security, and response time—are met under realistic conditions.

User acceptance testing (UAT) is particularly important from an assurance perspective. The IS auditor reviews whether business users participate in UAT to validate that the system fulfills business needs. Acceptance criteria must be documented prior to testing to prevent subjective approvals. Sign-off from business stakeholders signifies readiness for deployment.

Regression testing confirms that new changes or fixes do not disrupt existing functionalities. The auditor ensures that regression test libraries are maintained and reused, preserving continuity across releases. Automated testing tools enhance consistency, but governance requires oversight to validate scripts and results. Testing results must be documented, and defects must be categorized by severity and tracked to resolution.

The IS auditor verifies that test environments mirror production configurations as closely as possible, isolating test data from live data to prevent contamination. Data masking techniques should be applied when using production data for testing to maintain confidentiality. Proper governance ensures that test results drive objective go-live decisions rather than schedule pressures or political influence.

System Implementation and Deployment Governance

Implementation is the transition from development to production. The IS auditor assesses whether deployment follows approved cutover plans, rollback procedures, and communication strategies. Deployment governance minimizes disruption and ensures that the system enters operation in a controlled manner.

Auditors review implementation plans for detailed schedules, assigned responsibilities, and pre-implementation checkpoints. A "go/no-go" decision meeting should occur before release, where risk assessments and readiness criteria are evaluated. The auditor confirms that sign-off from business and IT leadership is obtained prior to deployment.

Change management governance during implementation ensures traceability. Only authorized personnel should migrate code or configurations to production. The auditor evaluates whether dual control mechanisms exist to prevent unauthorized changes—typically requiring one individual to prepare and another to approve or execute deployments.

Training and documentation also fall within implementation governance. The auditor ensures that end-users receive adequate training and that system manuals are accessible and current. Post-deployment support arrangements, including help desk coverage and escalation paths, should be defined.

Auditors also examine data migration controls, confirming that extraction, transformation, and loading (ETL) processes maintain completeness and accuracy. Parallel runs—operating new and old systems concurrently—provide assurance of data and process equivalence. Implementation concludes only when validation demonstrates that business objectives are met and stability is achieved.

Post-Implementation Review and Benefit Realization

A post-implementation review (PIR) assesses whether the system performs as intended, achieves expected benefits, and operates under effective controls. The IS auditor verifies that PIRs are scheduled after sufficient operational experience has accumulated. This review phase closes the feedback loop, feeding lessons learned into future projects.

The auditor examines metrics comparing projected versus actual outcomes—cost savings, efficiency improvements, user satisfaction, and risk reduction. Deviations must be analyzed to determine root causes, whether in requirements definition, development, or governance oversight.

Control performance evaluation is another PIR focus. The auditor ensures that logical access, segregation of duties, and change management controls remain effective post-deployment. If temporary controls were used during transition, auditors verify that permanent ones have replaced them.

The PIR process reinforces governance accountability. Findings should be reported to steering committees and integrated into organizational knowledge repositories. Weaknesses identified during review must lead to policy or methodology refinements, demonstrating a culture of continuous improvement.

Application Controls and Embedded Auditing

Application controls safeguard data integrity, accuracy, and completeness at the system level. The IS auditor distinguishes between input, processing, and output controls. Input controls ensure that only valid, authorized data enters the system. Processing controls verify that transactions execute correctly, while output controls confirm that results reach intended recipients accurately and securely.

Auditors assess whether systems include automated validation checks, such as range verification, sequence checks, and referential integrity enforcement. Error handling and exception reporting are equally important; governance requires that anomalies trigger alerts for timely investigation.

Embedded auditing refers to the integration of audit routines within application systems. The IS auditor reviews whether audit trails capture key activities, including data entry, modifications, approvals, and system access. These logs must be tamper-resistant and retained per policy. Embedded audit modules can generate exception reports automatically, facilitating continuous assurance.

Governance over application controls requires periodic review and calibration. As systems evolve, control configurations may lose relevance or effectiveness. The auditor ensures that control testing is part of change management, maintaining ongoing confidence in application reliability.

Agile and DevOps Environments

Modern development practices emphasize speed and adaptability through Agile and DevOps methodologies. The IS auditor must assess how governance and control principles adapt within these rapid iteration models.

In Agile environments, projects are divided into short cycles called sprints. Governance focuses on ensuring that iterative development maintains traceability, documentation, and risk management. The auditor examines sprint backlogs, user stories, and acceptance criteria to confirm that they align with overarching business objectives. Even with flexibility, mandatory checkpoints—security reviews, testing verification, and approvals—must remain intact.

DevOps extends Agile by integrating development and operations, automating deployment pipelines, and enabling continuous delivery. The IS auditor verifies that automation does not bypass essential controls. For example, continuous integration systems must enforce version control and testing standards before approving production releases.

Governance over DevOps includes segregation of duties within automated workflows, access control for pipeline configuration, and monitoring for unauthorized code pushes. The auditor ensures that governance metrics—such as deployment frequency, failure rates, and recovery times—are reviewed at appropriate management levels.

Outsourced Development and Third-Party Integration

When system development is outsourced, governance must ensure accountability and quality. The IS auditor reviews contracts for explicit requirements covering deliverables, milestones, testing rights, and security obligations. Outsourced development introduces additional risks related to intellectual property, confidentiality, and dependency on external expertise.

Auditors verify that organizations maintain oversight through regular status reports, code reviews, and acceptance testing. Right-to-audit clauses must permit inspection of vendor processes and controls. The auditor examines evidence of vendor compliance with secure development standards and ensures that vulnerabilities discovered during testing are remediated promptly.

Integration of third-party components, such as APIs or open-source libraries, also requires governance oversight. The IS auditor ensures that licensing obligations are respected and that third-party code undergoes security and compatibility testing before inclusion.

Supply chain governance extends to verifying the integrity of code sources through mechanisms such as digital signatures and hash validation. The auditor confirms that component inventories—software bills of materials—are maintained to support vulnerability management and compliance tracking.

System Maintenance and Change Management

Once systems are operational, maintenance governance ensures stability, performance, and compliance. The IS auditor evaluates whether the organization maintains documented change management procedures covering requests, approvals, testing, and implementation.

Routine maintenance, including patches and upgrades, must follow structured approval workflows. The auditor ensures that emergency changes are logged, reviewed retrospectively, and do not bypass testing. Version tracking and rollback capabilities provide assurance that changes can be reversed without data loss.

Auditors also verify monitoring processes for identifying performance degradation, capacity constraints, or configuration drift. Maintenance governance requires proactive planning—preventive maintenance schedules, hardware lifecycle tracking, and software end-of-support monitoring.

Change management governance integrates with risk management. The auditor examines whether risk assessments accompany significant changes, and whether residual risk is communicated to governance bodies. Documentation must demonstrate that business continuity considerations, such as backup validation, are incorporated into every change cycle.

Configuration and Release Management

Configuration management maintains integrity across system components. The IS auditor reviews whether configuration baselines are established and protected. Automated tools, such as configuration management databases (CMDBs), provide visibility into asset relationships and dependencies.

Governance requires that configuration changes undergo formal approval and testing before implementation. The auditor verifies that access to configuration repositories is restricted and monitored. Unauthorized alterations can introduce vulnerabilities or disrupt service availability.

Release management ensures that new or updated software enters production through controlled channels. The auditor reviews release documentation, including testing evidence, deployment checklists, and backout procedures. Governance must enforce coordination between development, testing, and operations teams, supported by communication plans to affected stakeholders.

Post-release reviews assess whether deployments achieved intended results without introducing defects or instability. Findings should inform continuous improvement of release governance processes.

Data Conversion and Migration Controls

Data conversion and migration represent critical junctures in system implementation where errors can compromise integrity, availability, and reliability. The IS auditor's role is to ensure that data migration from legacy systems to new environments occurs under strict control, preserving completeness, accuracy, and validity.

Migration typically involves three primary stages: extraction, transformation, and loading (ETL). During extraction, data is pulled from source systems. The auditor verifies whether extraction routines are documented, tested, and restricted to authorized personnel. Governance requires reconciliation reports to confirm that record counts and control totals match between source and staging environments.

Transformation involves cleansing, mapping, and formatting data to meet target schema requirements. The IS auditor reviews transformation rules for correctness, documentation, and approval. Inconsistent or undocumented transformations introduce risk of data corruption or misclassification. The auditor ensures that data quality controls—duplicate detection, validation, and standardization—are embedded in the transformation logic.

Loading transfers processed data into the target system. The auditor ensures that this step includes validation routines comparing pre- and post-load control totals, hash totals, and sampling verification. Any discrepancies must trigger investigation before final acceptance. Data migration logs must be retained to support audit trails and accountability.

Auditors also verify whether test migrations precede the final cutover. Pilot migrations identify data compatibility and performance issues under controlled conditions. The auditor confirms that rollback plans exist, ensuring recovery if migration fails. For sensitive information, encryption during transfer and secure storage in transit environments prevent unauthorized access or tampering.

Successful data migration concludes only when business stakeholders validate that data is usable, accurate, and accessible in the new system. The auditor ensures that sign-off occurs formally, supported by reconciliation evidence and exception resolution documentation.

System Integration Governance

Integration governance oversees how new systems interact with existing applications, databases, and infrastructure. The IS auditor evaluates whether governance frameworks define standards for interface design, data exchange, and dependency management. Poorly managed integration can create inconsistencies, duplicate data, or security vulnerabilities.

Auditors examine integration architecture diagrams to confirm completeness and accuracy. Interface control documents (ICDs) should specify data elements, transmission frequency, validation rules, and error-handling procedures. The absence of formal ICDs increases the likelihood of undetected communication errors or data mismatches.

Governance mandates testing of all interfaces before production deployment. The auditor reviews test results verifying message integrity, transaction completeness, and system performance under load. Where systems communicate through APIs or middleware, the auditor ensures that authentication and encryption standards are enforced consistently across components.

Integration security controls are paramount. The auditor examines whether tokens, keys, or certificates used for authentication are protected and rotated periodically. Logging of interface activities enables traceability of cross-system transactions. Integration points are frequent attack vectors, so continuous monitoring of interface health and traffic anomalies forms part of operational governance.

Post-integration reviews must confirm that all systems maintain consistent data states and that process handoffs occur without loss or duplication. The IS auditor validates whether monitoring dashboards provide near real-time visibility into interface performance, error rates, and throughput.

Implementation Risk Management

Implementation inherently introduces risk—ranging from cost overruns and schedule delays to data loss or business disruption. Governance must ensure that these risks are identified, assessed, and mitigated proactively. The IS auditor evaluates whether risk management processes are integrated into project governance throughout the SDLC rather than confined to isolated checkpoints.

Auditors review risk registers documenting technical, operational, and strategic risks. Each entry should include likelihood, impact, mitigation actions, and ownership. High-priority risks require escalation to steering committees. The auditor ensures that mitigation actions are tracked and verified for effectiveness.

Contingency and fallback plans form part of risk management. The auditor checks whether rollback procedures exist for failed implementations and whether backup integrity is validated. Scenario testing—such as failover simulations or system recovery exercises—demonstrates preparedness.

Governance requires independent assurance for major implementations. The auditor reviews whether internal audit, external consultants, or risk management teams perform periodic reviews to verify compliance with methodology and controls. Large-scale projects should have phase-gate reviews, where continuation depends on risk assessment outcomes.

Change in scope remains a common risk. The auditor ensures that change control processes require risk reassessment for every scope modification. Lack of such reassessment often results in underestimated impacts and project derailment.

The auditor must also consider cultural and human factors. Resistance to change, inadequate training, and communication breakdowns often contribute to implementation failure. Governance bodies should oversee change management strategies addressing these human dimensions through engagement, feedback, and education.

Post-Deployment Evaluation and Control Sustainability

Once a system is live, governance transitions from implementation oversight to operational assurance. Post-deployment evaluation determines whether performance, controls, and benefits remain sustainable. The IS auditor ensures that evaluations are scheduled periodically after go-live, capturing both early stabilization issues and long-term control performance.

Auditors examine operational metrics—availability, transaction accuracy, incident rates, and user satisfaction. Deviations from expected levels must be analyzed to identify root causes. Early identification of instability allows management to implement corrective actions before issues escalate.

Control sustainability refers to the ongoing effectiveness of controls after deployment. The IS auditor verifies whether maintenance procedures preserve configuration integrity, whether security settings remain enforced, and whether change management continues under governance oversight. Continuous monitoring tools—log analytics, performance dashboards, and alert systems—support sustainability by detecting anomalies automatically.

Auditors also review user feedback mechanisms and help desk logs to identify recurring issues that may signal systemic weaknesses. Governance must ensure that lessons from post-deployment evaluation inform policy updates, training programs, and control refinement.

Quality Assurance and Continuous Improvement

Quality assurance (QA) in system development extends beyond defect detection; it establishes a culture of continuous improvement. The IS auditor assesses whether QA is institutionalized as an independent function with authority to enforce standards. QA should monitor adherence to methodologies, evaluate deliverable quality, and provide feedback for process enhancement.

Auditors verify whether QA metrics—defect density, customer-reported errors, and compliance deviations—are analyzed for trends. The organization should use these insights to refine its SDLC, update checklists, and enhance training. Continuous improvement loops align with frameworks such as COBIT's "Monitor, Evaluate, and Assess" processes and ITIL's continual improvement model.

The auditor ensures that management commits resources to QA activities and that lessons learned from audits and reviews feed back into governance structures. Sustainable quality arises from institutional learning, not reactive correction.

Knowledge Transfer and Operational Handover

Effective system implementation concludes with structured knowledge transfer to operational teams. The IS auditor evaluates whether governance frameworks mandate documentation handover, training sessions, and support readiness assessments. Knowledge transfer prevents operational disruption and dependency on project teams after go-live.

Auditors review evidence of system documentation—architecture diagrams, user manuals, and troubleshooting guides—and ensure accessibility through central repositories. Training records should confirm that support staff understand processes, escalation paths, and maintenance tasks.

Handover governance requires formal sign-off by operations management, signifying readiness to assume control. The auditor ensures that unresolved defects or pending enhancements are documented and tracked in operational queues. This structured transition protects continuity and accountability.

Implementation Audits and Assurance Reviews

Implementation audits provide independent validation of project governance, control design, and outcome realization. The IS auditor performing such audits assesses whether project governance frameworks were followed and whether controls functioned effectively at each stage.

Auditors collect evidence through interviews, document reviews, and testing of controls such as approvals, segregation of duties, and change authorization. The audit report should link findings to risk impact, providing actionable recommendations for improvement.

Governance committees must review implementation audit results and oversee remediation. When recurring deficiencies appear across multiple projects, governance should mandate systemic reforms—updating methodologies, strengthening oversight, or enhancing training. Implementation audits thus serve as catalysts for institutional learning.

Emerging Trends in System Acquisition and Development Governance

Modern system development increasingly relies on emerging technologies such as artificial intelligence, low-code platforms, and cloud-native architectures. The IS auditor must adapt governance evaluation techniques to these evolving paradigms.

In AI systems, governance focuses on algorithm transparency, data ethics, and model validation. The auditor ensures that bias detection, explainability, and accountability frameworks are established. For low-code environments, governance must verify that citizen developers follow security and quality standards equivalent to professional developers.

Cloud-native development introduces continuous deployment pipelines, requiring automated governance controls for version management, vulnerability scanning, and policy enforcement. The IS auditor ensures that governance adapts to automation by validating configuration scripts and verifying segregation between development and production environments.

By maintaining vigilance over these emerging domains, the IS auditor helps enterprises innovate securely and responsibly.

Control Integration with Business Processes

Once a system is in production, its effectiveness depends on how well its controls integrate with business processes. The IS auditor evaluates whether automated controls embedded in the system align with manual controls operated by business users. Integration ensures that transactions are authorized, processed, and recorded correctly, maintaining the integrity of financial and operational data.

Auditors review process documentation and workflow diagrams to confirm that system configurations reflect approved business procedures. Segregation of duties (SoD) must be built into application logic, preventing users from executing conflicting roles such as initiating and approving the same transaction. Governance requires periodic SoD reviews and automated rule enforcement where feasible.

The auditor ensures that controls remain aligned as business processes evolve. Configuration changes, reorganizations, or policy updates can inadvertently disable or bypass established safeguards. Governance mandates continuous communication between IT and business management to synchronize control objectives.

Integrated control design also promotes efficiency. For example, automated reconciliations reduce manual intervention and error risk. The IS auditor verifies that such automation is validated for accuracy, logged for traceability, and monitored for exceptions. Control integration strengthens accountability while supporting compliance with internal and external regulatory frameworks.

Auditors further assess whether management dashboards consolidate control performance indicators, providing decision-makers with visibility into exceptions, risk events, and remediation status. This alignment of control information with business metrics enhances governance transparency and responsiveness.

Post-Implementation Monitoring and Continuous Assurance

Post-implementation monitoring ensures that newly deployed systems continue to perform as intended under real-world conditions. The IS auditor evaluates whether monitoring mechanisms capture operational, security, and compliance metrics. Governance dictates that these metrics are reviewed regularly by responsible managers and escalated to oversight bodies when thresholds are breached.

Automated monitoring tools—such as application performance monitoring (APM) systems, log analytics, and security information and event management (SIEM) platforms—support continuous assurance. The auditor reviews whether these systems are properly configured, generate timely alerts, and feed into structured incident management workflows.

Auditors confirm that monitoring data informs proactive decision-making rather than reactive crisis management. Performance baselines should be established and refined over time, allowing trend analysis to predict issues before they impact business operations. Governance requires retention of monitoring logs for forensic and compliance purposes, with access controlled to prevent manipulation.

Continuous assurance represents an evolution of traditional periodic audits. Through data analytics and automation, auditors can validate control operation in near real time. Governance frameworks such as COBIT advocate embedding continuous control monitoring into system design, ensuring that assurance activities are ongoing rather than episodic.

The IS auditor ensures that continuous monitoring outputs—alerts, trend reports, and anomaly detections—are reviewed by governance committees, confirming alignment with enterprise risk tolerance. This proactive oversight reduces audit latency and enhances resilience.

Control Reassessment and Optimization

Controls are not static; they must evolve with changes in technology, business strategy, and regulation. The IS auditor reviews whether governance structures mandate regular reassessment of control design and effectiveness. Control optimization seeks to balance assurance strength with operational efficiency, avoiding redundancy and unnecessary complexity.

Auditors evaluate periodic control self-assessments conducted by process owners. These self-assessments, combined with audit testing, provide comprehensive insight into control performance. Governance committees should receive summary reports highlighting improvement opportunities and resource requirements.

Optimization may involve automation of manual controls, consolidation of overlapping controls, or retirement of obsolete measures. The auditor ensures that any change to control structures follows proper change management and risk evaluation procedures.

Control metrics—such as frequency of incidents, test pass rates, and cost-to-control ratios—support governance decisions about refinement priorities. The auditor validates that these metrics are accurate and actionable. A mature control optimization process transforms compliance into continuous improvement, strengthening both assurance and agility.

Governance of User Access and Authorization Post-Deployment

User access governance remains critical after system implementation. The IS auditor verifies that access rights correspond to job responsibilities and that provisioning follows formal authorization workflows. Role-based access control (RBAC) simplifies governance by standardizing permissions according to function rather than individual assignment.

Auditors confirm that access reviews occur periodically, ensuring that former employees or role-changed personnel no longer retain inappropriate privileges. Automated access certification tools enhance efficiency and accuracy, but governance oversight must validate their completeness.

The principle of least privilege governs access management. The IS auditor reviews segregation between administrative, development, and operational roles. Elevated access should be time-bound and logged through privileged access management (PAM) solutions.

Post-deployment, access governance also encompasses integration with identity management systems. Single sign-on (SSO) and multifactor authentication (MFA) provide centralized and secure control, but auditors must confirm configuration consistency across connected applications.

In addition to preventive controls, detective measures—such as audit trails and anomaly detection—ensure transparency. The IS auditor verifies that logs record access attempts, configuration changes, and privileged actions with sufficient detail to support investigations. Governance committees must review periodic access control metrics to ensure compliance with policy and regulatory standards.

Data Protection and Privacy in System Implementation

Modern information systems must comply with data protection and privacy requirements from the earliest design stages. The IS auditor ensures that governance frameworks enforce privacy-by-design principles and that compliance obligations are embedded into technical specifications.

Auditors review whether data classification guides security controls—encryption, masking, or restricted sharing—based on sensitivity. Privacy impact assessments (PIAs) identify potential violations and must be conducted during acquisition or development. Governance requires PIA results to be reviewed by data protection officers or equivalent authorities before system approval.

Data minimization, retention limits, and consent management are integral governance requirements. The auditor examines whether the system enforces automatic data purging after retention periods and whether user consent mechanisms comply with applicable regulations. Audit trails of consent capture and withdrawal must be maintained.

Incident response governance also applies to privacy. The auditor confirms that breach notification procedures meet legal timeframes and that response roles are predefined. Regular testing of these procedures ensures organizational readiness.

Privacy governance transcends compliance; it builds stakeholder trust. The IS auditor's evaluation ensures that data protection remains a core system attribute rather than an external compliance exercise.

Audit Trails and Forensic Readiness

Audit trails are indispensable for accountability, nonrepudiation, and forensic analysis. The IS auditor reviews whether systems generate comprehensive, tamper-resistant logs that record critical events such as access, data modification, and administrative actions.

Governance requires that audit logging configurations are standardized and periodically verified. Log retention policies must align with legal and business requirements. The auditor ensures that log data is stored securely—preferably in centralized repositories protected by encryption and access controls.

Forensic readiness refers to the organization's ability to collect, preserve, and analyze digital evidence efficiently in case of investigation. The IS auditor verifies whether governance frameworks define responsibilities, preservation methods, and chain-of-custody procedures.

Automation supports audit trail analysis through correlation tools that identify anomalies or policy violations. The auditor ensures that exception alerts are reviewed by appropriate personnel and escalated according to governance protocols.

Strong audit trail governance enhances transparency, strengthens deterrence, and enables rapid response to incidents.

Sustainability of System Controls and Lifecycle

Every system has a lifecycle—from initiation to retirement—and governance must ensure that controls remain effective throughout. The IS auditor evaluates whether periodic lifecycle reviews assess continued business relevance, cost-effectiveness, and security posture.

As systems age, components may become unsupported, creating vulnerabilities. The auditor ensures that governance mandates timely upgrades or decommissioning. Lifecycle governance includes end-of-life (EOL) planning that covers data migration, archival, and secure disposal.

Control sustainability requires ongoing funding and management attention. The auditor reviews whether governance committees monitor control maintenance budgets and ensure allocation for patches, training, and compliance renewals.

Lifecycle reviews also identify opportunities for innovation. Systems reaching diminishing returns may be candidates for modernization through automation or cloud migration. Governance maturity is reflected in proactive rather than reactive lifecycle management.

Chapter 4: Information Systems Operations and Business Resilience

Introduction

Domain 4 of the CISA framework focuses on the governance, management, and control of information systems operations and the mechanisms that ensure continuity and resilience. Once systems are developed and implemented, they must be operated securely, efficiently, and predictably to support organizational objectives. The IS auditor's task in this domain is to evaluate whether operational controls sustain performance, reliability, and security while preparing the enterprise for interruptions through robust continuity and recovery processes.

Operations management involves managing resources—people, processes, and technology—to deliver consistent service. The auditor assesses whether operating procedures are standardized, whether incidents are handled promptly, and whether capacity, performance, and problem management processes align with service-level requirements.

Business resilience, meanwhile, ensures that critical operations can withstand and recover from disruptions, whether caused by system failures, cyberattacks, or natural disasters. The IS auditor verifies that resilience is built into daily operations and that continuity plans are tested, updated, and governed at the highest levels.

Operational Governance and Control Frameworks

Operational governance translates strategy into repeatable and monitored activities. The IS auditor evaluates whether the enterprise has defined operational objectives aligned with business goals, supported by frameworks such as ITIL, COBIT, or ISO 20000. Governance ensures accountability for operations through defined roles, metrics, and performance reviews.

Operations policies must cover system monitoring, scheduling, incident management, and maintenance. The auditor reviews whether procedures are documented, accessible, and approved by management. Operational metrics—uptime, incident closure rate, and service-level compliance—provide visibility into performance. Governance bodies should receive regular operational dashboards summarizing these indicators.

Auditors also examine the organizational structure to confirm segregation of duties between operations, development, and security teams. Excessive overlap may lead to unauthorized changes or weakened controls. Governance committees must ensure that operational accountability is distributed clearly, with escalation paths for exceptions or incidents.

Job Scheduling and Production Processing Controls

Automated job scheduling and batch processing form the backbone of many enterprise operations. The IS auditor assesses whether job control systems ensure timely and complete execution of tasks. Schedules must be reviewed for dependency accuracy and capacity constraints to prevent cascading failures.

Auditors verify that scheduling systems maintain logs of job initiation, completion, and exception events. Errors should trigger alerts to operators and generate incident tickets for investigation. Governance requires that failed jobs are reviewed and rerun according to documented procedures.

Production data handling must follow strict control principles. The auditor ensures that only authorized personnel can submit, modify, or cancel jobs. Version control for scripts and parameter files prevents unauthorized or erroneous execution. Governance should enforce pre-deployment testing of scheduling changes to maintain stability.

Auditors confirm reconciliation between batch results and input totals to ensure completeness. Unprocessed or partially processed transactions should be flagged automatically for follow-up. These controls collectively preserve accuracy, timeliness, and reliability of production processing.

Incident and Problem Management

Incident management governs response to unplanned service interruptions, while problem management focuses on identifying and eliminating root causes. The IS auditor evaluates whether the organization's incident response framework defines classification levels, escalation procedures, and response time targets aligned with service-level agreements (SLAs).

Auditors review incident logs to assess timeliness of detection, response, and resolution. Metrics such as mean time to detect (MTTD) and mean time to resolve (MTTR) indicate operational maturity. Governance requires trend analysis to identify recurring issues that warrant problem management investigation.

Problem management processes must capture root cause analyses and corrective actions. The IS auditor examines whether lessons learned are documented and integrated into change management and risk registers. Governance bodies should review periodic summaries of high-impact incidents and corresponding preventive measures.

Effective incident governance also includes communication protocols. The auditor confirms that stakeholders, including customers and management, receive timely updates during disruptions. Coordination with information security teams ensures unified response to cyber-related incidents.

Auditors assess whether post-incident reviews occur for major disruptions. These reviews evaluate performance against objectives, identifying process improvements and control enhancements to prevent recurrence.

Change and Patch Management in Operations

Operational change management controls ensure system stability by regulating modifications to production environments. The IS auditor verifies whether change requests are formally submitted, risk-assessed, tested, and approved before implementation. Unauthorized or emergency changes represent significant governance weaknesses.

Auditors review change logs to confirm completeness and traceability. Governance requires segregation between requestors, implementers, and approvers to prevent conflicts of interest. Documentation should include test evidence, backout plans, and approval signatures.

Patch management governs the application of updates to software, firmware, and operating systems. The IS auditor ensures that patch evaluation considers compatibility, security, and downtime implications. Governance mandates periodic vulnerability scans to identify missing patches and ensure timely remediation.

Automated patch management tools can enhance efficiency but require oversight. The auditor confirms that exceptions—such as deferred patches for legacy systems—are documented, risk-accepted, and monitored. Patch governance should integrate with change management, maintaining synchronization between approval and implementation processes.

Backup Management and Data Recovery

Backups form the foundation of resilience and data integrity. The IS auditor evaluates whether backup policies specify scope, frequency, retention, and storage media. Governance ensures that backups are verified through regular restoration tests.

Auditors verify that critical data, system configurations, and application binaries are included in backup cycles. Backup procedures should cover both full and incremental strategies to optimize recovery time and storage efficiency. Encryption of backup media protects confidentiality, particularly when stored offsite or in cloud repositories.

Physical and logical separation of backup copies mitigates risk of simultaneous loss from incidents such as ransomware or site disasters. The IS auditor ensures that backup success and failure reports are reviewed daily and that discrepancies trigger immediate investigation.

Governance requires periodic validation through test restores, confirming both technical functionality and business usability of recovered data. Restoration testing should simulate real scenarios, verifying recovery time objective (RTO) and recovery point objective (RPO) compliance.

Auditors also confirm that obsolete backups are disposed of securely to prevent data leakage. Backup management governance demonstrates organizational preparedness and discipline in safeguarding information continuity.

Performance and Capacity Management

Performance and capacity management ensure that systems meet service expectations under varying workloads. The IS auditor evaluates whether performance baselines exist and whether monitoring tools collect metrics such as CPU utilization, response time, and transaction throughput.

Capacity planning anticipates future resource requirements based on growth trends. The auditor verifies whether forecasting models incorporate business expansion, seasonal peaks, and technology upgrades.

Governance requires regular capacity review meetings where performance data informs investment and optimization decisions.

Performance deviations should trigger root cause analysis. The auditor reviews whether alerts escalate automatically when thresholds are breached and whether corrective actions—such as tuning, scaling, or resource reallocation—are documented.

Auditors confirm that performance metrics are reported to governance committees alongside cost metrics, enabling balanced evaluation of efficiency and expenditure. Proactive capacity management reflects mature operational governance, preventing disruptions from resource shortages or overutilization.

Service-Level Management and Reporting

Service-level management (SLM) ensures that IT services deliver consistent value aligned with business expectations. The IS auditor examines whether service-level agreements define measurable metrics such as availability, response time, and resolution time.

Governance requires that SLAs are reviewed and updated regularly to reflect changing business priorities. The auditor verifies that operational reports measure performance against SLA targets and that exceptions trigger corrective actions. Persistent deviations indicate either unrealistic targets or operational weaknesses requiring governance intervention.

SLM governance also involves customer communication. The IS auditor ensures that service reports are shared with stakeholders transparently, promoting accountability. Periodic service reviews between IT and business units foster collaboration and continuous improvement.

Configuration Management and Asset Control

Configuration management maintains accurate records of IT assets and their interdependencies. The IS auditor verifies whether a configuration management database (CMDB) exists and is maintained consistently.

The CMDB should record asset attributes—hardware, software, version, and location—along with relationships among systems. Governance requires that changes to configurations are authorized and documented through integrated change management processes.

Auditors assess whether configuration audits occur periodically to reconcile actual versus recorded states. Discrepancies may indicate unauthorized modifications or incomplete documentation.

Asset control governance extends to lifecycle management, ensuring timely procurement, maintenance, and disposal of IT assets. The IS auditor confirms that decommissioning procedures include secure data wiping and regulatory compliance verification.

Configuration management maturity enables efficient troubleshooting, informed risk analysis, and dependable service continuity.

Information Security Operations

Information security operations form the continuous defensive layer that protects systems and data during daily activities. The IS auditor evaluates whether operational security practices are embedded within standard operating procedures and whether governance ensures ongoing alignment between operational controls and security objectives.

The foundation of security operations lies in access management, monitoring, and incident response. The auditor reviews whether security operations centers (SOCs) or equivalent functions monitor system logs, network traffic, and endpoint alerts in real time. Monitoring must be continuous, with event correlation and anomaly detection supporting early warning capabilities. Governance requires that detected security events follow escalation procedures defined in incident response plans.

The IS auditor also verifies whether privileged access to production systems is governed by strict controls. Administrative actions—such as configuration changes or patch deployment—must be logged and reviewed periodically. Role-based access segregation prevents administrators from approving or auditing their own actions.

Auditors assess whether vulnerability management integrates with operational patch cycles. Continuous scanning tools should identify weaknesses, assign severity levels, and track remediation progress. Governance committees must receive summaries of outstanding vulnerabilities and risk acceptance decisions.

Operational security further includes endpoint protection, antivirus management, and intrusion detection systems. The auditor evaluates whether updates are automated and monitored for success. Weakness in signature updates or threat intelligence feeds can undermine defense effectiveness.

Security awareness in operations remains essential. The IS auditor verifies that training programs emphasize phishing prevention, secure data handling, and incident reporting. Governance requires that completion rates and test results are tracked as key performance indicators.

Security operations should not exist in isolation; integration with change, incident, and problem management ensures a holistic approach to risk reduction.

Job Monitoring and Automation Governance

Modern enterprises rely heavily on automated job scheduling and robotic process automation (RPA) to manage complex workloads. The IS auditor evaluates whether governance frameworks ensure control, accountability, and traceability within these automated environments.

Automation introduces efficiency but also risk if controls are weak. The auditor reviews whether automated processes include logging, exception handling, and verification steps. Governance dictates that automated tasks operate under unique service accounts with limited privileges, and that their credentials are protected through vaulting or encryption.

Auditors examine change management for automation scripts. Any modification to scheduling parameters or RPA logic must undergo testing and approval before deployment. Version control ensures rollback capability and historical traceability.

Monitoring dashboards should provide visibility into automation performance, including completion rates, error trends, and throughput. Governance committees should review automation metrics alongside manual process performance to confirm continued business alignment.

The auditor also assesses whether controls prevent automation from bypassing key approvals or validations. For example, automated data transfers must still enforce segregation of duties and reconciliation checks. Mature automation governance balances autonomy with oversight, ensuring that human accountability remains central to decision-making.

Business Continuity Planning (BCP)

Business continuity planning ensures that the organization can sustain critical operations during and after a disruption. The IS auditor evaluates whether continuity governance establishes clear ownership, periodic testing, and alignment with enterprise risk management.

A robust BCP framework begins with a **business impact analysis (BIA)**. The auditor verifies that the BIA identifies critical processes, recovery priorities, and dependencies across technology, personnel, and facilities. The BIA should define recovery time objectives (RTOs) and recovery point objectives (RPOs) consistent with business tolerance for downtime and data loss.

Continuity strategies must address both preventive and reactive measures. The IS auditor reviews documented strategies—such as alternate processing sites, redundant networks, and cloud-based failover systems. Governance ensures that strategies are approved by senior management and updated as business conditions change.

The auditor examines the completeness of continuity plans: contact lists, escalation hierarchies, communication protocols, and resource inventories. Plans must integrate with incident response and crisis management frameworks to enable coordinated action during disruptions.

Testing and exercising form the backbone of continuity assurance. The IS auditor reviews test schedules, results, and lessons learned. Tests should include table-top simulations, technical failovers, and full-scale recovery drills. Governance requires that deficiencies identified during tests are tracked and resolved.

Auditors also ensure that continuity awareness extends across the organization through training and communication programs. Employees must understand their roles and know where to access continuity procedures during emergencies.

Disaster Recovery Oversight

Disaster recovery (DR) is a specialized component of business continuity focusing on restoring IT services after catastrophic failures. The IS auditor evaluates whether DR governance ensures preparedness, coordination, and technical resilience.

The auditor reviews DR policies defining scope, activation criteria, and roles. Recovery plans should cover infrastructure, applications, data, and networks. Governance mandates that recovery procedures are current, tested, and synchronized with system changes.

Auditors confirm that DR environments—whether alternate sites, cloud backups, or high-availability clusters—are maintained and tested regularly. Testing frequency should align with system criticality; mission-critical applications require at least annual validation.

The auditor verifies that offsite backup locations are geographically diverse and protected from environmental and security risks. Connectivity between primary and recovery sites must be verified, with documented recovery sequences to minimize downtime.

Governance requires detailed documentation of dependencies, including third-party services. The IS auditor checks whether contractual agreements guarantee provider participation during recovery exercises.

Testing results must include measured recovery times, data integrity validation, and post-test evaluations. Governance bodies should receive summary reports comparing achieved versus target RTOs and RPOs. Deviations must prompt corrective actions and budget adjustments.

Auditors also assess DR training programs for technical teams. Recovery success relies on personnel competence as much as infrastructure readiness. Governance maturity is reflected in coordinated, well-rehearsed recovery operations that restore service confidently under pressure.

Operations Documentation and Knowledge Management

Comprehensive documentation sustains operational continuity and knowledge retention. The IS auditor reviews whether procedures, configurations, and troubleshooting guides are updated and accessible to authorized personnel.

Operational manuals should cover system startup and shutdown, error handling, job recovery, and emergency response. Governance ensures version control and periodic review to reflect changes in infrastructure and policy.

The auditor verifies that documentation repositories are secure yet easily retrievable during incidents. Knowledge sharing mechanisms—such as wikis, ticketing systems, and lessons-learned databases—support collaboration and efficiency.

Succession planning forms part of knowledge governance. The auditor ensures that key operational roles have trained backups, preventing single points of failure in expertise. Cross-training and rotation programs demonstrate mature human resource governance in operations.

Monitoring, Logging, and Event Correlation

Monitoring and logging provide operational visibility, enabling proactive management and forensic analysis. The IS auditor evaluates whether monitoring coverage includes all critical systems, applications, and network components.

Logs must capture essential details—user activities, configuration changes, errors, and system performance. The auditor ensures that logs are protected from alteration and retained per policy. Time synchronization across systems supports accurate event correlation.

Centralized monitoring platforms, such as SIEM systems, aggregate logs from multiple sources. The auditor verifies that correlation rules detect patterns indicative of anomalies or potential failures. Governance requires defined escalation paths for alerts, ensuring prompt response.

Auditors also evaluate performance dashboards for accuracy and relevance. Overly complex or irrelevant metrics can obscure critical warnings. Governance bodies should periodically review monitoring configurations to align them with evolving business and risk priorities.

Monitoring maturity manifests in predictive capability—the ability to anticipate and mitigate issues before impact. The IS auditor assesses whether trend analyses and capacity forecasts feed into governance reports, linking monitoring outcomes to strategic decision-making.

Resilience Through Redundancy and High Availability

Operational resilience is achieved through redundancy and high-availability architectures. The IS auditor examines whether governance mandates redundancy for critical infrastructure components—servers, power supplies, storage arrays, and network links.

Auditors verify that failover mechanisms, such as clustering or load balancing, are configured, tested, and monitored. Governance ensures that automatic failover does not compromise data consistency or transaction integrity.

The auditor also evaluates power and environmental controls, including uninterruptible power supplies (UPS), generators, and climate regulation. Facility-level redundancy is essential for maintaining operations during external disruptions.

Cloud adoption introduces new resilience models through distributed architectures and geographic replication. The IS auditor ensures that governance frameworks validate cloud providers' redundancy claims through service reports and independent audits.

Resilience governance must balance cost and criticality. The auditor reviews whether redundancy levels are justified by risk assessments and business impact analyses. Excessive redundancy without corresponding risk justification represents inefficiency, while insufficient redundancy undermines continuity.

Operational Risk Monitoring and Reporting

Operational risk monitoring provides continuous visibility into threats that may affect service delivery, data integrity, and system reliability. The IS auditor evaluates whether governance frameworks integrate operational risk management with incident, change, and performance processes to maintain holistic oversight.

The auditor reviews whether key risk indicators (KRIs) are defined and tracked across operational domains—system availability, backup success rates, patch compliance, and security incident frequency. KRIs must be measurable, time-bound, and directly linked to enterprise risk appetite. Governance committees should review KRI dashboards regularly, ensuring that deviations trigger immediate analysis and mitigation.

Auditors examine how operational risk data is aggregated and escalated. A mature governance process includes structured reporting lines from operational teams to executive risk committees. Each report should contain both quantitative metrics and qualitative assessments, describing root causes and proposed responses.

The IS auditor also assesses whether risk treatment plans are tracked through closure. Unresolved or repetitive risks indicate weak accountability or ineffective controls. Governance should enforce timelines and ownership for mitigation.

Continuous improvement is vital. Risk trend analysis supports strategic forecasting, helping the enterprise prioritize control investment. The IS auditor ensures that lessons from operational incidents inform future risk assessments and policy revisions.

Third-Party and Outsourcing Oversight in Operations

Operational functions often rely on external vendors for infrastructure hosting, cloud services, or managed support. The IS auditor evaluates whether governance frameworks extend accountability to these third parties through well-defined contracts, service-level agreements (SLAs), and monitoring mechanisms.

Auditors review outsourcing policies detailing vendor selection, onboarding, and ongoing performance evaluation. Each contract must specify deliverables, uptime guarantees, security responsibilities, and audit rights. The auditor ensures that oversight responsibilities are formally assigned within the organization—typically to vendor management or procurement functions.

Governance requires continuous monitoring of vendor performance through periodic reports and independent assessments. The IS auditor verifies whether SLA compliance is reviewed, exceptions are escalated, and corrective actions are documented. Key vendor metrics—such as incident response time, service quality, and compliance posture—should appear in governance dashboards.

Third-party risk management integrates security, operational, and regulatory perspectives. The IS auditor reviews vendor risk assessments that analyze data handling, privacy compliance, and business continuity readiness. Vendors supporting critical operations must demonstrate tested recovery capabilities aligned with enterprise requirements.

Governance also mandates offboarding procedures to ensure secure termination of services. The auditor confirms that data retrieval, access revocation, and confidentiality obligations are completed upon contract expiration. Strong third-party oversight ensures that external dependencies do not become uncontrolled risk vectors.

Environmental and Physical Security Controls

Information systems operations depend on physical infrastructure, making environmental controls essential for availability and safety. The IS auditor evaluates whether facilities hosting critical systems maintain physical protection, environmental regulation, and emergency readiness.

Physical access controls must prevent unauthorized entry to data centers and control rooms. The auditor reviews whether access is managed through badges, biometrics, or multifactor authentication, with logs retained for audit. Visitors should be escorted and recorded in access registers. Governance requires periodic access reviews to ensure continued validity of authorizations.

Environmental controls safeguard against heat, humidity, and power fluctuations. The IS auditor checks for redundant HVAC systems, humidity sensors, and power conditioning equipment. Governance mandates maintenance schedules and automated alerts for environmental thresholds.

Power continuity is achieved through uninterruptible power supplies (UPS), backup generators, and dual power feeds. The auditor ensures that these components undergo regular testing and that fuel and maintenance records are maintained.

Fire detection and suppression systems—smoke sensors, fire-resistant walls, and gas-based extinguishers—must be operationally tested and compliant with safety standards. The IS auditor ensures that fire drills and evacuation procedures are conducted regularly.

Governance extends to physical layout considerations: separation of high-voltage areas, cabling management, and flood protection. Security awareness for facility staff complements technical controls, ensuring that operational safety remains a shared responsibility.

Operational Compliance and Regulatory Alignment

Operations must comply with internal policies and external regulations governing data management, safety, and service delivery. The IS auditor reviews whether operational teams track regulatory requirements relevant to their activities, such as data localization, financial reporting, and critical infrastructure protection.

Compliance governance includes assigning accountability for monitoring legal and industry changes. The auditor ensures that compliance officers or risk managers communicate updates to operations teams and verify implementation. Failure to incorporate regulatory changes into operational procedures can expose the organization to penalties and reputational harm.

Operational documentation—procedures, logs, and reports—must support auditability. The IS auditor confirms that records are retained for mandated periods and that evidence of compliance (such as access reviews or security test results) is available for inspection.

Periodic compliance reviews or certifications (e.g., ISO 20000 for service management, ISO 27001 for security management) provide independent assurance. Governance requires management to track corrective actions from such audits to completion.

The auditor also verifies whether the organization conducts regular control self-assessments to evaluate operational adherence to policies. These self-assessments strengthen ownership and readiness for external audits.

Operational Metrics and Continuous Improvement

Performance measurement and feedback loops are essential for operational excellence. The IS auditor examines whether key performance indicators (KPIs) reflect efficiency, effectiveness, and quality across operations. Examples include mean incident resolution time, system uptime percentage, job completion accuracy, and user satisfaction scores.

Governance mandates periodic review of KPIs by operations leadership. The IS auditor verifies that metrics are aligned with business outcomes and adjusted as strategic priorities evolve. Overemphasis on quantitative metrics without qualitative interpretation may lead to misleading conclusions, so balanced scorecards integrating multiple perspectives are recommended.

Continuous improvement governance involves structured initiatives that analyze performance data and implement targeted enhancements. The IS auditor reviews whether improvement plans are documented, approved, and tracked for impact. Lessons learned from incidents, audits, and user feedback should feed into policy and process revisions.

Automation, analytics, and artificial intelligence increasingly support operational improvement. The auditor ensures that automation initiatives maintain transparency and do not compromise control effectiveness. Governance requires validation of algorithmic decisions impacting system management or incident prioritization.

Ultimately, continuous improvement governance transforms operations from reactive management to proactive optimization.

Training, Awareness, and Competency Management

People remain the most critical component of reliable operations. The IS auditor evaluates whether governance frameworks establish formal training programs, competency assessments, and succession planning for operational staff.

Auditors review records of technical certifications, onboarding training, and refresher courses covering new tools and procedures. Governance should require training in incident handling, change management, backup procedures, and emergency response.

Awareness programs reinforce security and control consciousness. The IS auditor ensures that periodic reminders, briefings, and simulations maintain employee readiness. Effectiveness should be measured through participation rates, quiz results, and behavioral indicators such as timely incident reporting.

Competency governance includes defining skill matrices and career progression paths for key operational roles. Cross-training mitigates the risk of knowledge concentration. The auditor verifies that critical positions have designated backups capable of performing essential tasks during absences or crises.

The presence of documented training frameworks and management oversight demonstrates maturity in operational human resource governance.

Chapter 5: Protection of Information Assets

Introduction to Information Asset Protection

Information assets include all data, systems, and supporting resources that hold value to the organization. Protecting these assets requires a comprehensive, layered defense approach encompassing governance, policy enforcement, physical and logical security, and incident response readiness.

The IS auditor assesses whether the organization maintains an enterprise-wide information security program approved by senior management and integrated into overall governance. Security policies should define objectives, roles, and responsibilities for protecting data. Procedures and standards must translate policies into actionable control mechanisms across business units.

A mature protection program recognizes that information security is not solely an IT issue but an organizational imperative. Governance ensures that accountability for data protection extends from board members to individual users. The auditor evaluates whether management demonstrates commitment through resource allocation, ongoing awareness campaigns, and performance measurement.

Auditors also examine whether security objectives are risk-based, ensuring that control efforts focus on the most critical information and systems. Protection effectiveness is measured by the degree to which identified threats are mitigated and vulnerabilities reduced to acceptable levels.

Information Security Governance and Strategy

Effective protection begins with a robust governance structure that defines how information security decisions are made and how responsibilities are distributed. The IS auditor evaluates whether the organization has established a security governance framework that aligns with business strategy, legal obligations, and risk appetite.

Governance must define roles such as the Chief Information Security Officer (CISO), data owners, custodians, and users. Each role carries specific accountability: the CISO oversees policy and compliance; data owners define access and classification; custodians implement controls; and users adhere to usage guidelines. The auditor verifies that these roles are clearly documented and communicated.

A security strategy outlines long-term objectives for protecting assets and defines how emerging risks and technologies will be managed. The IS auditor ensures that strategic planning includes threat assessments, resource requirements, and performance indicators. Periodic updates reflect evolving business models, regulatory changes, and technological advances.

Governance oversight must include executive and board-level reporting. The auditor reviews whether metrics such as incident rates, compliance posture, and risk exposure are presented to leadership for review and decision-making. This visibility ensures accountability and reinforces the enterprise's commitment to safeguarding its assets.

Information Classification and Ownership

Classification provides the foundation for determining how information should be handled and protected. The IS auditor verifies whether the organization maintains an information classification policy that categorizes data based on sensitivity, value, and regulatory requirements.

Typical classification levels include public, internal, confidential, and restricted. The auditor evaluates whether these levels are clearly defined and consistently applied across systems and processes. Data owners should determine classifications based on business impact and compliance needs.

Once classified, information must have assigned owners responsible for authorizing access, approving changes, and overseeing retention and disposal. The auditor ensures that ownership responsibilities are documented and reviewed periodically. Custodians—such as IT administrators—must enforce controls according to the data owner's requirements but not alter classifications without authorization.

The auditor also reviews whether labeling mechanisms—metadata, document markings, or automated tagging—support consistent enforcement. Misclassified or unlabeled data increases risk of unauthorized exposure or noncompliance.

Governance mandates that classification drives protection levels. For example, confidential data must require encryption, multi-factor authentication, and restricted sharing. Public data may require fewer controls but must still be monitored to prevent unauthorized modification.

Access Control and Identity Management

Access control safeguards ensure that only authorized individuals or systems can access specific resources. The IS auditor evaluates whether identity and access management (IAM) frameworks enforce authentication, authorization, and accountability across the enterprise.

Authentication verifies identity through mechanisms such as passwords, smart cards, or biometrics. The auditor ensures that policies require strong credentials, multifactor authentication (MFA) for sensitive systems, and secure password management practices including complexity, expiry, and reuse prevention.

Authorization governs what authenticated users can do. The auditor examines whether access rights are granted based on least privilege and job role through role-based access control (RBAC) or attribute-based access control (ABAC). Access provisioning must follow formal requests, managerial approval, and documentation.

Auditors review periodic access recertifications, ensuring that inactive or unnecessary accounts are removed. Governance requires that terminations trigger immediate revocation of system privileges.

Accountability is achieved through audit trails and monitoring. The IS auditor verifies whether system logs record user actions such as logins, file access, and configuration changes. Logs must be reviewed regularly for anomalies or violations.

Identity management extends to privileged accounts and service identities. Governance demands segregation between operational and administrative roles, and usage of privileged access management (PAM) tools to control elevated credentials.

The auditor also ensures that IAM integrates with HR processes—so onboarding, transfers, and exits automatically update access entitlements.

Network Security and Perimeter Defense

Network protection forms the first technical barrier against unauthorized access. The IS auditor examines whether network architecture follows defense-in-depth principles, incorporating segmentation, redundancy, and layered controls.

Firewalls must regulate traffic between internal and external networks, enforcing least-privilege access through rulesets regularly reviewed for accuracy. The auditor ensures that rule changes follow approval and testing processes. Intrusion detection and prevention systems (IDS/IPS) should monitor network activity, detect anomalies, and block or alert on suspicious behavior.

The auditor verifies encryption use for data in transit through protocols like TLS or VPN. Secure network design requires demilitarized zones (DMZs) for public-facing servers, separation of management networks, and limited remote access paths.

Wireless networks demand additional scrutiny. The IS auditor confirms use of strong encryption (e.g., WPA3), authentication, and periodic scanning for rogue access points.

Governance requires continuous monitoring of network logs, vulnerability scans, and patch compliance for routers, switches, and firewalls. The auditor checks whether penetration tests validate network defense effectiveness.

Network segmentation—dividing sensitive systems from general traffic—reduces breach impact. The IS auditor ensures segmentation aligns with data classification and risk profiles.

Cryptographic Management

Cryptography underpins confidentiality, integrity, and authenticity. The IS auditor verifies whether the organization maintains policies governing encryption standards, key management, and usage.

Encryption must protect sensitive data both at rest and in transit. The auditor ensures that approved algorithms and key lengths meet industry standards, and that deprecated methods are phased out promptly.

Key management is critical. The IS auditor reviews whether keys are generated securely, distributed under dual control, stored encrypted, rotated regularly, and revoked when compromised or expired. Governance requires maintaining key inventories and audit trails of key lifecycle events.

Digital signatures and certificates authenticate entities and ensure data integrity. The auditor checks whether certificate authorities (CAs) are trusted and whether expired or revoked certificates are removed from systems.

Cryptographic governance also includes data masking and tokenization for non-production environments. The IS auditor verifies that masked data cannot be reverse-engineered and that cryptographic processes are performance-tested to avoid operational bottlenecks.

Mismanagement of cryptography can nullify even the strongest controls. Thus, auditors must confirm both technical compliance and procedural rigor in handling cryptographic materials.

Security Architecture and Defense-in-Depth

Security architecture defines the structure through which an organization applies multiple, coordinated layers of protection across its information systems. The IS auditor evaluates whether this architecture aligns with enterprise risk appetite, business goals, and regulatory obligations while maintaining consistent principles of confidentiality, integrity, and availability.

Defense-in-depth requires overlapping controls that collectively reduce risk if one layer fails. The IS auditor examines the distribution of these controls—physical, technical, and administrative—and ensures that no single point of failure exists. Examples include layered network segmentation, multi-factor authentication, secure coding, and endpoint protection.

Auditors review architecture documentation, such as diagrams, data flow maps, and trust boundaries, to confirm that design decisions reflect sound security practices. Governance requires that architecture reviews occur before major system deployments or significant changes, ensuring that vulnerabilities are identified early.

Configuration baselines and hardening standards form part of architectural governance. The IS auditor ensures that all systems, devices, and applications follow minimum-security configurations defined by corporate or industry benchmarks (e.g., CIS, NIST). Periodic validation ensures consistency between documented baselines and operational reality.

Architecture must also include monitoring and detection mechanisms. The auditor verifies that log aggregation, intrusion detection, and behavioral analytics tools integrate cohesively across all architectural layers. Security architecture is not static—it evolves as threats, technologies, and business processes change. Governance must enforce periodic reassessment to maintain relevance.

A mature defense-in-depth model integrates physical security (locked server rooms, surveillance, visitor controls), technical defenses (firewalls, encryption, endpoint protection), and administrative controls (policies, training, segregation of duties). The IS auditor confirms that all three dimensions are harmonized, forming a unified and proactive security posture.

Security Awareness and Training Programs

Human behavior remains the most unpredictable element in information security. The IS auditor evaluates whether the organization's security awareness program educates all employees—technical and non-technical—on their responsibilities for protecting information assets.

Governance mandates periodic training sessions, tailored by role and risk exposure. For example, developers receive secure coding training, while finance personnel focus on fraud and data handling awareness. The auditor ensures that awareness materials are updated regularly to reflect new threats such as phishing, ransomware, or social engineering.

Measurement of effectiveness is critical. The IS auditor reviews training completion rates, test scores, and simulated attack results. Organizations often conduct phishing simulations to gauge resilience; governance requires analysis of outcomes and targeted follow-up for improvement.

Awareness must extend to contractors and third parties with system access. The auditor confirms that onboarding processes include mandatory security briefings and that contractual agreements stipulate compliance with organizational security policies.

Governance structures—often led by a security awareness coordinator—must report metrics to senior management, highlighting trends and residual risks. Continuous reinforcement through newsletters, posters, and campaigns maintains engagement beyond formal sessions.

The auditor recognizes that awareness is not a one-time event but a sustained effort cultivating a security-conscious culture. Employees who understand both the *why* and *how* of security controls become active participants in asset protection.

Data Loss Prevention (DLP) and Information Handling Controls

Data loss prevention mechanisms ensure that sensitive information does not leave the organization's control unintentionally or maliciously. The IS auditor examines whether DLP technologies and policies monitor data in use, in motion, and at rest across endpoints, networks, and cloud platforms.

The auditor reviews policy configurations defining what constitutes sensitive data—such as personal identifiers, financial records, or intellectual property—and verifies that DLP tools use accurate patterns to detect and block unauthorized transfers. Governance requires alignment between DLP policies and data classification levels.

Auditors evaluate whether alerts from DLP systems are reviewed promptly and whether escalation workflows exist for potential incidents. Excessive false positives may reduce effectiveness; therefore, tuning and governance review are necessary.

Data handling controls complement DLP. The IS auditor ensures that removable media use is restricted, email encryption is enforced for sensitive content, and file-sharing platforms implement access control and audit logs. Cloud data governance requires monitoring for unauthorized uploads and third-party integrations.

Governance oversight includes periodic audits of DLP configurations, incident trends, and policy exceptions. Management must analyze whether DLP effectively reduces risk without impeding productivity.

A robust DLP strategy demonstrates the organization's ability to maintain control over its information assets even as data flows extend beyond traditional network boundaries.

Endpoint Protection and Malware Defense

Endpoints—including laptops, mobile devices, and workstations—represent frequent entry points for cyberattacks. The IS auditor assesses whether endpoint security controls prevent, detect, and remediate malicious activity.

Antivirus and antimalware solutions must be centrally managed, ensuring consistent configuration, signature updates, and reporting. The IS auditor verifies that update failures generate alerts and that outdated devices are remediated promptly. Governance requires periodic compliance reports on endpoint protection coverage.

The auditor examines whether devices are hardened with restricted administrative privileges, secure boot settings, and disk encryption. Removable media controls, such as disabling USB ports or enforcing encryption, reduce data exfiltration risks.

Patch management on endpoints remains vital. The IS auditor ensures that operating systems and applications receive timely updates and that patch deployment is tracked through compliance dashboards. Endpoints missing critical patches must be isolated or remediated per policy.

Mobile device management (MDM) extends endpoint governance to smartphones and tablets. The auditor verifies that MDM enforces authentication, remote wipe, and application control.

Behavioral detection—such as endpoint detection and response (EDR) systems—adds advanced defense capabilities by identifying unusual activity. Governance mandates integration between EDR and central security monitoring for coordinated incident response.

Endpoint protection is effective only when paired with user awareness, least-privilege enforcement, and continuous monitoring. The IS auditor ensures that all three dimensions operate under unified governance policies.

Incident Detection and Response Governance

Incident response (IR) governance ensures the organization can detect, contain, and recover from security events swiftly and effectively. The IS auditor reviews whether an incident response plan (IRP) exists, is approved by management, and aligns with business continuity and disaster recovery frameworks.

Detection begins with monitoring systems—SIEM platforms, IDS/IPS sensors, and anomaly analytics. The auditor ensures that alerts are triaged by trained analysts and that severity levels dictate escalation timing. Governance requires 24/7 monitoring for critical systems or compensating measures if full coverage is impractical.

The IRP must define incident categories (e.g., malware, data breach, unauthorized access), response teams, communication protocols, and evidence-handling procedures. The IS auditor examines whether team roles are assigned—incident commander, communications lead, forensic analyst—and whether contact lists are current.

Auditors review incident records for timeliness, root cause analysis, and remediation actions. Major incidents must include post-incident reviews identifying lessons learned and control improvements. Governance committees should receive regular summaries of incident trends and key metrics such as mean time to contain (MTTC) and mean time to recover (MTTR).

Coordination with legal, compliance, and communications departments ensures consistent messaging and regulatory reporting during breaches. The auditor ensures that breach notification obligations under data protection laws are documented and rehearsed.

Testing of the incident response process—through simulations, tabletop exercises, or live drills—validates readiness. Governance requires documentation of results and remediation of observed gaps.

An effective incident response capability transforms crises into learning opportunities, demonstrating resilience and governance maturity.

Physical Security and Environmental Protection of Assets

While logical security safeguards data, physical controls protect the infrastructure hosting that data. The IS auditor evaluates whether physical security aligns with the organization's risk profile and environmental requirements.

Access to server rooms, data centers, and communication closets must be restricted and logged. Surveillance cameras, alarms, and security personnel provide deterrence and detection. The auditor ensures that physical access logs are reviewed and that exceptions trigger investigations.

Environmental protections—temperature control, humidity regulation, fire suppression, and flood prevention—complement physical access security. The IS auditor checks maintenance schedules and alert mechanisms.

Asset tagging and inventory reconciliation maintain visibility of hardware, preventing unauthorized removal. Governance requires audits of physical asset inventories and secure disposal of retired equipment through certified destruction or degaussing processes.

Physical security extends to portable devices. The auditor verifies that laptops and mobile devices employ encryption, cable locks, and secure transport procedures.

Governance oversight integrates physical and logical controls within unified risk management frameworks. Physical compromise often precedes digital exploitation; thus, both must operate under the same governance discipline.

Vulnerability Management

Vulnerability management forms the foundation of proactive security. It ensures that weaknesses in systems, applications, and configurations are identified, prioritized, and remediated before they can be exploited. The IS auditor evaluates whether the organization maintains a documented vulnerability management policy defining scope, frequency, tools, and responsibilities.

Regular scanning of network devices, servers, endpoints, and applications is essential. The auditor reviews whether automated vulnerability scanners operate on a defined schedule and whether results are validated to eliminate false positives. Governance requires risk-based prioritization, with critical vulnerabilities addressed first according to severity metrics such as CVSS scores.

Auditors examine patch and remediation workflows. Vulnerabilities must be tracked from identification through resolution, with ownership assigned to technical teams and progress monitored by governance committees. Exceptions—such as delayed remediation due to operational dependencies—must be documented, justified, and approved by management.

The IS auditor verifies whether vulnerability management integrates with change and configuration management. All remediation actions should follow proper testing, approval, and rollback procedures. Integration with threat intelligence feeds allows the organization to focus on vulnerabilities actively exploited in the wild, improving prioritization accuracy.

Governance oversight includes periodic reporting to senior management summarizing vulnerability trends, open items, and mean time to remediate (MTTR). Mature programs also perform vulnerability correlation across assets to identify systemic weaknesses—such as outdated libraries or misconfigured templates—requiring architectural correction.

Auditors assess whether penetration testing complements vulnerability scanning, validating whether identified weaknesses are exploitable. The absence of coordinated vulnerability management signals a reactive rather than preventive security posture.

Penetration Testing and Red Team Exercises

Penetration testing validates the effectiveness of security controls by simulating real-world attack scenarios. The IS auditor evaluates whether governance frameworks define testing frequency, scope, and approval processes to ensure that activities are safe, authorized, and repeatable.

The auditor confirms that tests cover critical systems, network perimeters, applications, and social engineering vectors. Penetration testers—whether internal or external—must operate under signed agreements specifying permitted techniques, data handling, and reporting obligations. Governance requires segregation between testers and system administrators to maintain independence.

Test results should detail vulnerabilities exploited, data accessed, and controls bypassed. The IS auditor reviews reports for completeness and ensures that remediation actions are documented and tracked to closure

Following a penetration test, management must assess both the direct findings and the systemic weaknesses that allowed exploitation. The IS auditor evaluates whether governance committees review test results, assign accountability for remediation, and verify closure of high-risk items within defined timeframes.

Red team exercises extend penetration testing by assessing detection and response capabilities in real time. Unlike traditional testing, red teams mimic persistent adversaries using stealth tactics over longer periods, while blue teams (defenders) attempt to identify and mitigate attacks. The IS auditor ensures that red team engagements are sanctioned by senior leadership, coordinated to avoid operational disruption, and followed by collaborative debriefs between offensive and defensive teams.

Governance oversight of red team programs should emphasize lessons learned and control improvement rather than blame. Post-engagement reports must capture not only exploited vulnerabilities but also procedural insights—such as delayed response or ineffective alerting. The IS auditor confirms that these insights feed back into incident response playbooks, awareness training, and technology enhancements.

Penetration and red team activities are most valuable when integrated into a continuous improvement cycle. Governance requires scheduling follow-up tests to confirm remediation effectiveness and to benchmark maturity over time. These exercises also provide the board with a realistic view of organizational resilience against sophisticated attacks.

Security Monitoring and Continuous Detection

Security monitoring ensures that anomalies, policy violations, and intrusions are detected promptly and investigated thoroughly. The IS auditor reviews whether the enterprise operates a centralized monitoring function, often through a Security Operations Center (SOC) or managed security service provider (MSSP).

Governance mandates that monitoring scope includes critical infrastructure, servers, endpoints, applications, and network traffic. The auditor verifies whether event logs are aggregated into a Security Information and Event Management (SIEM) system capable of correlation, alerting, and reporting.

Key performance indicators for monitoring—such as mean time to detect (MTTD), false-positive rate, and incident closure efficiency—must be defined and reviewed regularly by management. The IS auditor ensures these metrics align with business risk priorities and are reported in governance dashboards.

Automated detection through behavioral analytics and machine learning enhances monitoring capability. The auditor confirms that such systems are tuned properly and that human analysts review high-priority alerts to prevent overreliance on automation.

Monitoring must also cover insider threats. The IS auditor evaluates whether user behavior analytics (UBA) tools identify deviations from normal activity patterns, such as unusual data access or login anomalies. Governance requires that alerts involving privileged accounts trigger immediate investigation.

Security monitoring extends beyond detection to proactive threat hunting. The auditor ensures that analysts conduct targeted searches based on emerging indicators of compromise (IOCs) or threat intelligence feeds. Governance must define documentation and review requirements for threat-hunting activities, maintaining evidence of actions and findings.

Continuous detection maturity is achieved when monitoring evolves into a feedback loop: incidents inform improved detection rules, and analytics drive early warning of future risks. The IS auditor confirms that this loop functions under formal governance and that management evaluates its efficiency through regular performance reviews.

Cloud Security Governance

Cloud computing introduces new dimensions of risk and shared responsibility. The IS auditor assesses whether the organization's cloud security governance ensures accountability across all service models—Infrastructure as a Service (IaaS), Platform as a Service (PaaS), and Software as a Service (SaaS).

Governance begins with clear documentation of shared responsibilities between the organization and cloud providers. The auditor verifies whether policies delineate which party manages controls related to data protection, access management, and incident response. Ambiguity in these boundaries often leads to compliance gaps.

The IS auditor examines whether due diligence precedes cloud adoption, including vendor risk assessments, security certifications (such as ISO 27017 or SOC 2), and contractual right-to-audit clauses. Governance requires continuous oversight of provider performance through dashboards, audit reports, and service-level metrics.

Data protection in the cloud must comply with organizational classification policies. The auditor ensures that sensitive data is encrypted before leaving enterprise boundaries and that encryption keys remain under organizational control. Identity federation, multifactor authentication, and conditional access policies strengthen cloud access governance.

Cloud monitoring and logging are equally critical. The IS auditor verifies whether logs are centralized, tamper-resistant, and integrated with the enterprise SIEM for unified visibility. Governance must require timely review of anomalies, such as unauthorized configuration changes or excessive data downloads.

Misconfigurations are the most common cloud vulnerability. The auditor ensures governance enforces configuration baselines, continuous compliance scanning, and approval workflows for major changes. Automated tools should flag deviations from standards such as CIS Benchmarks.

Cloud exit strategy governance ensures portability and reversibility. The IS auditor checks whether contracts define data return, deletion, and transition processes to avoid vendor lock-in or data loss.

Effective cloud security governance enables organizations to innovate securely while maintaining control and compliance in distributed environments.

Data Privacy and Regulatory Compliance

Data privacy governance ensures that the organization respects individuals' rights and complies with applicable regulations such as the GDPR, HIPAA, or other jurisdictional privacy laws. The IS auditor evaluates whether privacy principles—lawfulness, fairness, transparency, purpose limitation, data minimization, and accountability—are embedded into business processes.

The auditor verifies whether a data protection officer (DPO) or equivalent role oversees privacy compliance, supported by clearly defined reporting lines and authority. Privacy policies must be communicated to all employees and made available to data subjects as required by law.

Auditors examine whether data inventories identify what personal data is collected, processed, shared, and stored. Each processing activity should have a documented legal basis, such as consent or contractual necessity. Governance requires that data retention schedules enforce deletion once purposes are fulfilled or legal limits reached.

Consent management must be transparent and auditable. The IS auditor ensures that consent capture, withdrawal, and modification are tracked systematically. Privacy impact assessments (PIAs) must be conducted for new projects or technologies posing high privacy risks.

Cross-border data transfers require additional scrutiny. Governance mandates safeguards such as standard contractual clauses or approved frameworks to ensure compliance. The IS auditor reviews whether these mechanisms are documented and monitored for changes in legal adequacy.

Incident response for personal data breaches must meet legal notification timelines. The auditor verifies whether breach assessment and reporting procedures align with regulatory requirements and whether evidence of compliance (notifications, communications, and remediation actions) is retained.

Governance bodies should receive periodic privacy compliance reports, including metrics on data subject requests, training completion, and audit results. Privacy governance thus transforms compliance from a reactive burden into a proactive trust-building discipline.

Security Metrics, Reporting, and Continuous Improvement

Measuring the performance of security controls is essential to validate their effectiveness and guide future investments. The IS auditor evaluates whether the organization defines key security metrics linked to objectives and risk tolerance.

Common metrics include incident response times, patch compliance rates, access review completion, and vulnerability remediation percentages. The auditor ensures that these metrics are collected consistently, analyzed for trends, and reported to governance committees.

Governance must ensure that metrics drive decisions rather than serve as static reports. For example, recurring incidents involving the same root cause should prompt policy or design revisions. Metrics should also evaluate cultural aspects—such as training participation and user behavior—to provide a holistic view of security performance.

The IS auditor confirms that continuous improvement cycles are formalized: assess, implement, monitor, and refine. Security programs must adapt to emerging threats and technological evolution through scheduled reviews and maturity assessments.

Benchmarking against frameworks like COBIT, NIST CSF, and ISO 27001 helps identify improvement opportunities. Governance bodies should set measurable goals—such as reducing incident detection time or increasing automation coverage—and monitor progress toward these targets.

Continuous improvement governance demonstrates an organization's commitment to resilience, accountability, and transparency.

Emerging Technologies and Security Trends

Emerging technologies continuously reshape the security landscape, presenting both opportunities and new risks that auditors must understand to maintain effective oversight. The IS auditor evaluates whether governance structures anticipate these changes and integrate emerging technologies into strategic planning with appropriate risk controls.

Artificial Intelligence and Machine Learning (AI/ML) play increasingly important roles in automation, predictive analytics, and threat detection. The auditor ensures that governance policies address ethical use, data quality, and algorithm transparency. AI systems trained on biased or incomplete data can produce inaccurate outcomes or introduce new vulnerabilities. Governance requires independent validation of models, data lineage documentation, and defined accountability for AI-driven decisions that impact security or compliance.

Internet of Things (IoT) devices extend enterprise connectivity to sensors, industrial machinery, and consumer products. The IS auditor reviews whether IoT security governance enforces network segmentation, secure firmware updates, and authentication for all devices. Because IoT devices often lack native security controls, compensating measures such as gateway firewalls and continuous monitoring become essential. Governance must also include inventory management, ensuring that all connected devices are tracked and periodically assessed for vulnerabilities.

Blockchain and Distributed Ledger Technologies (DLT) introduce immutable transaction recording and decentralized architectures. The auditor examines whether governance frameworks ensure key management, consensus algorithm security, and privacy compliance for stored data. Smart contracts require rigorous code audits to prevent exploitation. Governance committees should define criteria for blockchain use cases, verifying business justification and interoperability with existing systems.

Cloud-native architectures—including containerization and microservices—offer flexibility but increase complexity. The IS auditor assesses whether governance mandates image signing, runtime monitoring, and container orchestration security. Configuration management and vulnerability scanning tools must operate continuously in these dynamic environments.

Zero Trust Architecture (ZTA) represents a major shift from perimeter-based defense to identity-centric controls. The IS auditor confirms that zero trust principles—verification of every access request, least privilege enforcement, and continuous monitoring—are embedded into network design and identity management frameworks. Governance ensures that implementation follows an incremental, risk-based roadmap with measurable milestones.

Quantum computing presents future risks to encryption algorithms. The auditor evaluates whether the organization monitors advancements in post-quantum cryptography and includes migration planning in its long-term security strategy. Governance committees must stay informed of emerging standards to ensure timely adaptation.

Finally, the IS auditor ensures that continuous learning and technology scanning processes exist. Governance should establish innovation councils or risk forums tasked with reviewing technological trends and integrating insights into enterprise planning. Organizations that treat emerging technologies as both opportunities and responsibilities maintain strategic advantage while minimizing exposure.

Information Security Auditing

Information security auditing validates that controls are effectively designed, implemented, and maintained. The IS auditor assesses whether security audits follow a structured, repeatable methodology aligned with recognized standards such as ISACA's IS Audit and Assurance Guidelines or ISO 19011.

Audit planning begins with defining objectives, scope, and criteria. The IS auditor verifies that audit plans prioritize high-risk areas, such as privileged access management, data protection, and incident response. Governance requires annual risk assessments to inform audit coverage and resource allocation.

Evidence collection must follow reliable and ethical methods. The auditor ensures that sampling, interviews, system inspections, and data analysis produce verifiable results. Objectivity and independence are essential; therefore, auditors must not assess controls they designed or operate. Governance enforces segregation between operational teams and audit functions.

Audit findings must be risk-rated, actionable, and clearly communicated. The IS auditor reviews whether reports include impact analysis, recommendations, and management responses. Governance requires that audit committees track remediation progress, confirm closure of critical issues, and escalate unresolved items to senior management or the board.

Continuous auditing and data analytics enhance oversight by providing near-real-time insight into security control performance. The IS auditor ensures that automated audit tools—such as log analysis or configuration monitoring—are properly calibrated and integrated into assurance workflows.

Governance also mandates quality assurance reviews of the audit process itself. Peer evaluations and external assessments verify compliance with professional standards and promote improvement.

Effective auditing transforms governance from reactive compliance checking to proactive assurance. It validates that protection mechanisms operate as intended and supports continuous improvement across all domains of information security.

Security Integration with Enterprise Governance

Information security must operate as an integral component of enterprise governance, not an isolated technical discipline. The IS auditor evaluates whether security objectives are aligned with corporate strategy, risk management, and compliance frameworks.

Governance integration begins with board oversight. The auditor ensures that the board receives periodic updates on cyber risk posture, investment priorities, and major incidents. Clear reporting lines between the CISO, CIO, and risk committees enable informed decision-making.

Enterprise risk management (ERM) frameworks must incorporate information security risks alongside financial, operational, and reputational risks. The IS auditor confirms that risk appetite statements define acceptable exposure levels for cyber threats and that mitigation strategies align with business tolerance.

Security should also support innovation rather than constrain it. The auditor examines whether governance structures promote collaboration between security, IT, and business units during digital transformation projects. Security-by-design principles must be embedded into project governance, ensuring risk controls are included early in system lifecycles.

Integration extends to vendor management, legal compliance, and human resources. Governance must ensure that third-party contracts include security clauses, privacy obligations, and audit rights. Security awareness and ethical conduct are reinforced through HR onboarding and performance evaluation processes.

The IS auditor evaluates whether enterprise governance metrics include security KPIs, making protection performance part of organizational success criteria. Mature governance integrates cybersecurity into strategic planning, resource allocation, and culture, creating a resilient and trusted organization.

Strategic Security Planning and Investment Governance

Long-term protection of information assets requires forward-looking planning and sustainable investment. The IS auditor reviews whether security budgeting and prioritization processes align with risk-based decision-making and measurable outcomes.

Governance demands that security initiatives undergo cost-benefit analysis, linking proposed controls to specific risk reductions or compliance requirements. The auditor ensures that budgets cover not only technology but also training, incident response, and continuous improvement.

The IS auditor assesses whether investment governance includes lifecycle management for security tools—procurement, maintenance, review, and decommissioning. Tools that no longer align with current threats or business needs must be retired responsibly.

Periodic strategic reviews assess whether security spending remains aligned with organizational growth and technological change. Governance committees should evaluate performance indicators such as reduced incident frequency, improved recovery times, or audit findings closure rates.

The auditor also verifies whether innovation budgets support emerging technology evaluations and pilot programs, ensuring proactive adaptation to future risks. Transparent prioritization, measurable benefits, and executive sponsorship define mature investment governance.

Chapter 6: Practice Questions

Question (1-100)

Q1. Which of the following best describes the main purpose of an IS audit?

A. Detect fraud within financial systems

B. Evaluate compliance with security policies

C. Assess whether information systems safeguard assets and maintain data integrity

D. Verify user satisfaction with IT services

Q2. Which of the following steps should be performed first when planning an IS audit?

A. Identify the audit universe

B. Define the audit objectives

C. Develop audit programs

D. Gather evidence

Q3. The most important reason to use risk-based audit planning is to:

A. Ensure all systems are reviewed annually

B. Comply with ISACA audit standards

C. Focus audit resources on areas of highest impact

D. Reduce total audit cost

Q4. Which of the following best defines audit risk?

A. The risk that controls will fail

B. The risk that the auditor gives an incorrect opinion

C. The risk that management overrides controls

D. The inherent risk in information systems

Q5. When using Computer-Assisted Audit Techniques (CAATs), the auditor should first:

A. Verify the reliability of data

B. Design test scripts

C. Run the analysis

D. Prepare a report

Q6. What is the main advantage of using Computer-Assisted Audit Techniques (CAATs) during audit testing?

A. They eliminate the need for manual checks

B. They allow 100 percent testing of data populations

C. They ensure compliance with audit standards

D. They reduce sampling errors

Q7. Which audit documentation provides the primary support for audit findings and conclusions?

A. Audit program

B. Management letter

C. Audit charter

D. Work papers

Q8. The IS audit function's independence is best achieved when it:

A. Reports directly to the CIO

B. Reports to the board or audit committee

C. Reports to IT management

D. Reports to external auditors

Q9. An IS auditor finds evidence of fraud. The auditor's first course of action should be to:

A. Suspend the audit

B. Inform senior management immediately

C. Collect sufficient evidence to substantiate the finding

D. Report directly to law enforcement

Q10. Which of the following types of audit evidence provides the strongest support?

A. Verbal statements from employees
B. System-generated logs
C. Direct observation by the auditor
D. Copies of management reports

Q11. Which ISACA standard mandates due professional care in audit work?

A. Standard 1202
B. Standard 1001
C. Standard 1401
D. Standard 2201

Q12. The IS auditor's use of sampling is primarily intended to:

A. Increase audit efficiency
B. Eliminate the need for CAATs
C. Reduce audit scope
D. Avoid substantive testing

Q13. Which of the following is most essential when developing an audit program?

A. Understanding business processes and risks
B. Availability of audit staff
C. Input from IT management
D. Prior audit results

Q14. An IS auditor performing a post-implementation review should focus primarily on:

A. Project budgeting accuracy
B. System uptime metrics
C. Achievement of business objectives
D. User training effectiveness

Q15. During an IS audit, what ensures that the auditor's work is repeatable and traceable?

A. Supervision notes
B. Work paper documentation standards
C. Management review
D. Quality assurance checklists

Q16. Which is the best control to ensure independence of the IS audit function?

A. Annual rotation of audit staff
B. Audit charter approved by the board
C. Internal policy signed by the CIO
D. Peer reviews by IT teams

Q17. When testing automated controls, the auditor should place greatest reliance on:

A. Evidence from re-performance
B. Inquiry of system users
C. Review of system documentation
D. Inspection of access logs

Q18. In determining materiality for an IS audit, the auditor should primarily consider:

A. Total asset value
B. Potential impact on business objectives
C. Size of IT department
D. Number of systems affected

Q19. Which of the following should be included in the audit closing meeting?

A. Discussion of unresolved findings

B. Approval of audit objectives
C. Assignment of new audits
D. Review of audit charter

Q20. The primary purpose of audit follow-up activities is to:

A. Reassess audit scope
B. Ensure corrective actions are implemented
C. Evaluate audit staff performance
D. Recalculate risk ratings

Q21. Which of the following provides the best evidence that audit findings are being addressed appropriately by management?

A. Verbal confirmation from process owners
B. Signed management responses in the audit report
C. Evidence of corrective actions implemented
D. An updated audit plan

Q22. Which of the following would be the most effective way for an IS auditor to verify that a security control is functioning as intended?

A. Review security policy documentation
B. Interview IT security personnel
C. Perform an independent test of the control
D. Review previous audit reports

Q23. Which of the following should be the IS auditor's primary consideration when evaluating audit evidence?

A. The cost of obtaining the evidence
B. The relevance and reliability of the evidence
C. The volume of evidence collected
D. The timing of evidence collection

Q24. When assessing the adequacy of IT governance, the IS auditor should primarily determine whether:

A. IT goals align with business objectives
B. IT management reports to the CIO
C. IT policies are documented and approved
D. Project budgets are within limits

Q25. The IS auditor is reviewing audit logs and discovers gaps in system activity. What should the auditor do first?

A. Report the issue immediately to management
B. Determine the cause and potential impact of the gaps
C. Recommend implementing a new logging tool
D. Reperform tests using alternative logs

Q26. An IS auditor notes that user access reviews are not being conducted periodically. What should be the auditor's primary concern?

A. Reduced efficiency in IT operations
B. Poor documentation practices
C. Increased risk of unauthorized access
D. Delays in application updates

Q27. Which of the following would provide the best assurance that backup data can be restored successfully?

A. Reviewing backup logs
B. Performing test restores periodically

C. Verifying backup schedules
D. Checking storage capacity

Q28. When evaluating segregation of duties within IT operations, the IS auditor's primary objective is to ensure that:

A. Efficiency in workflow is maximized
B. No single individual can both initiate and approve a transaction
C. Each employee has backup responsibilities
D. IT management performs periodic reviews

Q29. Which of the following is the most effective control to ensure the integrity of audit evidence stored electronically?

A. Restricting access rights to audit files
B. Maintaining paper copies of all evidence
C. Using encrypted storage with access logs
D. Storing evidence on the auditor's local drive

Q30. An IS auditor is reviewing the effectiveness of incident response procedures. Which of the following provides the best evidence of their adequacy?

A. Documentation of response steps
B. Results from recent incident simulations or drills
C. Existence of an incident response policy
D. Management approval of procedures

Q31. During an audit of IT change management, which finding should be of the greatest concern to the IS auditor?

A. Lack of documented approval for emergency changes
B. Missing version control labels on source code
C. Developers performing user acceptance testing
D. Incomplete post-implementation review forms

Q32. Which of the following is the best indicator that an internal audit function adheres to ISACA's IS Audit and Assurance Standards?

A. Regular quality reviews of audit work
B. Management satisfaction with audit results
C. Absence of audit findings in prior reports
D. Low audit turnover rates

Q33. When an IS auditor uses sampling to test transactions, the reliability of results is most dependent on:

A. The use of automated audit tools
B. The size and randomness of the sample
C. The auditor's experience
D. The volume of total transactions

Q34. Which of the following should the IS auditor review to verify that audit recommendations have been effectively implemented?

A. Updated policies and procedures
B. Evidence of corrected control deficiencies
C. Revised audit charter
D. Staff training records

Q35. The IS auditor's main objective in evaluating audit trails is to determine whether they:

A. Are retained for at least one year
B. Can support forensic investigations
C. Provide sufficient information to trace transactions

D. Are reviewed by management

Q36. Which of the following should an IS auditor consider most critical when evaluating audit scope?

A. Available audit staff

B. Time constraints

C. Organizational risk assessment results

D. Management expectations

Q37. An IS auditor discovers that system logs are not regularly reviewed. What is the potential risk?

A. Excessive system downtime

B. Unnoticed security incidents

C. Inefficient resource utilization

D. Delay in software upgrades

Q38. When performing an IS audit, which of the following should be the auditor's highest priority?

A. Identifying process improvements

B. Detecting control weaknesses that pose business risk

C. Verifying user satisfaction with IT services

D. Ensuring all audit procedures are followed exactly

Q39. Which of the following actions would best help maintain audit quality across engagements?

A. Using standard audit work paper templates

B. Conducting staff performance evaluations

C. Rotating audit staff annually

D. Increasing audit sample sizes

Q40. What is the primary benefit of maintaining an audit risk assessment on an ongoing basis?

A. It reduces the total number of audits required annually

B. It allows dynamic prioritization of audits as risks evolve

C. It ensures every system is audited at least once a year

D. It fulfills ISACA compliance requirements

Q41. Which of the following best ensures the credibility of audit findings?

A. Management review of the audit report

B. Evidence supported by sufficient documentation

C. Auditor experience with similar audits

D. Agreement with auditees on findings

Q42. Which of the following would most likely indicate a weakness in the IS audit function?

A. Audit recommendations are not implemented

B. Audit scope is approved by senior management

C. Audit results are communicated timely

D. Audit work follows ISACA standards

Q43. What is the most important reason for maintaining detailed audit documentation?

A. It supports future training for new auditors

B. It provides evidence of compliance with standards

C. It allows external reviewers to replicate audit work

D. It serves as historical reference for similar audits

Q44. Which of the following provides the best assurance that audit tools and techniques are producing accurate results?

A. Performing tool validation and control testing

B. Using tools approved by management

C. Using tools with recent vendor updates

D. Comparing results with those of external auditors

Q45. Which of the following should an IS auditor review to ensure effective monitoring of critical IT processes?
A. Service level agreements and related performance metrics
B. Organizational charts and job descriptions
C. Change management request forms
D. Disaster recovery policy documents
Q46. Which of the following is the best way for an IS auditor to confirm that controls are operating effectively?
A. Conduct interviews with control owners
B. Perform re-performance or observation testing
C. Review control design documentation
D. Analyze internal audit reports
Q47. Which of the following would most likely reduce the reliability of an audit conclusion?
A. Incomplete evidence collection
B. Minor documentation errors
C. Extended audit duration
D. Rotation of audit staff
Q48. Which of the following should an IS auditor review to ensure that the audit plan aligns with enterprise goals?
A. Strategic IT plan
B. Audit budget
C. IT organizational structure
D. IT user satisfaction surveys
Q49. When developing an annual audit plan, the most important input for prioritizing audit engagements is:
A. Management's concerns
B. Results of the enterprise risk assessment
C. Availability of audit resources
D. Last year's audit findings
Q50. Which of the following should be the IS auditor's primary concern when reviewing the audit universe?
A. That it covers all auditable areas within the enterprise
B. That it is approved by senior management
C. That it includes only IT processes
D. That it aligns with financial audit schedules
Q51. Which of the following factors most affects the reliability of evidence obtained through observation?
A. The auditor's experience
B. The presence of the auditee during observation
C. The timing and frequency of the observation
D. The use of observation checklists
Q52. Which of the following is the most important element of an effective audit follow-up process?
A. Formal tracking and reporting of corrective actions
B. Regular rotation of follow-up auditors
C. Communication of unresolved issues to IT management
D. Archiving of audit work papers
Q53. Which of the following conditions would be most significant when evaluating IT audit resource needs?

A. The frequency of IT system changes
B. The size of the organization
C. The skill levels required for specialized audits
D. The cost of external consultants

Q54. What is the main benefit of an IS audit charter?
A. It defines the audit methodology in detail
B. It provides authority and independence to the audit function
C. It describes the organization's IT risk appetite
D. It establishes audit report formats

Q55. Which of the following factors should an IS auditor consider first when determining the frequency of audits for a specific system?
A. The system's financial importance
B. The level of risk associated with the system
C. The age of the system
D. The number of users

Q56. When evaluating audit evidence gathered through interviews, the IS auditor should primarily:
A. Give full weight to responses from senior management
B. Treat responses as supporting information requiring corroboration
C. Disregard them if they conflict with documentation
D. Consider them more reliable than automated data

Q57. Which of the following would be the most effective method for an IS auditor to identify unauthorized program changes?
A. Reviewing change management logs and approvals
B. Interviewing development staff
C. Examining application user manuals
D. Reviewing IT policies

Q58. Which of the following provides the greatest assurance that an IS audit function is meeting its objectives?
A. Positive feedback from auditees
B. Periodic external quality assessments
C. Reduced number of audit findings
D. Timely completion of audit plans

Q59. An IS auditor is preparing to audit a new enterprise resource planning (ERP) system. Which of the following should be reviewed first?
A. User access control settings
B. Change management procedures
C. Business process documentation
D. Application interface controls

Q60. Which of the following is the best evidence that an IS audit engagement was conducted according to professional standards?
A. Management's acceptance of audit findings
B. Existence of approved audit programs and signed work papers
C. Positive results from a follow-up audit
D. An absence of auditor errors in the final report

Q61. Which of the following best describes the primary objective of IT governance?
A. To ensure IT investments are cost-efficient
B. To align IT strategy with business objectives
C. To centralize control over IT decision-making

D. To standardize IT operational procedures

Q62. An IS auditor reviewing IT governance should be most concerned if:

A. The CIO attends board meetings only quarterly
B. The IT steering committee meets biannually
C. IT policies have not been updated in six months
D. IT objectives are not linked to strategic business goals

Q63. Which of the following is the best indicator of effective IT governance?

A. High IT project success rates
B. Clear accountability for IT risk and performance
C. Regular audits of IT systems
D. Frequent board reports on IT budgets

Q64. When reviewing an organization's IT steering committee, an IS auditor should be most concerned if:

A. Meeting minutes are not formally approved
B. Business representation is minimal compared to IT staff
C. The committee uses informal communication
D. The CIO chairs the committee

Q65. Which of the following roles should be responsible for approving IT policies?

A. IT management
B. The IT steering committee
C. The board of directors or equivalent governance body
D. The audit committee

Q66. Which of the following would best demonstrate management's commitment to effective IT governance?

A. Allocating sufficient funding for IT projects
B. Establishing and enforcing IT performance metrics
C. Conducting periodic IT risk assessments
D. Creating detailed IT policies and procedures

Q67. The IS auditor is assessing IT risk management practices. Which of the following would be the strongest indicator of maturity?

A. Reactive handling of incidents as they occur
B. Annual risk assessments conducted by external consultants
C. Continuous risk monitoring integrated into business processes
D. Separate risk registers for each department

Q68. Which of the following is the primary purpose of an IT strategy committee?

A. To approve project budgets
B. To provide oversight and direction for IT strategy
C. To review technical issues with IT operations
D. To evaluate post-implementation reviews

Q69. Which of the following best helps ensure IT delivers value to the business?

A. Implementing a chargeback model
B. Adopting a formal IT governance framework
C. Maintaining a centralized IT department
D. Reducing technology costs

Q70. Which of the following provides the most objective measure of IT governance effectiveness?

A. Employee satisfaction surveys
B. Benchmarking IT performance against peers
C. Internal management opinion reports

D. Reduction in IT audit findings

Q71. An IS auditor finds that IT risk management and enterprise risk management (ERM) are separate with minimal coordination. What should be the auditor's main concern?

A. Duplication of risk registers
B. Inefficient use of IT resources
C. Misalignment between IT and business risk priorities
D. Reduced documentation of mitigation actions

Q72. Which of the following best indicates that IT governance is operating effectively?

A. IT and business leaders jointly define project priorities
B. IT budget variances are less than 5 percent
C. The CIO prepares quarterly reports for the board
D. There is no backlog of IT projects

Q73. Which of the following is the best indicator that IT value delivery processes are effective?

A. Increased IT project approval rate
B. Achievement of key performance targets for IT services
C. Frequent changes in IT leadership
D. Reduction in IT operational costs

Q74. Which of the following most effectively supports governance of enterprise IT?

A. A well-defined IT organizational structure
B. A centralized IT help desk
C. A distributed development team
D. An informal risk communication network

Q75. The IS auditor is assessing IT policy management. Which issue would be most concerning?

A. Policies are reviewed every 18 months instead of annually
B. Policies are not approved by senior management
C. Policies contain references to multiple standards
D. Policies are written in highly technical language

Q76. Which of the following would provide the best evidence that IT governance practices are integrated into enterprise governance?

A. IT key performance indicators are part of the enterprise scorecard
B. IT management reports directly to the CIO
C. IT steering committee meets monthly
D. The board receives quarterly IT financial updates

Q77. When evaluating IT governance effectiveness, which of the following should an IS auditor assess first?

A. The maturity of IT management processes
B. The alignment of IT goals with enterprise strategy
C. The frequency of IT audits
D. The size of the IT governance committee

Q78. Which of the following demonstrates effective IT resource management within governance practices?

A. Maintaining a skills inventory and capacity management plan
B. Outsourcing all IT functions to reduce cost
C. Reducing IT staff turnover through bonuses
D. Implementing a strict change approval process

Q79. Which of the following is the most appropriate role for the board of directors in IT governance?

A. Approving the IT budget
B. Overseeing IT risk management and strategic alignment

C. Managing daily IT operations
D. Authorizing user access privileges

Q80. Which of the following is the primary purpose of COBIT within IT governance?
A. To define IT organizational structures
B. To provide a framework for aligning IT goals with business objectives
C. To establish performance-based pay for IT staff
D. To prescribe technical configurations for IT systems

Q81. Which of the following provides the strongest evidence of effective IT performance management?
A. IT projects consistently meet their deadlines
B. IT staff receive annual performance reviews
C. Performance metrics are tied to business outcomes
D. Help desk response times are within service targets

Q82. The IS auditor is reviewing an organization's IT governance model and notes that risk management responsibilities are not clearly assigned. What is the most significant risk?
A. Inefficient resource utilization
B. Inconsistent handling of IT risks across departments
C. Increased IT operating costs
D. Reduced management reporting frequency

Q83. Which of the following best demonstrates management's accountability for IT governance outcomes?
A. Documented IT governance policies
B. Inclusion of IT performance metrics in executive scorecards
C. Annual IT policy reviews by the CIO
D. Appointment of a steering committee chair

Q84. Which of the following would be the most concerning finding during a review of IT strategic planning?
A. The IT plan does not reference specific performance indicators
B. The IT plan is reviewed every two years
C. The IT plan includes budget estimates for three years
D. The IT plan references multiple frameworks

Q85. Which of the following is the primary purpose of an IT balanced scorecard?
A. To evaluate IT personnel performance
B. To measure IT's contribution to business goals
C. To track help desk performance trends
D. To document IT audit results

Q86. The IS auditor observes that IT risk reporting is handled only within the IT department. What is the main governance concern?
A. Incomplete alignment of IT risks with enterprise risks
B. Inefficient IT reporting structure
C. Lack of technical expertise in risk management
D. Duplication of reporting at multiple levels

Q87. Which of the following is the best indicator of effective IT portfolio management?
A. Projects are prioritized based on business value and risk
B. The IT department meets its budget annually
C. The number of ongoing projects remains constant
D. Project sponsors are assigned for every initiative

Q88. Which of the following most effectively promotes IT governance awareness across the enterprise?
A. Annual IT risk training for all staff
B. Publication of IT policies on the intranet
C. Regular communication of governance objectives and metrics
D. Formal IT committee meeting minutes
Q89. Which of the following best ensures that IT governance processes remain relevant over time?
A. Conducting regular governance maturity assessments
B. Rotating IT leadership every three years
C. Aligning IT strategy to emerging technology trends
D. Increasing IT audit frequency
Q90. Which of the following is most critical to ensure IT policies are effectively implemented?
A. Management approval of the policies
B. Regular policy awareness and training programs
C. Inclusion of policies in the employee handbook
D. Audit verification of policy compliance
Q91. Which of the following should be of greatest concern to an IS auditor reviewing IT strategic planning?
A. The IT plan focuses primarily on technology upgrades
B. The plan includes goals aligned with business strategy
C. The IT plan is reviewed by both business and IT leaders
D. The IT plan incorporates risk assessments
Q92. Which of the following best ensures that IT projects support enterprise strategy?
A. Approval by the IT steering committee
B. Linkage of project objectives to strategic business goals
C. Regular project cost-benefit analyses
D. Adoption of an agile project management approach
Q93. Which of the following would be the most important metric for measuring the success of IT governance implementation?
A. Reduction in the number of IT incidents
B. Increased business satisfaction with IT services
C. Percentage of IT projects delivering expected business benefits
D. Reduction in IT operational costs
Q94. Which of the following roles is primarily responsible for monitoring IT governance effectiveness?
A. Chief Information Officer (CIO)
B. Chief Executive Officer (CEO)
C. Internal audit
D. IT steering committee
Q95. Which of the following would provide the most reliable evidence of IT governance alignment with corporate strategy?
A. Inclusion of IT goals in the corporate balanced scorecard
B. Quarterly IT performance reports
C. Regular internal audit assessments
D. Management's approval of IT budgets
Q96. An IS auditor finds that IT risk reports are prepared but not reviewed by business management. What is the most significant implication?
A. IT may not receive adequate budget allocations
B. IT risks may not be properly integrated into enterprise risk decisions

C. The IT department is not following reporting procedures
D. The risk register may become outdated

Q97. Which of the following is the most important factor in defining IT performance metrics?

A. Alignment with business goals
B. Benchmark comparison data
C. Availability of reporting tools
D. Industry best practices

Q98. Which of the following governance issues poses the greatest risk to IT strategic alignment?

A. Frequent turnover in IT management
B. Lack of a documented IT strategic plan
C. Inconsistent use of project management tools
D. Absence of an IT audit committee

Q99. Which of the following would best help ensure IT risk management supports enterprise risk management (ERM)?

A. Joint risk workshops involving business and IT
B. Regular updates to IT risk registers
C. Separate risk committees for IT and business
D. IT management review of risk dashboards

Q100. Which of the following is the most significant indicator of strong IT governance maturity?

A. Defined accountability for IT-related decisions
B. Minimal IT budget variances year over year
C. Stable IT organizational structure
D. Increased number of IT audits completed

Answer Key and Explanation (1-100)

Q1. Answer: C

Explanation: The main purpose of an IS audit is to assess whether information systems safeguard assets, maintain data integrity, and support organizational objectives, ensuring controls effectively mitigate risk and that information is reliable for decision-making. Option A is incorrect because fraud detection is incidental and falls within forensic auditing, not the broader assurance scope of IS auditing. Option B is too narrow as compliance checks are only one component of a comprehensive IS audit. Option D is irrelevant because user satisfaction is a service management goal, not an assurance objective of IS auditing.

Q2. Answer: B

Explanation: Defining audit objectives is the first and most critical step because it establishes the audit's purpose, scope, and focus, ensuring resources are directed to high-risk areas aligned with organizational goals. Option A refers to identifying the audit universe, which is part of annual planning rather than an individual engagement. Option C is incorrect because audit programs are developed after the objectives have been set. Option D is premature since evidence gathering belongs to the execution phase, not the planning phase.

Q3. Answer: C

Explanation: Risk-based audit planning focuses limited audit resources on processes and systems with the highest potential impact on business objectives, improving assurance value and efficiency. Option A is incorrect because reviewing all systems annually ignores varying risk levels and is not resource-efficient. Option B misstates the rationale since compliance with standards is expected but not the primary driver of risk-based planning. Option D is secondary because while cost efficiency may result, the purpose is to align audit priorities with risk exposure, not to reduce expense.

Q4. Answer: B

Explanation: Audit risk refers to the possibility that an auditor expresses an inappropriate opinion when material misstatements or control deficiencies exist, resulting from a combination of inherent, control, and detection risks. Option A is incorrect because it represents only control risk, one component of audit risk. Option C describes a cause of control failure rather than audit risk itself. Option D represents inherent risk, another component, but it does not encompass the full definition of audit risk.

Q5. Answer: A

Explanation: The auditor should first verify that the data used for CAATs is accurate, complete, and reliable to ensure that any analysis produces valid results and conclusions. Option B is incorrect because designing test scripts occurs after confirming data reliability; otherwise, tests may be irrelevant or flawed. Option C is also incorrect since running the analysis before verification could lead to misleading or invalid results. Option D is premature because reporting occurs only after evidence has been gathered, analyzed, and validated.

Q6. Answer: B

Explanation: The main advantage of CAATs is that they allow the auditor to test entire data populations rather than relying solely on samples, providing more comprehensive assurance and accuracy in identifying control weaknesses. Option A is incorrect because manual procedures are still required for qualitative judgments and verifying control design. Option C is incorrect since CAATs support audit work but do not by themselves ensure compliance with standards. Option D, while partially true, is secondary because minimizing sampling error is a benefit of broader testing, not its primary objective.

Q7. Answer: D

Explanation: Work papers are the primary documentation supporting audit findings and conclusions as they contain the evidence, analyses, and rationale that validate results and demonstrate due professional care. Option A is incorrect because the audit program only lists planned audit steps but does not contain evidence. Option C is wrong since the audit charter defines authority and responsibility but does not substantiate individual findings. Option B is a summary communication to management and relies on work papers for factual support.

Q8. Answer: B

Explanation: Independence is best achieved when the IS audit function reports directly to the board or audit committee, ensuring objectivity, authority, and freedom from operational influence. Option A is incorrect because reporting to the CIO compromises independence by placing the auditor under IT management control. Option C is similar in that it subjects auditors to potential conflicts of interest when evaluating their supervisors' operations. Option D is incorrect because external auditors are independent entities, not an internal reporting channel for the IS audit function.

Q9. Answer: C

Explanation: The auditor should first collect and document sufficient, relevant evidence to substantiate the suspected fraud before escalating it to management, ensuring that conclusions are based on facts rather than assumptions. Option A is incorrect because halting the audit prematurely could interrupt evidence gathering. Option B is inappropriate until evidence has been verified, as premature reporting may lead to false allegations. Option D is incorrect because auditors must follow internal escalation procedures before contacting external authorities.

Q10. Answer: C

Explanation: Direct observation by the auditor provides the most reliable form of evidence because it is firsthand and cannot easily be manipulated, ensuring objective verification of control operation. Option A is weakest as verbal statements are subjective and not independently verifiable. Option B, while stronger, may be altered without proper controls and therefore requires validation. Option D is less reliable because management-generated reports could be biased or incomplete.

Q11. Answer: A

Explanation: ISACA Standard 1202 specifically requires auditors to exercise due professional care, applying diligence, competence, and judgment in all audit engagements to maintain quality and credibility. Option B is incorrect because Standard 1001 defines the purpose and scope of IS audit standards but does not address care. Option C refers to follow-up activities rather than performance standards. Option D is associated with audit planning, not professional care.

Q12. Answer: A

Explanation: Sampling is used to enhance audit efficiency by allowing auditors to draw reasonable conclusions about large data sets without testing every transaction, balancing assurance quality with time and cost constraints. Option B is incorrect because sampling and CAATs are complementary techniques, not substitutes. Option C is wrong because sampling does not reduce audit scope; it helps manage workload within that scope. Option D is incorrect since sampling often supports substantive testing rather than replaces it.

Q13. Answer: A

Explanation: Understanding business processes and related risks is fundamental to designing an effective audit program that targets key control areas and delivers relevant assurance. Option B is incorrect because staffing considerations affect scheduling, not program content. Option C provides valuable insight but cannot replace risk-based knowledge. Option D can guide focus areas but is secondary to a current risk assessment of business processes.

Q14. Answer: C

Explanation: The auditor's main focus during a post-implementation review is assessing whether the system meets its intended business objectives and delivers the expected value to the organization. Option A is incorrect because budget accuracy is a project management issue, not an audit goal. Option B, though relevant to operations, does not measure effectiveness in achieving strategic outcomes. Option D, while useful, is a training metric rather than a success indicator for the system itself.

Q15. Answer: B

Explanation: Work paper documentation standards ensure that audit procedures, evidence, and conclusions are clearly recorded, enabling another auditor to reproduce and verify the work performed. Option A is incorrect because supervision notes assist guidance but do not ensure full traceability. Option C represents external oversight, not internal audit traceability. Option D helps with consistency but cannot replace detailed documentation standards.

Q16. Answer: B

Explanation: A board-approved audit charter formally defines the IS audit function's purpose, authority, and independence, ensuring auditors operate free from management influence. Option A improves objectivity but does not guarantee structural independence. Option C undermines independence by placing control under IT management. Option D is inappropriate because IT peer reviews compromise impartiality.

Q17. Answer: A

Explanation: Re-performance provides the most reliable evidence when testing automated controls because it directly validates system functionality and control execution. Option B is incorrect since user inquiry offers subjective information. Option C is limited as documentation describes but does not prove control operation. Option D is supportive evidence but not conclusive by itself.

Q18. Answer: B

Explanation: Materiality is based on the potential impact an issue could have on business objectives, not just monetary value or operational size, ensuring findings are evaluated in a strategic context. Option A is too narrow since asset value alone does not capture risk implications. Option C is irrelevant because department size has no bearing on materiality. Option D may influence scope but not the material significance of findings.

Q19. Answer: A

Explanation: The closing meeting should include a discussion of unresolved findings and agreed-upon next steps to ensure management understands outstanding issues and corrective action plans. Option B is incorrect since audit objectives are defined during planning, not closing. Option C is unrelated and handled in audit scheduling. Option D is not relevant to closing discussions as the charter governs overall audit authority, not engagement details.

Q20. Answer: B

Explanation: The main goal of follow-up activities is to verify that management has implemented corrective actions to address previously identified audit findings, thereby reducing residual risk. Option A is incorrect because scope reassessment belongs to planning for future audits. Option C is a management function unrelated to follow-up objectives. Option D may occur later but is not the purpose of the follow-up itself.

Q21. Answer: C

Explanation: The most reliable evidence that audit findings are being addressed is the existence of documented corrective actions that have been implemented and verified, demonstrating that management has effectively mitigated the identified risks. Option A is unreliable because verbal confirmation lacks supporting proof. Option B indicates acknowledgment but not actual resolution. Option D relates to future planning rather than direct evidence of remediation.

Q22. Answer: C

Explanation: Performing an independent test of the control provides direct and objective assurance that the control operates as intended, validating both its design and effectiveness. Option A is incorrect because reviewing documentation only confirms design, not operation. Option B provides insight but is subjective and may be biased. Option D can offer context but relies on historical information that may be outdated.

Q23. Answer: B

Explanation: The auditor should focus on the relevance and reliability of audit evidence to ensure conclusions are supported by valid, objective data that aligns with the audit objectives. Option A is incorrect because cost should not outweigh the need for credible assurance. Option C emphasizes quantity over quality, which may lead to misleading results. Option D is a procedural factor but secondary to evidence quality.

Q24. Answer: A

Explanation: The auditor's key focus in evaluating IT governance is verifying that IT goals align with and support the organization's overall business objectives, ensuring that technology enables strategic outcomes. Option B is incorrect because reporting lines alone do not demonstrate governance effectiveness. Option C is supportive but insufficient without alignment evidence. Option D is operational and not directly indicative of governance adequacy.

Q25. Answer: B

Explanation: The auditor should first investigate and determine the cause and impact of the missing log data to assess whether it represents a control weakness, system failure, or deliberate manipulation. Option A is premature since reporting without analysis may create unnecessary concern. Option C may be appropriate later but only after the cause is known. Option D is an investigative step but should follow root-cause determination.

Q26. Answer: C

Explanation: The absence of periodic user access reviews heightens the risk of unauthorized access and potential data breaches, undermining control over sensitive systems. Option A is incorrect because operational efficiency is less critical than security in this context. Option B, while true, is a secondary documentation issue. Option D is unrelated to access management controls.

Q27. Answer: B

Explanation: Performing periodic test restores is the only way to confirm that backups can be successfully recovered and that both data integrity and system restoration procedures work as intended. Option A is incorrect because reviewing backup logs only confirms completion, not recoverability. Option C verifies process scheduling but not functionality. Option D relates to resource management, not assurance of restoration capability.

Q28. Answer: B

Explanation: The goal of segregation of duties is to prevent fraud and error by ensuring no individual has end-to-end control over a process, such as both initiating and approving a transaction. Option A is incorrect because efficiency is not the primary concern in control design. Option C is more about continuity planning than segregation. Option D, while good practice, is a monitoring activity rather than a preventive control principle.

Q29. Answer: C

Explanation: Using encrypted storage combined with detailed access logging provides strong assurance that electronic audit evidence remains secure, unaltered, and traceable. Option A offers basic protection but lacks encryption and tracking features. Option B is less efficient and vulnerable to loss or damage. Option D introduces significant risk, as local drives may not have proper security or backups.

Q30. Answer: B

Explanation: Results from recent incident response simulations provide direct evidence of procedural effectiveness by demonstrating how well teams handle real scenarios. Option A shows structure but not performance. Option C indicates that policies exist but not that they are functional. Option D ensures oversight but does not confirm operational adequacy.

Q31. Answer: A

Explanation: Lack of documented approval for emergency changes is most concerning because it creates opportunities for unauthorized or untested changes that can introduce serious system vulnerabilities. Option B represents a procedural issue that affects tracking but not authorization. Option C violates segregation principles but may have compensating controls. Option D reflects administrative weakness but not necessarily risk of immediate impact.

Q32. Answer: A

Explanation: Regular quality reviews ensure that audit work complies with professional standards and that due professional care and consistency are maintained across engagements. Option B is subjective and does not guarantee adherence to standards. Option C may simply indicate inadequate testing rather than quality. Option D relates to staffing, not compliance with audit methodology.

Q33. Answer: B

Explanation: The reliability of audit sampling results depends primarily on selecting an adequately sized and truly random sample to ensure representative conclusions. Option A can assist but cannot replace proper statistical design. Option C contributes to interpretation quality but not sample reliability. Option D impacts calculation of size, not reliability itself.

Q34. Answer: B

Explanation: Reviewing tangible evidence that control deficiencies have been corrected is the most reliable method to confirm implementation and risk mitigation. Option A supports sustainability but does not prove execution. Option C is unrelated to specific findings. Option D shows awareness training but not control effectiveness.

Q35. Answer: C

Explanation: The main purpose of audit trails is to enable transaction tracing and verification from initiation to completion, ensuring accountability and integrity. Option A defines retention policy, not adequacy. Option B is a secondary benefit but not the primary objective. Option D reflects monitoring but not audit trail completeness.

Q36. Answer: C

Explanation: The auditor should base the scope on the organization's risk assessment to ensure that high-risk areas receive sufficient attention and audit coverage. Option A affects logistics, not content. Option B may influence scheduling but cannot dictate scope. Option D is important for alignment but must not override risk priorities.

Q37. Answer: B

Explanation: Failure to review system logs regularly increases the risk that security incidents, policy violations, or unauthorized activities will go undetected, compromising system integrity. Option A could result from unrelated operational issues. Option C concerns performance rather than security. Option D is unrelated to log review.

Q38. Answer: B

Explanation: The auditor's top priority is identifying control weaknesses that pose significant business risks, as addressing them provides the greatest assurance value. Option A is beneficial but secondary. Option C is service-level oriented, not assurance-focused. Option D reflects procedural compliance, which should not outweigh risk significance.

Q39. Answer: A

Explanation: Standardized work paper templates ensure consistency, completeness, and uniform documentation quality across engagements, facilitating review and adherence to standards. Option B is a personnel management activity, not a quality control measure. Option C promotes objectivity but not documentation quality. Option D affects testing depth, not consistency of process.

Q40. Answer: B

Explanation: Maintaining a continuous audit risk assessment enables the auditor to adjust priorities and coverage dynamically as organizational and external risks evolve, improving relevance and responsiveness. Option A may occur incidentally but is not the purpose. Option C is inflexible and not risk-driven. Option D is incorrect because ISACA standards recommend but do not mandate specific frequencies.

Q41. Answer: B
Explanation: Audit findings are credible only when supported by sufficient, relevant, and reliable evidence that can stand independent verification and demonstrates due professional care. Option A ensures oversight but does not establish credibility of the findings themselves. Option C may improve quality but cannot substitute for proper evidence. Option D is not required since findings may be valid even without management agreement.
Q42. Answer: A
Explanation: A consistent lack of implementation of audit recommendations suggests that audit findings are not impactful or actionable, reflecting limited effectiveness of the IS audit function. Option B is normal and part of governance approval. Option C reflects good practice, not a weakness. Option D demonstrates compliance with professional standards and is therefore a strength.
Q43. Answer: C
Explanation: The key purpose of detailed audit documentation is to provide a clear audit trail that enables another qualified professional to replicate and validate the auditor's work and conclusions. Option A is a secondary benefit related to learning. Option B is true but focuses on compliance rather than professional verification. Option D is helpful for reference but not the primary justification for thorough documentation.
Q44. Answer: A
Explanation: Tool validation and control testing confirm that the audit tools function as intended and produce accurate results under controlled conditions, ensuring audit reliability. Option B focuses on administrative approval, not technical accuracy. Option C supports maintenance but does not confirm correct operation. Option D may help comparison but cannot replace direct validation.
Q45. Answer: A
Explanation: Reviewing service level agreements and related performance metrics ensures that critical IT processes are monitored and measured against agreed objectives, providing transparency and accountability. Option B provides context but not monitoring evidence. Option C relates to change control, not process monitoring. Option D focuses on resilience planning rather than operational oversight.
Q46. Answer: B
Explanation: Re-performance or direct observation testing provides firsthand assurance that a control operates as intended, producing reliable and unbiased evidence of effectiveness. Option A yields subjective input that requires verification. Option C confirms design but not operation. Option D may indicate control results but is indirect evidence.
Q47. Answer: A
Explanation: Incomplete evidence collection weakens the audit foundation by preventing the auditor from reaching conclusions supported by sufficient and appropriate information. Option B may require correction but doesn't necessarily affect reliability. Option C affects efficiency, not validity. Option D can improve objectivity rather than diminish it.
Q48. Answer: A
Explanation: Reviewing the strategic IT plan allows the auditor to align audit priorities with organizational goals, ensuring audit activities address key risks to achieving those objectives. Option B is administrative and does not reflect alignment. Option C shows structure but not strategic direction. Option D provides perception data unrelated to alignment.
Q49. Answer: B
Explanation: The enterprise risk assessment provides the most objective and comprehensive view of organizational risk, allowing the auditor to prioritize engagements effectively based on potential business impact. Option A is valuable but subjective. Option C influences scheduling, not priority. Option D may guide planning but reflects past rather than emerging risks.

Q50. Answer: A
Explanation: The audit universe should comprehensively include all auditable areas, processes, and systems within the enterprise to ensure full risk coverage and effective planning. Option B ensures oversight but not completeness. Option C is incorrect because IS audits must integrate both IT and business processes. Option D is irrelevant unless financial dependencies exist.
Q51. Answer: C
Explanation: The reliability of observational evidence depends on observing the process at appropriate times and under normal conditions to ensure accurate representation of control operation. Option A influences interpretation but not reliability. Option B can alter behavior and thus distort results. Option D improves structure but does not ensure valid timing.
Q52. Answer: A
Explanation: A formal tracking and reporting mechanism ensures that corrective actions are monitored until completion and unresolved issues are escalated appropriately, strengthening audit accountability. Option B is procedural and not essential to follow-up effectiveness. Option C is necessary but a step within tracking. Option D is a recordkeeping function unrelated to corrective action management.
Q53. Answer: C
Explanation: The complexity and specialization of audits determine the skill levels required, which directly influences resource planning and competency needs. Option A affects timing but not fundamental capability. Option B is a general factor, not specific to audit scope. Option D relates to budget rather than core resource adequacy.
Q54. Answer: B
Explanation: The IS audit charter formally grants the audit function its authority, independence, and responsibility, allowing auditors to perform their duties objectively and without interference. Option A is incorrect because methodologies are detailed in audit manuals or procedures, not the charter. Option C relates to governance, not audit authorization. Option D concerns administrative presentation, not structural independence.
Q55. Answer: B
Explanation: Audit frequency should be based primarily on risk level, ensuring that high-risk systems receive more frequent and thorough reviews, while low-risk systems are audited less often. Option A is a component of risk but not the sole factor. Option C may affect control maturity but not necessarily risk exposure. Option D influences access considerations but does not dictate audit frequency.
Q56. Answer: B
Explanation: Interview results are considered supporting evidence that must be corroborated through observation, documentation review, or testing to confirm accuracy and reliability. Option A risks bias since authority does not ensure truth. Option C is too dismissive, as contradictions should be investigated. Option D is incorrect because automated or system-based data are generally more reliable than verbal statements.
Q57. Answer: A
Explanation: Reviewing change management logs and approvals directly reveals whether changes were properly authorized, documented, and tested before implementation, making it the most effective detection method. Option B may provide insight but lacks evidence. Option C focuses on documentation that does not reflect real-time changes. Option D outlines procedures but does not confirm execution.
Q58. Answer: B
Explanation: Independent external quality assessments provide objective assurance that the audit function complies with professional standards and effectively meets its goals. Option A is subjective and not a performance measure. Option C could indicate superficial audits rather than success. Option D measures efficiency but not audit effectiveness.
Q59. Answer: C

Explanation: Reviewing business process documentation first helps the auditor understand the system's functional objectives and control requirements, providing a foundation for evaluating the appropriateness of subsequent technical controls. Option A and D are vital but follow understanding of process context. Option B relates to maintenance controls, not initial understanding of system purpose.

Q60. Answer: B

Explanation: Approved audit programs and properly signed work papers demonstrate compliance with professional standards, proper supervision, and execution of planned procedures, providing verifiable proof of adherence. Option A shows cooperation but not conformity with standards. Option C reflects outcome improvement but not process quality. Option D is desirable yet insufficient to evidence standard compliance.

Q61. Answer: B

Explanation: The core goal of IT governance is to align IT strategy with business objectives, ensuring that IT enables the achievement of organizational goals and delivers value while managing risks effectively. Option A focuses only on cost, not alignment. Option C is too restrictive and may conflict with decentralized models. Option D pertains to IT management practices, not governance alignment.

Q62. Answer: D

Explanation: The absence of linkage between IT and business goals indicates a fundamental governance weakness, as IT may deliver outputs misaligned with strategic needs. Option A is less critical as board interaction frequency may vary. Option C reflects maintenance issues, not strategic failure. Option B is procedural but does not necessarily impair alignment.

Q63. Answer: B

Explanation: Clear accountability for IT risk and performance demonstrates that governance mechanisms define responsibility and oversight for IT outcomes. Option A measures success but may lack governance structure. Option C is a control activity, not governance evidence. Option D shows financial oversight but not holistic accountability.

Q64. Answer: B

Explanation: Limited business representation reduces the committee's ability to ensure IT initiatives align with strategic objectives, undermining governance balance. Option A is procedural and does not directly affect governance quality. Option C may affect documentation but not structure. Option D is acceptable if the committee maintains business oversight and accountability.

Q65. Answer: C

Explanation: The board or equivalent governance body should approve IT policies to ensure alignment with enterprise strategy and accountability for IT-related risks. Option A may draft policies but lacks governing authority. Option B advises on strategy but does not hold formal approval power. Option D oversees assurance, not policy creation.

Q66. Answer: B

Explanation: Implementing and enforcing IT performance metrics demonstrates that management actively monitors outcomes, ensuring IT delivers value and supports strategic objectives. Option A shows support but not governance. Option C is necessary but tactical. Option D is procedural rather than performance-driven.

Q67. Answer: C

Explanation: Integrating continuous risk monitoring into business processes reflects mature risk management that is proactive and embedded in operations. Option A is ad hoc and immature. Option B shows periodic attention but lacks integration. Option D causes fragmentation and reduces enterprise-wide visibility.

Q68. Answer: B

Explanation: The IT strategy committee provides oversight and direction to ensure IT strategy aligns with enterprise goals and delivers value through governance structures. Option A is a management task.

Option C is too operational for a strategic body. Option D is part of audit or performance management, not strategic direction.

Q69. Answer: B

Explanation: A formal IT governance framework, such as COBIT, ensures that IT investments, performance, and risks are managed systematically to deliver business value. Option A helps with cost transparency but not governance. Option C is structural, not strategic. Option D may save money but can reduce IT capability if misapplied.

Q70. Answer: B

Explanation: Benchmarking against peer organizations offers objective, quantifiable evidence of governance performance relative to industry standards. Option A is subjective and narrow. Option C lacks independence. Option D may indicate improvement but could also result from reduced audit scope or frequency.

Q71. Answer: C

Explanation: When IT risk management operates independently from ERM, risk priorities may diverge, causing misalignment and potential exposure of critical business processes. Option A is a byproduct, not the core issue. Option B is secondary and operational. Option D may occur but is less significant than strategic misalignment.

Q72. Answer: A

Explanation: Jointly defined project priorities demonstrate strategic alignment between IT and business, ensuring governance decisions reflect enterprise objectives. Option B focuses on financial control, not alignment. Option C reflects communication, not shared governance. Option D may indicate low demand or poor planning, not necessarily effectiveness.

Q73. Answer: B

Explanation: Meeting or exceeding IT performance targets shows that IT services are delivering expected value in alignment with business objectives. Option A may indicate lax approval standards. Option C suggests instability. Option D may be favorable but could come at the expense of service quality.

Q74. Answer: A

Explanation: A clear IT organizational structure with defined roles, responsibilities, and accountability supports effective governance and decision-making. Option B improves operations, not governance. Option C promotes agility but may weaken oversight. Option D lacks formality and control.

Q75. Answer: B

Explanation: The absence of senior management approval undermines the legitimacy and authority of IT policies, indicating weak governance and lack of oversight at the enterprise level. Option A may represent a procedural delay but not a governance failure. Option C could cause minor confusion yet still support compliance. Option D may reduce clarity but does not compromise policy governance.

Q76. Answer: A

Explanation: Including IT key performance indicators in the enterprise scorecard confirms that IT governance is embedded in overall corporate governance and measured alongside business performance. Option B describes reporting structure, not integration. Option C reflects frequency of oversight but not integration. Option D is financial oversight, not strategic alignment.

Q77. Answer: B

Explanation: The starting point for evaluating IT governance is determining whether IT goals are aligned with enterprise strategy, as alignment drives all other governance and management activities. Option A is secondary and focuses on execution. Option C is an audit management detail, not a governance indicator. Option D is administrative and has no direct correlation with effectiveness.

Q78. Answer: A

Explanation: Maintaining a current skills inventory and capacity plan demonstrates proactive management of IT human resources, ensuring that IT capabilities align with strategic needs. Option B prioritizes cost over capability. Option C is beneficial for morale but not a governance measure. Option D relates to change control, not resource governance.

Q79. Answer: B

Explanation: The board's role is to oversee IT risk management and ensure IT strategy supports overall business objectives, providing top-level governance and accountability. Option A is a component of oversight but not the full role. Option C is managerial and operational, outside the board's responsibility. Option D is administrative and far below governance scope.

Q80. Answer: B

Explanation: COBIT provides a comprehensive governance framework that aligns IT goals with business objectives while ensuring effective risk management, resource optimization, and value delivery. Option A is an element but not COBIT's central purpose. Option C relates to HR management, not governance. Option D pertains to technical standards, which COBIT does not define.

Q81. Answer: C

Explanation: Effective IT performance management links IT metrics to business outcomes, demonstrating that IT contributes directly to organizational goals and value delivery. Option A measures timeliness but not value. Option B is an HR process rather than performance management at the enterprise level. Option D is operational and does not reflect strategic performance alignment.

Q82. Answer: B

Explanation: Without clear ownership, IT risk management becomes inconsistent, leading to gaps, duplicated efforts, and potential oversight of critical risks. Option A may result but is less severe than inconsistent treatment. Option C focuses on cost, not risk alignment. Option D affects visibility but not risk mitigation itself.

Q83. Answer: B

Explanation: Including IT performance metrics in executive scorecards makes management directly accountable for IT outcomes and integration with business performance. Option A indicates structure but not accountability. Option C ensures maintenance but not ownership. Option D establishes leadership but not measurable accountability.

Q84. Answer: A

Explanation: The absence of measurable performance indicators prevents tracking progress toward strategic objectives, undermining governance and accountability. Option B may reduce agility but not alignment. Option C is a sound financial planning practice. Option D is not problematic if frameworks are integrated appropriately.

Q85. Answer: B

Explanation: The IT balanced scorecard translates IT objectives into measurable indicators linked to business goals, promoting alignment and value realization. Option A is a human resources function. Option C focuses too narrowly on operations. Option D concerns audit outcomes, not strategic measurement.

Q86. Answer: A

Explanation: When IT risks are reported only within IT, they may not be incorporated into enterprise-level risk assessments, leading to misalignment and potential underestimation of business impact. Option B is procedural, not strategic. Option C concerns skill but not governance. Option D is irrelevant since risk underreporting is the primary issue.

Q87. Answer: A

Explanation: Prioritizing IT projects according to business value and risk ensures optimal allocation of resources and supports governance objectives for value delivery. Option B measures efficiency, not governance quality. Option C may indicate stagnation, not balance. Option D shows accountability but not strategic prioritization.

Q88. Answer: C

Explanation: Continuous communication of governance objectives, roles, and performance metrics builds enterprise-wide awareness and reinforces the importance of IT governance integration. Option A increases awareness but focuses only on risk. Option B ensures accessibility but not understanding. Option D is administrative and limited in audience.

Q89. Answer: A

Explanation: Regular governance maturity assessments enable the organization to evaluate and improve governance structures continuously, keeping them aligned with evolving needs and standards. Option B may harm continuity. Option C supports innovation but not governance effectiveness. Option D focuses on assurance, not governance adaptation.

Q90. Answer: B

Explanation: Policy awareness and training ensure employees understand and apply policies consistently, making them effective in practice. Option A grants authority but not adoption. Option C improves accessibility but not comprehension. Option D is reactive and validates implementation after the fact.

Q91. Answer: A

Explanation: A strategic plan that focuses mainly on technology upgrades reflects a tactical rather than strategic orientation, suggesting that IT investments may not align with business priorities or deliver measurable value. Option B indicates good alignment and is not a concern. Option C shows governance participation and oversight. Option D strengthens planning by addressing risk and therefore supports, not weakens, strategy.

Q92. Answer: B

Explanation: Ensuring that each IT project explicitly links its objectives to the organization's strategic goals provides the strongest assurance of alignment and value contribution. Option A provides oversight but cannot ensure alignment by itself. Option C supports financial justification but not strategic fit. Option D enhances flexibility but does not guarantee strategic connection.

Q93. Answer: C

Explanation: The percentage of IT projects achieving expected business benefits directly measures governance effectiveness by showing that IT investments consistently deliver strategic value. Option A reflects control improvements, not governance success. Option B is a useful perception measure but subjective. Option D may indicate efficiency but could result from budget cuts, not governance maturity.

Q94. Answer: D

Explanation: The IT steering committee oversees and monitors IT governance effectiveness, ensuring that IT objectives align with strategic priorities and that performance is measured and managed. Option A executes governance but does not monitor it independently. Option B provides ultimate accountability but delegates monitoring. Option C evaluates governance as assurance, not as part of ongoing oversight.

Q95. Answer: A

Explanation: Integrating IT goals into the corporate balanced scorecard confirms that IT objectives are explicitly tied to strategic business priorities and monitored through shared performance metrics. Option B provides operational data, not alignment proof. Option C assesses compliance but not alignment directly. Option D ensures funding but not strategic integration.

Q96. Answer: B

Explanation: Without business management review, IT risks remain siloed, preventing holistic enterprise risk management and potentially leading to unmitigated business exposure. Option A is a secondary financial outcome. Option C focuses on compliance, not governance. Option D is an administrative result, not the core governance concern.

Q97. Answer: A

Explanation: Performance metrics must be directly aligned with business goals to ensure that IT performance measurement reflects strategic contribution and relevance. Option B supports context but not purpose. Option C affects execution, not design. Option D guides selection but cannot substitute for alignment with enterprise objectives.

Q98. Answer: B

Explanation: Without a documented IT strategic plan, IT direction becomes fragmented, resulting in projects and initiatives that fail to align with business goals. Option A affects stability but not necessarily alignment. Option C impacts project control, not strategy. Option D affects oversight but is less critical than having no defined plan.

Q99. Answer: A

Explanation: Joint risk workshops involving both business and IT foster shared understanding and integration of IT risk within enterprise risk frameworks, ensuring consistent prioritization and response. Option B focuses on maintenance, not alignment. Option C perpetuates silos rather than integration. Option D provides visibility but not collaboration.

Q100. Answer: A

Explanation: Clear accountability for IT decisions ensures that responsibilities are assigned and enforced across all levels, reflecting mature governance and effective oversight. Option B is financial, not governance-based. Option C may indicate stability but not maturity. Option D reflects audit coverage, not governance capability.

Question (101-200)

Q101. Which of the following best helps ensure that IT delivers value to the business?

A. Establishing clear IT governance objectives
B. Conducting annual IT staff performance reviews
C. Reviewing IT vendor contracts annually
D. Implementing cost-saving measures across IT

Q102. Which of the following would most likely indicate a breakdown in IT governance?

A. IT projects are consistently delivered late and over budget
B. The CIO reports directly to the CEO
C. The organization uses multiple IT governance frameworks
D. IT performance is reviewed monthly by senior management

Q103. Which of the following is the most critical success factor for implementing IT governance?

A. Commitment and involvement from senior management
B. Appointment of a governance framework administrator
C. Regular IT staff communication sessions
D. Adoption of a common software platform

Q104. An IS auditor finds that IT governance responsibilities are shared informally among several departments. What is the key risk?

A. Overlapping duties and duplication of effort
B. Misalignment of IT and business priorities
C. Insufficient IT funding allocations
D. Increased staff turnover in IT departments

Q105. Which of the following should be the IS auditor's main concern when IT strategic objectives are set independently of business objectives?

A. Inconsistent IT performance metrics
B. Increased IT costs without business justification
C. Misalignment resulting in wasted IT investments
D. Limited oversight by executive management

Q106. Which of the following is the primary benefit of integrating IT risk management with enterprise risk management (ERM)?

A. Easier consolidation of risk reports
B. Consistent risk prioritization and mitigation across the enterprise
C. Reduction in audit frequency
D. Improved IT budget planning

Q107. Which of the following should be reviewed first when evaluating IT governance practices?

A. IT policies and standards
B. IT strategic plan
C. IT organization chart
D. IT operating budget

Q108. Which of the following is the most effective way for the board of directors to monitor IT performance?

A. Reviewing IT performance dashboards aligned to key business metrics
B. Approving IT policies annually
C. Receiving quarterly IT expenditure reports
D. Conducting periodic IT staff evaluations

Q109. An IS auditor finds that the IT steering committee meets regularly but does not document decisions. What is the most significant concern?

A. Lack of accountability and traceability for governance actions
B. Inefficient use of committee time
C. Poor attendance from key stakeholders
D. Excessive focus on operational issues

Q110. Which of the following best supports effective IT resource optimization?

A. Periodic reallocation of IT staff to projects
B. Monitoring of IT resource utilization through KPIs
C. Decentralized IT budgeting process
D. Outsourcing non-core IT activities

Q111. Which of the following would be the most reliable indicator that IT governance is delivering expected results?

A. Reduction in audit findings related to IT
B. Achievement of targeted IT value delivery outcomes
C. Decrease in IT operational costs
D. Improved satisfaction ratings from IT employees

Q112. Which of the following should be the IS auditor's main concern if IT governance reporting is based solely on self-assessments by IT management?

A. Reports may lack objectivity and independent verification
B. The cost of governance activities may increase
C. The reporting process may take longer than expected
D. Senior management may not understand technical language

Q113. Which of the following is the best indicator of an organization's IT governance maturity?

A. Existence of an IT governance committee
B. Integration of IT performance management with business performance
C. Periodic IT compliance audits
D. Existence of IT risk policies

Q114. Which of the following should be established first to ensure effective IT governance implementation?

A. Defined roles and responsibilities for IT governance participants
B. Key performance indicators for IT operations
C. A centralized IT budgeting process
D. IT audit and compliance schedules

Q115. Which of the following would most likely improve IT governance communication across the enterprise?

A. Publishing a quarterly IT governance newsletter
B. Mandating IT governance training for new employees
C. Holding cross-functional governance awareness workshops
D. Displaying IT dashboards on the company intranet

Q116. Which of the following best demonstrates effective IT risk governance?

A. Regular updates to the IT risk register
B. Board-level oversight of IT risk exposure and response
C. Annual risk management training sessions
D. Detailed IT incident reporting procedures

Q117. Which of the following would provide the best assurance that IT strategic alignment is effective?

A. All IT projects require a business case and sponsor approval
B. The IT department submits annual strategic reports
C. The CIO presents IT results to the audit committee

D. IT policies are reviewed annually

Q118. An IS auditor reviewing IT governance notes that key performance indicators (KPIs) are not updated for two years. What is the most likely risk?

A. KPIs no longer reflect current strategic priorities
B. Audit effort may increase
C. IT staff may misunderstand policy objectives
D. System configurations may become outdated

Q119. Which of the following is the best method to evaluate IT governance effectiveness objectively?

A. Benchmarking against recognized frameworks such as COBIT
B. Conducting internal surveys among IT users
C. Measuring IT cost reduction percentages
D. Tracking IT service desk performance trends

Q120. Which of the following should be the IS auditor's primary focus when assessing IT governance policies?

A. Whether policies are aligned with business objectives
B. Whether policies are concise and easy to read
C. Whether policies are reviewed semi-annually
D. Whether policies include detailed technical standards

Q121. Which of the following would be the most significant risk if IT governance roles and responsibilities are not clearly defined?

A. Delays in project completion
B. Conflicts and duplication in decision-making
C. Overreliance on external service providers
D. Inadequate documentation of IT procedures

Q122. Which of the following best supports effective IT performance measurement?

A. Establishing key performance indicators linked to business objectives
B. Reviewing IT employee performance annually
C. Conducting monthly financial variance reports
D. Implementing automated monitoring tools

Q123. Which of the following would most likely cause IT governance to fail in achieving its objectives?

A. Lack of board-level involvement in IT oversight
B. Limited use of technology standards
C. Decentralized IT operations
D. Frequent IT policy updates

Q124. An IS auditor finds that IT performance reports are produced but not distributed to business managers. What is the most critical issue?

A. Inefficient use of reporting resources
B. Lack of business awareness of IT value and risk
C. Incomplete audit trail of IT operations
D. Potential duplication of report content

Q125. Which of the following would provide the strongest assurance that IT governance objectives are achieved?

A. Periodic independent governance assessments
B. Annual IT staff performance evaluations
C. Comprehensive IT budgeting procedures
D. Documented escalation protocols for incidents

Q126. Which of the following best demonstrates management accountability in IT governance?

A. Frequent IT staff meetings

B. Regular submission of technical reports to the board
C. Formal assignment of IT performance ownership to business units
D. Existence of detailed IT procedures
Q127. Which of the following would most improve IT governance maturity?
A. Integrating IT performance and risk reporting into enterprise dashboards
B. Establishing separate governance for IT operations
C. Expanding the IT budget to include emerging technologies
D. Increasing the frequency of IT steering committee meetings
Q128. Which of the following would be the best evidence that IT governance is value-driven?
A. Projects are prioritized based on expected business benefits
B. IT expenditures are below the industry average
C. The IT department consistently meets project deadlines
D. The number of open IT issues is decreasing
Q129. Which of the following is the most important requirement for IT governance reporting?
A. Reports must be concise and visually clear
B. Reports must link IT performance to business outcomes
C. Reports must include all technical metrics
D. Reports must follow a consistent format
Q130. An IS auditor finds that the IT risk management function reports to the CIO. What is the main governance concern?
A. Lack of independence in IT risk oversight
B. Inefficiency in risk reporting cycles
C. Duplication of audit responsibilities
D. Incomplete tracking of control gaps
Q131. Which of the following most effectively ensures that IT resources are used optimally?
A. Regular resource utilization analysis
B. Business case approval for all IT initiatives
C. Periodic rotation of IT project teams
D. Outsourcing non-core IT processes
Q132. Which of the following governance controls best ensures that IT decisions support strategic priorities?
A. The existence of an IT steering committee
B. Regular alignment reviews between IT and business leadership
C. Defined escalation procedures for project issues
D. Standardized IT budgeting templates
Q133. Which of the following should be the IS auditor's highest concern when evaluating IT governance effectiveness?
A. Lack of integration between IT risk and enterprise risk
B. Delays in IT policy updates
C. Absence of user satisfaction metrics
D. Multiple IT governance frameworks in use
Q134. Which of the following is the best indicator of IT governance process effectiveness?
A. Continuous improvement mechanisms are in place
B. IT audit findings are minimal
C. The IT budget remains stable
D. Technical documentation is frequently updated
Q135. Which of the following would be the most appropriate recommendation to strengthen IT governance?

A. Establish key risk indicators aligned with business objectives
B. Increase IT staff training on technical standards
C. Create additional IT operating policies
D. Automate IT service management workflows

Q136. Which of the following best describes the primary objective of IT governance within an enterprise?

A. Ensuring that all IT projects are delivered on time and within budget
B. Aligning IT initiatives with business objectives and managing IT-related risk
C. Maintaining compliance with international security frameworks
D. Reducing IT operational costs through outsourcing

Q137. Which committee typically provides direction for IT strategic initiatives and ensures IT investments support enterprise goals?

A. Audit Committee
B. IT Steering Committee
C. Risk Management Committee
D. Information Security Committee

Q138. According to COBIT 2019, what is the key distinction between governance and management objectives?

A. Governance focuses on execution, management on direction
B. Governance ensures objectives are met, management sets them
C. Governance evaluates and directs; management plans and executes
D. Governance is tactical, management is strategic

Q139. Which IT governance framework was developed by ISACA to guide alignment of IT with enterprise objectives?

A. ITIL
B. COBIT
C. ISO 27001
D. TOGAF

Q140. A Balanced Scorecard in IT governance primarily helps to:

A. Quantify financial return on IT investments only
B. Translate strategic objectives into measurable performance indicators
C. Evaluate security incident response metrics
D. Assign project roles and responsibilities

Q141. When assessing IT policies, the auditor should FIRST ensure that:

A. They are aligned with organizational objectives and regulations
B. They have been approved by the IT department
C. They are documented on the intranet
D. They include incident response steps

Q142. Which principle best supports effective segregation of duties in IT operations?

A. All developers should deploy their own code for accountability
B. Privileged access should rotate among team members monthly
C. Development and production responsibilities should be separated
D. Auditors should approve all change requests

Q143. What is the PRIMARY purpose of enterprise architecture in IT governance?

A. Define security policies
B. Map technology components to business processes for alignment
C. Document network diagrams
D. Measure financial ROI of projects

Q144. A chief information officer (CIO) reports directly to the chief financial officer (CFO). This structure most likely indicates:
A. Balanced governance alignment
B. Potential conflict with enterprise strategic alignment
C. Ideal segregation of duties
D. Strong security oversight
Q145. Which of the following is MOST important for effective vendor management?
A. Reviewing invoices for accuracy
B. Establishing service-level agreements (SLAs) with measurable KPIs
C. Having monthly social meetings with vendors
D. Ensuring vendors use identical hardware platforms
Q146. Which metric best reflects governance performance according to the COBIT 2019 implementation lifecycle?
A. Number of servers patched
B. IT budget variance percentage
C. Achievement of stakeholder-driven benefit-realization goals
D. Headcount in IT department
Q147. An organization's risk-management program should PRIMARILY aim to:
A. Eliminate all threats to information assets
B. Identify, assess, and treat risks to acceptable levels
C. Assign risk ownership to the audit function
D. Increase control complexity to ensure coverage
Q148. Which document defines expected behavior and responsibilities for IT users and staff?
A. Strategic Plan
B. Information Security Policy
C. Project Charter
D. Network Diagram
Q149. Which function is responsible for defining and monitoring quality objectives for IT processes?
A. Quality Management
B. System Operations
C. Internal Audit
D. Human Resources
Q150. When auditing outsourced IT services, an IS auditor should FIRST:
A. Review the vendor's SOC (Type II) report
B. Examine the vendor's financial statements
C. Evaluate contract terms and governance responsibilities
D. Interview user department managers
Q151. Which model is often used to assess process maturity for governance capability?
A. IDEAL model
B. Deming cycle (PDCA)
C. CMMI maturity model
D. Waterfall model
Q152. Who should approve the enterprise IT strategy before implementation?
A. Chief Information Officer (CIO)
B. Board of Directors or equivalent governing body
C. Chief Information Security Officer (CISO)
D. IT Steering Committee Chair
Q153. In IT resource management, which practice best ensures optimization of human resources?

A. Regular skills assessment and training aligned to strategy
B. Hiring based on referrals only
C. Cross-training without documentation
D. Allowing departments to hire freely without IT oversight

Q154. The IDEAL model used in IT governance improvement initiatives consists of which sequence?

A. Initiate, Develop, Execute, Assess, Leverage
B. Initiating, Diagnosing, Establishing, Acting, Learning
C. Identify, Design, Evaluate, Audit, Learn
D. Implement, Deliver, Execute, Analyze, Loop

Q155. Which of the following best demonstrates the principle of "enterprise governance of information and technology (EGIT)" from COBIT 2019?

A. IT department sets its own objectives independent of business
B. Board evaluates stakeholder needs and monitors IT performance against strategy
C. CIO manages daily incidents and help-desk tickets
D. Auditors document security policies for users

Q156. Which of the following best describes the role of senior management in IT governance?

A. Managing day-to-day IT operations
B. Drafting technical procedures for end users
C. Reviewing code changes before deployment
D. Approving and sponsoring IT initiatives to ensure alignment with business goals

Q157. Which of the following best supports enterprise-level IT decision-making?

A. Centralizing all IT budget control in the finance department
B. Establishing clearly defined IT decision rights and accountability structures
C. Limiting IT discussions to technical staff
D. Outsourcing all governance activities to consultants

Q158. An IS auditor evaluating IT governance should FIRST review:

A. IT budget and expense reports
B. The IT strategic plan and alignment with business objectives
C. Change management logs
D. Security awareness training attendance

Q159. Which governance principle ensures IT decisions are made at the appropriate organizational level?

A. Accountability
B. Transparency
C. Decision rights
D. Due diligence

Q160. Which of the following metrics BEST indicates that IT is effectively supporting business objectives?

A. System uptime percentage
B. Percentage of IT projects aligned to strategic goals
C. Number of employees in IT
D. Number of open audit findings

Q161. Which governance mechanism ensures effective two-way communication between business units and IT?

A. Change Advisory Board (CAB)
B. IT Steering Committee
C. Audit Working Group
D. Information Security Team

Q162. Which of the following is MOST critical when establishing IT governance policies?
A. Ensuring they align with corporate governance and regulatory requirements
B. Ensuring they are concise and brief
C. Ensuring they are written by technical staff only
D. Ensuring they include every operational detail
Q163. What is the PRIMARY reason for implementing an IT governance framework such as COBIT?
A. To standardize daily IT operations
B. To establish accountability and align IT activities with enterprise objectives
C. To define job descriptions for IT staff
D. To automate business processes
Q164. Which of the following best describes the purpose of a RACI chart in IT governance?
A. To identify risk appetite levels
B. To clarify roles and responsibilities across stakeholders
C. To document business process flow
D. To list IT control objectives
Q165. Which of the following best reflects an effective IT governance maturity level?
A. Policies are ad hoc and undocumented
B. IT decisions are reactive and isolated
C. IT and business strategies are fully integrated and measured
D. Management has not yet defined decision rights
Q166. Which of the following BEST demonstrates accountability in IT governance?
A. Clearly documented IT roles and reporting lines
B. Detailed system configuration manuals
C. Complex change-management approval chains
D. Numerous audit trails for minor activities
Q167. In a governance context, the term "value delivery" primarily refers to:
A. The cost efficiency of IT operations
B. The extent to which IT investments produce desired business outcomes
C. The percentage of IT projects completed on time
D. The speed of help-desk response times
Q168. Which IT governance mechanism defines how management performance is evaluated and rewarded?
A. Compensation and incentive structure
B. Strategic alignment framework
C. Balanced scorecard
D. Organizational chart
Q169. Which of the following governance approaches gives the CIO primary decision rights for IT infrastructure while business units control application choices?
A. Business monarchy
B. IT monarchy
C. Federal governance model
D. Feudal governance model
Q170. Which of the following best indicates weak IT governance?
A. Frequent executive reviews of IT investments
B. Clear documentation of IT policies and decision rights
C. IT initiatives pursued without business case justification
D. Defined metrics linking IT projects to enterprise KPIs

Q171. In the COBIT 2019 framework, which component defines how policies and procedures are put into practice?
A. Governance objectives
B. Governance and management processes
C. Principles and policies
D. Organizational structures
Q172. What is the PRIMARY advantage of defining an IT governance charter?
A. It provides a static record of IT decisions
B. It outlines governance scope, roles, authority, and accountability framework
C. It serves as a technical configuration baseline
D. It lists all IT systems in the organization
Q173. Which of the following best ensures that IT risk is appropriately addressed within corporate governance?
A. Establishing an independent IT risk management function
B. Implementing additional firewalls
C. Conducting vulnerability scans weekly
D. Having the IT manager handle all risk responses alone
Q174. Which of the following is a key input to the IT strategic planning process?
A. Lessons learned from past project performance
B. Daily incident management reports
C. Backup restoration logs
D. Hardware asset inventory
Q175. Which of the following best describes the "IT principles" component of governance as defined by Weill and Ross?
A. Technical configuration standards
B. High-level statements about the role of IT in the business
C. Step-by-step procedures for operations
D. Metrics used to measure performance
Q176. Which of the following best demonstrates effective IT resource management?
A. Assigning every developer multiple concurrent projects without planning
B. Periodically evaluating IT assets and capabilities to ensure optimal utilization
C. Outsourcing all IT functions without review
D. Allowing departments to acquire technology independently
Q177. Which of the following BEST supports continuous improvement in IT governance?
A. Performing one-time audits of IT processes
B. Establishing key performance indicators (KPIs) and regularly reviewing results
C. Maintaining static policies regardless of business change
D. Delegating all improvements to external consultants
Q178. Which of the following is MOST important when defining IT governance roles?
A. Ensuring each role is linked to measurable accountability
B. Assigning overlapping responsibilities for flexibility
C. Giving all decision authority to technical managers
D. Minimizing executive involvement to reduce bureaucracy
Q179. Which of the following is a key output of IT portfolio management under governance?
A. List of employees by department
B. Prioritized investment list aligned with enterprise value objectives
C. Server uptime statistics
D. Daily incident reports

Q180. Which of the following governance practices ensures that IT investments remain relevant over time?
A. Conducting post-implementation reviews of major projects
B. Outsourcing project monitoring to vendors
C. Avoiding documentation to save time
D. Setting budgets once at project start and never revising
Q181. Which of the following best characterizes IT principles in governance frameworks?
A. Tactical system-specific procedures
B. Broad statements defining IT's role in achieving business success
C. Vendor-specific hardware standards
D. Regulatory compliance checklists
Q182. Which governance mechanism helps link business outcomes to IT performance metrics?
A. Balanced Scorecard
B. Gantt Chart
C. Data Flow Diagram
D. Regression Analysis
Q183. Which of the following is MOST critical when selecting IT performance indicators?
A. Indicators should be easily measurable and aligned to strategic objectives
B. Indicators should emphasize technical complexity
C. Indicators should change every week
D. Indicators should exclude non-financial measures
Q184. Which of the following best ensures IT risk is appropriately escalated to senior management?
A. Relying on ad hoc judgment of project managers
B. Informal discussions during staff meetings
C. Only reporting high-impact incidents annually
D. Defined risk thresholds and reporting protocols in governance policies
Q185. Which governance element directly supports regulatory compliance and accountability?
A. Documented policies and procedures
B. Unstructured verbal communication
C. Ad hoc project meetings
D. Isolated technical manuals
Q186. Which of the following roles typically ensures that IT governance processes remain effective and current?
A. Process owner
B. Database administrator
C. System operator
D. Application developer
Q187. Which of the following best supports IT governance during mergers or acquisitions?
A. Ignoring legacy systems until integration completes
B. Conducting a due-diligence assessment of IT alignment and risks
C. Automatically adopting the acquirer's IT policies without review
D. Disbanding governance committees temporarily
Q188. Which of the following best demonstrates management commitment to IT governance?
A. Assigning adequate budget and resources to governance initiatives
B. Delegating all governance responsibilities to external auditors
C. Avoiding participation in steering committees
D. Requiring quarterly cost-cutting in IT without evaluation
Q189. Which of the following should be the PRIMARY focus of an IT governance review?

A. Evaluating compliance with technical configurations
B. Assessing alignment between IT objectives and enterprise strategy
C. Counting the number of servers in use
D. Comparing IT staff compensation with market rates

Q190. In IT governance, "strategic alignment" refers to:
A. Synchronizing network configurations across all sites
B. Ensuring IT initiatives support and enable business objectives
C. Assigning identical budgets to all IT departments
D. Centralizing all IT operations under one team

Q191. Which of the following governance mechanisms is MOST useful for prioritizing IT investments?
A. Portfolio management process
B. Data backup schedule
C. Code review checklist
D. Incident response plan

Q192. Which of the following best ensures consistent decision-making across IT and business units?
A. Implementing multiple overlapping committees without coordination
B. Allowing each department to set its own IT rules
C. Establishing standardized governance policies and decision frameworks
D. Deferring all IT decisions to external consultants

Q193. Which of the following would be MOST useful for monitoring IT governance effectiveness?
A. Regular KPI and KRI reporting dashboards
B. Annual software license renewals
C. Daily system administration logs
D. Vendor product brochures

Q194. Which governance concept ensures that IT-related decisions are made transparently and can be justified to stakeholders?
A. Transparency and accountability
B. Complexity and flexibility
C. Independence and secrecy
D. Innovation and risk appetite

Q195. Which of the following best demonstrates the concept of "risk optimization" under COBIT 2019?
A. Eliminating all IT risks regardless of cost
B. Balancing potential risk exposure with business benefits and costs
C. Focusing solely on financial losses from IT incidents
D. Transferring all IT risks to third-party vendors

Q196. Which of the following most effectively ensures alignment between IT strategy and enterprise strategy?
A. Conducting quarterly IT risk assessments
B. Including IT leadership in corporate strategic planning sessions
C. Requiring IT to submit monthly technical reports
D. Outsourcing strategic planning to a consulting firm

Q197. Which of the following is a key output of effective IT governance?
A. Reduced audit frequency
B. Increased technical documentation volume
C. Improved business value realization from IT investments
D. Decreased employee training costs

Q198. Which of the following would BEST indicate a mature IT governance process?

A. Ad hoc decision-making by project teams
B. Regular reviews of governance metrics and continuous improvement initiatives
C. Informal approval of IT budgets by department heads
D. IT policies rewritten every few years without review

Q199. Which of the following best supports IT governance accountability?

A. Defining clear roles and documenting responsibilities in a RACI chart
B. Rotating IT leadership positions every quarter
C. Replacing written procedures with oral communication
D. Allowing teams to self-govern without oversight

Q200. Which of the following BEST helps ensure that IT delivers value to stakeholders?

A. Establishing a formal benefits realization process
B. Maintaining the same IT portfolio year after year
C. Outsourcing all high-risk projects
D. Avoiding metrics to focus on innovation

Answer Key and Explanation (101-200)

Q101. Answer: A

Explanation: Establishing clear IT governance objectives ensures that IT initiatives are directly aligned with strategic business outcomes, maximizing value delivery while maintaining control and accountability. Option B addresses personnel management, not governance. Option C focuses on procurement efficiency. Option D is financial but not necessarily value-driven.

Q102. Answer: A

Explanation: Consistent failure to deliver projects on time and within budget suggests ineffective governance, poor oversight, and weak alignment between IT and business objectives. Option B shows strong organizational positioning. Option C may reflect flexibility rather than weakness. Option D indicates active governance monitoring.

Q103. Answer: A

Explanation: Senior management commitment provides authority, resources, and enterprise-level engagement essential for effective governance implementation. Option B adds structure but not leadership. Option C promotes awareness but not enforcement. Option D focuses on technology, not governance processes.

Q104. Answer: B

Explanation: Informal distribution of IT governance responsibilities leads to fragmented decision-making and lack of strategic alignment between IT and business, the most serious governance weakness. Option A may occur but is secondary. Option C is a consequence, not the root cause. Option D is unrelated to governance structure.

Q105. Answer: C

Explanation: Misalignment between IT and business objectives results in wasted investments, redundant efforts, and systems that fail to support strategic goals. Option A is a byproduct of misalignment. Option B may occur but is a symptom, not the core issue. Option D represents governance oversight but is less directly damaging.

Q106. Answer: B

Explanation: Integrating IT risk management into ERM ensures consistent prioritization, assessment, and treatment of risks across the organization, improving enterprise resilience. Option A is administrative, not strategic. Option C is unrelated to risk integration. Option D is a side effect but not the primary benefit.

Q107. Answer: B

Explanation: The IT strategic plan establishes direction, goals, and governance principles, providing the foundation for assessing alignment and control structures. Option A reflects execution but not strategy. Option C provides role clarity but not governance effectiveness. Option D is operational and financial rather than strategic.

Q108. Answer: A

Explanation: IT performance dashboards that link metrics to business outcomes provide the board with relevant, real-time insight into IT's contribution to strategic goals. Option B ensures oversight but not continuous monitoring. Option C focuses on costs, not performance. Option D is operational, not a governance responsibility.

Q109. Answer: A

Explanation: Without documented decisions, governance accountability and traceability are compromised, reducing the ability to verify that decisions were made transparently and aligned with enterprise goals. Option B affects efficiency, not assurance. Option C may hinder input but is less critical. Option D concerns focus, not documentation.

Q110. Answer: B

Explanation: Monitoring IT resource utilization through key performance indicators ensures resources are allocated efficiently and aligned with strategic priorities. Option A may enhance flexibility but not control. Option C can fragment governance. Option D may improve focus but must be measured for performance, not assumed effective.

Q111. Answer: B

Explanation: Achieving targeted value delivery outcomes shows that IT governance effectively supports strategic objectives and ensures returns on IT investments. Option A may signal improved controls but not governance success. Option C is financial and does not ensure strategic value. Option D measures morale, not results.

Q112. Answer: A

Explanation: Self-assessments without independent validation risk bias, overstated compliance, and lack of objectivity in governance reporting. Option B concerns cost, not reliability. Option C affects timing, not assurance. Option D is a communication issue, not a reliability concern.

Q113. Answer: B

Explanation: Integrating IT and business performance management demonstrates mature governance that aligns IT contribution with enterprise outcomes. Option A reflects structure, not maturity. Option C ensures oversight but not integration. Option D is a prerequisite, not a sign of maturity.

Q114. Answer: A

Explanation: Defining roles and responsibilities creates the accountability framework required to execute governance processes consistently and effectively. Option B measures performance but assumes structure exists. Option C addresses finance, not governance foundations. Option D pertains to assurance, not implementation.

Q115. Answer: C

Explanation: Cross-functional workshops promote shared understanding and collaboration across departments, ensuring governance concepts are understood and applied consistently. Option A informs but does not engage. Option B targets new employees only. Option D shares information but lacks interaction.

Q116. Answer: B

Explanation: Board-level oversight ensures that IT risk is managed at the strategic level and aligned with business risk appetite, the hallmark of effective risk governance. Option A is operational and lacks governance authority. Option C is educational but not governance-driven. Option D focuses on reporting, not oversight.

Q117. Answer: A

Explanation: Requiring a business case and sponsor approval ensures each IT initiative directly supports business objectives and delivers measurable value. Option B shows reporting but not linkage. Option C provides visibility but not alignment proof. Option D reflects good governance practice but not alignment effectiveness.

Q118. Answer: A

Explanation: Outdated KPIs misalign performance tracking with evolving business strategies, leading to poor decision-making and ineffective governance oversight. Option B may occur but is secondary. Option C affects understanding but not governance directly. Option D is unrelated to metrics.

Q119. Answer: A

Explanation: Benchmarking against frameworks like COBIT provides an objective, standardized measure of governance maturity and alignment with best practices. Option B offers opinions, not standards-based evaluation. Option C focuses on cost rather than governance. Option D assesses operations, not governance performance.

Q120. Answer: A

Explanation: The auditor should focus on ensuring IT policies are aligned with business objectives, as alignment defines effective governance and supports enterprise strategy. Option B improves usability but not governance quality. Option C ensures maintenance but not relevance. Option D provides technical guidance, not governance alignment.

Q121. Answer: B

Explanation: Undefined roles and responsibilities cause overlapping authority, inconsistent decision-making, and a lack of accountability, severely weakening IT governance effectiveness. Option A may result but is a symptom rather than the main risk. Option C concerns sourcing, not governance clarity. Option D relates to process documentation, not decision accountability.

Q122. Answer: A

Explanation: Defining KPIs that directly link IT outcomes to business objectives ensures performance measurement reflects strategic contribution, not just activity tracking. Option B assesses individuals, not IT performance. Option C focuses on budget control, not alignment. Option D supports data collection but not measurement relevance.

Q123. Answer: A

Explanation: Without board-level engagement, IT governance lacks strategic authority and enterprise alignment, leading to poor accountability and ineffective oversight. Option B affects technical uniformity but not governance authority. Option C may increase complexity but not necessarily failure. Option D reflects active maintenance and is not a weakness.

Q124. Answer: B

Explanation: When business managers do not receive IT performance reports, they cannot assess IT's contribution to business value or risk exposure, undermining transparency and strategic decision-making. Option A is procedural. Option C pertains to data logging, not communication. Option D is minor and administrative.

Q125. Answer: A

Explanation: Independent governance assessments verify the adequacy and effectiveness of IT governance practices objectively, ensuring they achieve intended outcomes. Option B relates to HR oversight. Option C is administrative, not strategic. Option D concerns operational control, not governance assurance.

Q126. Answer: C

Explanation: Assigning ownership of IT performance to business units ensures that management is directly accountable for results and integration of IT with business value delivery. Option B reflects reporting, not accountability. Option A enhances communication but not ownership. Option D defines procedures, not responsibility.

Q127. Answer: A

Explanation: Integrating IT reporting into enterprise dashboards ensures visibility and alignment of IT performance and risk with business oversight, driving governance maturity. Option B fragments governance. Option C supports innovation but not maturity. Option D may help oversight but not structural improvement.

Q128. Answer: A

Explanation: Prioritizing projects by expected business benefits ensures IT resources deliver measurable value aligned with strategic goals, a key characteristic of value-driven governance. Option B focuses on cost control, not value. Option C measures efficiency, not strategic contribution. Option D concerns operations, not governance outcomes.

Q129. Answer: B

Explanation: The most critical aspect of governance reporting is demonstrating how IT performance supports or impacts business outcomes, ensuring relevance and value for decision-makers. Option A improves readability but not content significance. Option C creates overload without context. Option D adds consistency but not insight.

Q130. Answer: A

Explanation: When IT risk management reports to the CIO, independence is compromised because risks may be downplayed to protect IT interests, weakening enterprise-level governance. Option B concerns efficiency but not integrity. Option C is unrelated. Option D is an outcome, not the core governance issue.

Q131. Answer: B

Explanation: Requiring a business case for every IT initiative ensures that resources are allocated only to projects providing measurable value, optimizing utilization across the enterprise. Option A aids monitoring but lacks preventative control. Option C is staffing-related, not strategic. Option D may improve focus but doesn't guarantee optimization.

Q132. Answer: B

Explanation: Regular alignment reviews between IT and business leadership ensure decisions remain strategically consistent and adaptive to changes in organizational objectives. Option A provides structure but not continuous verification. Option C concerns project management, not governance alignment. Option D is administrative, not strategic.

Q133. Answer: A

Explanation: Without integration of IT and enterprise risk, governance loses alignment with the overall risk appetite, exposing the organization to unmanaged or misprioritized risks. Option B affects maintenance, not strategic oversight. Option C is beneficial but not critical to governance effectiveness. Option D may complicate consistency but not destroy alignment.

Q134. Answer: A

Explanation: Governance effectiveness is demonstrated by ongoing improvement mechanisms that assess and enhance governance processes, ensuring adaptability and sustained value delivery. Option B measures control performance, not governance maturity. Option C concerns finance, not governance quality. Option D supports operations but not oversight.

Q135. Answer: A

Explanation: Implementing key risk indicators tied to business objectives enhances governance by providing measurable insights into IT risk and performance alignment with strategy. Option B improves skills but not governance. Option C may increase bureaucracy. Option D improves efficiency but not oversight quality.

Q136. Answer: B

Explanation: The main goal of IT governance is to ensure that IT strategy aligns with enterprise objectives while managing risk so IT delivers value to stakeholders. This alignment drives accountability and value creation across the organization, as highlighted in COBIT 2019. Option A focuses narrowly on project delivery, which is a management concern rather than governance oversight. Option C represents a compliance subset of governance but lacks the strategic alignment aspect. Option D centers on cost reduction, which may be an outcome of efficiency but not the overarching purpose of governance.

Q137. Answer: B

Explanation: The IT Steering Committee brings together business and IT leaders to ensure that technology projects, priorities, and resources align with business strategies. It reviews investment portfolios and approves major initiatives to maintain strategic direction. The Audit Committee primarily oversees internal control and assurance, not strategic prioritization. The Risk Management Committee focuses on enterprise-wide risk posture, not IT project direction. The Information Security Committee deals with security-specific governance but lacks the enterprise investment oversight of an IT Steering Committee.

Q138. Answer: C

Explanation: COBIT 2019 explains that governance evaluates stakeholder needs, directs priorities, and monitors outcomes, while management plans, builds, runs, and monitors activities to meet governance directives. This distinction establishes a top-down accountability model within EGIT. Option A reverses their roles—execution belongs to management, not governance. Option B misstates the flow since governance defines direction rather than enforcing completion. Option D inverts scope because governance is strategic and management tactical.

Q139. Answer: B

Explanation: COBIT (Control Objectives for Information and Related Technology) was created by ISACA as a comprehensive framework for aligning IT and business goals while ensuring value delivery, resource optimization, and risk management. It integrates best practices from multiple standards into one governance model. ITIL, while widely used, focuses on service management processes, not full governance. ISO 27001 defines requirements for information-security management systems, a narrower domain. TOGAF centers on enterprise architecture design rather than overarching IT governance.

Q140. Answer: B

Explanation: The Balanced Scorecard converts strategic business objectives into quantifiable performance measures across financial, customer, process, and learning perspectives, allowing the board to monitor IT's contribution to enterprise value. It bridges qualitative strategy with operational metrics. Option A limits the scorecard to finance, missing its holistic intent. Option C is too narrow; incident metrics form just one element. Option D pertains to project management, not governance performance measurement.

Q141. Answer: A

Explanation: The auditor's initial focus is verifying that IT policies are consistent with business goals and legal or regulatory obligations, confirming top-level alignment before examining detail. This ensures governance coherence across all control areas. Option B checks authorization but may overlook enterprise misalignment. Option C ensures availability but not content validity. Option D represents an operational detail that matters after alignment is confirmed.

Q142. Answer: C

Explanation: Proper segregation of duties prevents unauthorized changes and fraud by ensuring developers cannot directly deploy or modify production code, maintaining independent review and control. This principle underpins secure governance and change management. Option A contradicts it by granting excessive authority to developers. Option B introduces operational instability and lacks control continuity. Option D confuses assurance with execution—auditors verify, not approve, operational changes.

Q143. Answer: B

Explanation: Enterprise architecture provides a structured blueprint that links IT systems, processes, and infrastructure to business strategy, enabling consistent alignment and informed investment decisions. It helps ensure governance transparency regarding dependencies and impacts. Option A is a subset function handled by information-security governance. Option C describes a technical artifact, not the architecture's purpose. Option D focuses on financial outcomes rather than the strategic alignment that architecture delivers.

Q144. Answer: B

Explanation: When the CIO reports to the CFO, IT may become finance-centric, prioritizing cost control over strategic innovation, creating misalignment with enterprise objectives. Effective governance recommends CIO participation at the executive or board level for balanced decision-making. Option A assumes alignment without considering reporting bias. Option C confuses reporting hierarchy with control segregation. Option D overstates the CFO's influence on security, which belongs to broader governance.

Q145. Answer: B

Explanation: SLAs with quantifiable KPIs form the cornerstone of vendor governance by defining expectations, accountability, and performance criteria that align with organizational goals. They enable consistent monitoring and escalation procedures. Option A addresses financial control but not service quality. Option C builds rapport but lacks enforceable metrics. Option D is irrelevant to contractual performance and may restrict innovation.

Q146. Answer: C

Explanation: Governance success is measured by value creation and benefit realization aligned with stakeholder expectations, the top layer of COBIT's objectives cascade. This shows whether IT delivers tangible business outcomes. Option A is an operational management metric unrelated to strategic goals. Option B measures cost control but not value. Option D is merely an input metric, not a governance result.

Q147. Answer: B

Explanation: The purpose of risk management is to systematically identify, analyze, and respond to risks so they remain within the organization's risk appetite while supporting objectives. This balanced approach ensures both protection and efficiency. Option A is unrealistic—risks can only be mitigated, not eliminated. Option C confuses roles since management owns risk, not auditors. Option D assumes more controls equal safety, which can erode agility and add cost.

Q148. Answer: B

Explanation: The information-security policy establishes acceptable-use guidelines and delineates employee responsibilities for safeguarding assets, forming the behavioral foundation of governance. It ensures consistency across all IT activities. The Strategic Plan outlines long-term objectives but not daily conduct. The Project Charter defines project scope only. The Network Diagram depicts topology, providing no behavioral direction.

Q149. Answer: A

Explanation: Quality Management ensures IT processes meet defined standards and continuously improve through metrics, feedback, and corrective actions, reinforcing governance accountability. It focuses on prevention and enhancement, not inspection alone. System Operations executes tasks but doesn't define quality frameworks. Internal Audit evaluates quality controls but does not manage them. Human Resources handles personnel issues, not IT process quality.

Q150. Answer: C

Explanation: Reviewing the contract clarifies control responsibilities, service levels, and audit rights—essential for scoping the engagement and determining reliance on vendor controls. This sets the foundation for subsequent audit procedures. Option A comes later to verify control assurance. Option B addresses financial viability but not operational accountability. Option D gathers user input but is secondary to understanding contractual obligations.

Q151. Answer: C

Explanation: The Capability Maturity Model Integration (CMMI) provides structured levels (1–5) to assess process capability and identify improvement paths within governance and management practices. It's directly referenced in COBIT. The IDEAL model outlines improvement stages but not maturity levels. PDCA supports continual improvement but lacks grading structure. Waterfall is a development methodology, not a governance assessment model.

Q152. Answer: B

Explanation: The board ensures the IT strategy aligns with organizational goals and risk appetite, providing top-level endorsement and accountability for outcomes. Governance authority rests here per ISACA standards. The CIO drafts and recommends but does not formally approve. The CISO's focus is limited to security strategy. The IT Steering Chair coordinates inputs but lacks enterprise authorization power.

Q153. Answer: A

Explanation: Continual skills assessments and targeted training ensure IT staff capabilities evolve with business strategy, maximizing productivity and reducing competency gaps. This approach ties workforce development to governance objectives. Option B limits diversity and skill verification. Option C lacks structure or records to evaluate effectiveness. Option D removes central control, creating misalignment and redundancy.

Q154. Answer: B

Explanation: The IDEAL model (Initiating, Diagnosing, Establishing, Acting, Learning) provides a structured lifecycle for process improvement in governance systems like COBIT and CMMI. It supports iterative refinement and maturity growth. Option A sounds similar but mislabels phases. Option C substitutes unrelated steps and omits continuous improvement. Option D repeats terms without formal methodological basis.

Q155. Answer: B

Explanation: EGIT requires the board to evaluate stakeholder expectations, direct IT strategy, and monitor performance to ensure value delivery and risk balance, the essence of top-level accountability. This aligns COBIT 2019's governance system principles. Option A contradicts alignment by isolating IT. Option C depicts operational management, not governance oversight. Option D reflects compliance documentation, not strategic evaluation.

Q156. Answer: D

Explanation: Senior management provides direction, approval, and sponsorship for IT initiatives, ensuring they align with corporate objectives and risk appetite. Their engagement ensures accountability and prioritization across IT and business units. Option A is operational and handled by line management. Option C is a technical function, not executive responsibility. Option B concerns documentation and user guidance, far below governance level.

Q157. Answer: B

Explanation: Defining decision rights clarifies who makes which IT decisions, how input is gathered, and how accountability is enforced — a fundamental aspect of effective governance (Weill & Ross, IT Governance). It ensures transparency and minimizes conflict. Option A overly centralizes control, reducing agility. Option C excludes key stakeholders from decisions. Option D undermines internal ownership and accountability.

Q158. Answer: B

Explanation: The IT strategic plan is the cornerstone of governance, showing how IT initiatives support enterprise goals. Reviewing it first allows the auditor to assess alignment and direction before examining operational evidence. Option A assesses financial control but not alignment. Option C is process-level evidence, not strategic. Option D is compliance-related and far narrower in scope.

Q159. Answer: C

Explanation: Decision rights define who has authority to make specific IT-related choices, ensuring alignment with expertise and accountability. This prevents confusion and overlap between business and IT leadership. Option A is the outcome of proper governance, not the mechanism itself. Option B supports openness but doesn't assign authority. Option D applies to ethical behavior, not structural governance design.

Q160. Answer: B

Explanation: Tracking the proportion of IT projects directly tied to strategic objectives shows alignment and value realization — the essence of governance success. It demonstrates IT's contribution to achieving enterprise outcomes. Option A measures availability but not alignment. Option C is a resource count, not a performance indicator. Option D measures compliance weakness, not positive value creation.

Q161. Answer: B

Explanation: The IT Steering Committee facilitates collaboration between business and IT leaders, aligning initiatives and resources while maintaining mutual understanding of priorities. It ensures that IT strategy reflects business needs and vice versa. Option A focuses on operational change control, not governance. Option C reviews audit issues, not strategic communication. Option D specializes in security governance, not overall business alignment.

Q162. Answer: A

Explanation: IT governance policies must integrate with corporate governance principles and meet regulatory expectations to ensure consistency and accountability throughout the enterprise. This alignment preserves coherence between business and IT. Option B emphasizes brevity over completeness. Option C limits input to technical perspectives, ignoring strategic oversight. Option D overloads policy with procedural details that belong elsewhere.

Q163. Answer: B

Explanation: COBIT and similar frameworks exist to provide structured principles for aligning IT with business goals while ensuring accountability, value delivery, and risk management. They bridge strategy and execution. Option A describes management-level processes. Option C pertains to HR management, not governance. Option D focuses on automation, which may result from governance but isn't its purpose.

Q164. Answer: B

Explanation: A RACI matrix (Responsible, Accountable, Consulted, Informed) ensures clarity in responsibilities for each governance activity, reducing overlap and confusion. It supports accountability and transparency. Option A refers to risk management documentation. Option C defines workflows, not accountability. Option D belongs to framework definition, not responsibility assignment.

Q165. Answer: C

Explanation: Mature governance means IT is fully embedded in business planning with clear metrics and performance tracking, ensuring continual value realization. This reflects COBIT Level 5 maturity. Options A and B show early, chaotic stages of governance. Option D indicates immaturity due to lack of structure.

Q166. Answer: A

Explanation: Accountability arises when individuals have defined responsibilities and clear reporting relationships for decision-making and performance outcomes. This creates traceability within governance. Option B is technical documentation, not organizational. Option C may hinder agility without improving accountability. Option D focuses on tracking actions, not assigning ownership.

Q167. Answer: B

Explanation: Value delivery ensures IT initiatives generate measurable business benefits aligned with enterprise objectives, a cornerstone of ISACA's governance principles. It emphasizes performance, not just efficiency. Option A reflects cost focus without assessing benefits. Option C tracks timeliness, not outcomes. Option D measures service efficiency, not strategic value.

Q168. Answer: A

Explanation: Governance includes linking incentives to achievement of IT and business objectives, ensuring accountability and motivation align with strategic goals. This supports consistent decision-making. Option B sets alignment but doesn't assign rewards. Option C monitors results but not compensation. Option D merely depicts hierarchy without evaluating performance.

Q169. Answer: C

Explanation: The federal model balances enterprise-wide IT control with local flexibility, assigning infrastructure decisions to central IT and application choices to business units. It promotes both standardization and responsiveness. Option A centralizes all IT authority in business executives. Option B does the same within IT alone. Option D decentralizes all authority, leading to fragmentation.

Q170. Answer: C

Explanation: Launching IT initiatives without a solid business case demonstrates poor alignment, lack of accountability, and governance immaturity. This practice leads to resource waste and unmanaged risk. Option A supports oversight. Option B and D both represent mature governance elements — documentation and measurable alignment.

Q171. Answer: B

Explanation: COBIT defines "processes" as organized sets of practices transforming governance objectives into actionable procedures and activities. They bridge policy intent with execution. Option A states outcomes, not implementation. Option C outlines guiding rules but not execution. Option D specifies decision hierarchies, not operational realization.

Q172. Answer: B

Explanation: The governance charter formalizes how IT governance functions, defining authority, roles, and responsibilities to ensure accountability and transparency. It serves as the foundational document for governance structures. Option A misrepresents it as a record, not a framework. Option C and D relate to technical documentation, not governance definition.

Q173. Answer: A

Explanation: A dedicated IT risk management function integrates IT risk into enterprise risk oversight, ensuring coordinated mitigation and reporting to governance bodies. It institutionalizes risk ownership and escalation. Options B and C are tactical controls, not governance functions. Option D centralizes risk handling improperly, reducing transparency.

Q174. Answer: A

Explanation: Incorporating lessons learned ensures that past successes and failures guide future planning, enhancing alignment and effectiveness of governance. This input links governance evaluation with strategic improvement. Option B is operational data, not strategic insight. Option C and D are technical artifacts unrelated to planning at the governance level.

Q175. Answer: B

Explanation: IT principles are enterprise-wide declarations defining how IT will support and enable the business, guiding all future decisions and investments. They shape cultural and strategic direction. Option A and C confuse principles with technical or procedural documentation. Option D measures outcomes but does not articulate guiding values.

Q176. Answer: B

Explanation: Effective IT resource management involves regular assessment of people, technology, and financial assets to ensure they are optimally deployed and aligned with organizational priorities. This promotes efficiency, cost control, and agility under governance oversight. Option A risks overextension and poor quality. Option C abandons oversight entirely, introducing risk. Option D fragments standards and increases redundancy.

Q177. Answer: B

Explanation: Defining and tracking KPIs enables organizations to measure progress toward governance goals and identify areas for refinement, supporting continuous improvement. It creates a feedback loop essential for maturity growth. Option A is episodic and reactive. Option C prevents adaptation. Option D removes internal accountability and long-term learning.

Q178. Answer: A

Explanation: Clear accountability ensures every role can be evaluated for performance and compliance with governance objectives, reinforcing transparency and control. This linkage drives responsibility throughout the enterprise. Option B fosters confusion and conflicts. Option C centralizes authority improperly. Option D weakens oversight and alignment with business strategy.

Q179. Answer: B

Explanation: Portfolio management delivers a prioritized set of IT programs and projects that maximize business value relative to risk and resource constraints. It reflects governance's role in aligning investments to strategic goals. Option A is unrelated personnel data. Option C and D are operational metrics, not governance deliverables.

Q180. Answer: A

Explanation: Post-implementation reviews assess whether completed projects achieved expected benefits and inform future decisions, ensuring continued relevance and accountability. They feed lessons back into governance cycles. Option B compromises independence. Option C erodes institutional learning. Option D ignores dynamic business realities.

Q181. Answer: B

Explanation: IT principles articulate top-level beliefs about how IT should enable the business, guiding all subsequent decisions and investments (Weill & Ross). They anchor governance philosophy. Option A deals with operations, not direction. Option C and D are implementation aids, not principle definitions.

Q182. Answer: A

Explanation: The Balanced Scorecard translates strategic goals into balanced metrics across perspectives, enabling monitoring of IT's contribution to business value. It aligns management actions with enterprise strategy. Option B tracks project timelines only. Option C maps data movement, not outcomes. Option D is a statistical tool, not a governance framework.

Q183. Answer: A

Explanation: Effective performance indicators must be measurable, consistent, and directly connected to enterprise goals so that governance can evaluate success objectively. Balanced measures provide both financial and qualitative insight. Option B creates bias toward IT detail over business relevance. Option C prevents trend analysis. Option D omits key value and customer metrics.

Q184. Answer: D

Explanation: Setting clear escalation criteria and formal reporting ensures timely awareness of significant risks at the appropriate level, maintaining enterprise oversight. This structure enhances responsiveness and accountability. Option B lacks documentation and formality. Option C delays risk response. Option A depends on individual discretion, undermining consistency.

Q185. Answer: A

Explanation: Comprehensive documentation codifies expectations, responsibilities, and evidence trails, ensuring compliance and traceability for audits and regulators. It also enables repeatability of governance processes. Option B lacks permanence. Option C is episodic and informal. Option D is too narrow in scope.

Q186. Answer: A

Explanation: The process owner is accountable for designing, monitoring, and improving a governance process so it continues to meet objectives and align with policy. This ensures sustained maturity. Options B–D execute technical tasks but do not own governance processes.

Q187. Answer: B

Explanation: Due-diligence reviews evaluate compatibility, risks, and governance structures to enable smooth integration and continued compliance. They preserve enterprise control during transition. Option A invites operational disruption. Option C risks adopting ineffective controls. Option D removes oversight when it is most needed.

Q188. Answer: A

Explanation: Providing sufficient funding, personnel, and executive attention to governance programs demonstrates real commitment to integrating IT with business strategy and maintaining oversight. It signals that leadership values governance as a strategic enabler, not a compliance burden. Option B shifts responsibility externally, undermining accountability. Option C reduces leadership visibility and influence. Option D focuses on short-term cost control rather than sustainable governance.

Q189. Answer: B

Explanation: Governance reviews focus on whether IT's goals, policies, and activities align with the organization's strategy and deliver value. This ensures technology enables business outcomes effectively. Option A targets technical operations, not strategic alignment. Option C is purely inventory data. Option D addresses HR competitiveness but not governance performance.

Q190. Answer: B

Explanation: Strategic alignment ensures every IT project and investment supports enterprise strategy, reinforcing shared goals and measurable outcomes. This is the first principle of governance per ISACA. Option A confuses technical standardization with strategy. Option C focuses on budget equality rather than alignment. Option D is structural centralization, not alignment.

Q191. Answer: A

Explanation: Portfolio management ranks potential IT initiatives by risk, return, and strategic fit, ensuring resources support the most valuable opportunities. It provides transparency and measurable decision-making. Options B, C, and D are operational controls, not prioritization tools.

Q192. Answer: C

Explanation: Standardized governance frameworks ensure all stakeholders follow the same principles, reducing conflicts and duplication. This fosters alignment and accountability enterprise-wide. Option B fragments control. Option A increases confusion. Option D removes internal ownership, weakening governance maturity.

Q193. Answer: A

Explanation: Dashboards showing key performance and risk indicators allow continuous monitoring of governance objectives, enabling proactive management and accountability. They provide visual, real-time oversight. Option B is administrative. Option C is operational and granular. Option D contains external marketing content irrelevant to governance.

Q194. Answer: A

Explanation: Transparency and accountability ensure decision-making processes are open, traceable, and defensible, fostering stakeholder confidence and regulatory trust. These are fundamental COBIT governance principles. Option B mixes unrelated traits. Option C contradicts open governance. Option D describes strategic qualities, not governance standards.

Q195. Answer: B

Explanation: Risk optimization in COBIT involves maintaining risk within acceptable levels while ensuring IT contributes maximum value relative to cost. It seeks equilibrium between risk appetite and opportunity. Option A is unrealistic and inefficient. Option C narrows risk to financial impact only. Option D abdicates responsibility and may create dependency risks.

Q196. Answer: B

Explanation: Involving IT leaders in enterprise strategic planning fosters continuous dialogue and ensures IT initiatives directly support business priorities. This collaboration strengthens shared accountability for outcomes. Option A assesses risks but does not drive strategic alignment. Option C is administrative, not strategic. Option D may provide insights but removes internal ownership of strategy.

Q197. Answer: C

Explanation: The main output of IT governance is measurable business value—achieved when IT resources, risks, and performance are managed to deliver strategic benefits. This is the "value delivery" principle of COBIT. Option A may occur secondarily but is not a direct goal. Option B and D focus on operational by-products rather than strategic outcomes.

Q198. Answer: B

Explanation: Regular performance reviews supported by defined metrics and improvement cycles signify maturity, ensuring governance evolves with business needs. This reflects proactive monitoring per COBIT's continuous improvement model. Option A and C reflect immature, reactive processes. Option D lacks feedback and validation mechanisms.

Q199. Answer: A

Explanation: A RACI chart clarifies who is responsible, accountable, consulted, and informed for each governance activity, ensuring visibility and traceability of decisions. It's a practical accountability mechanism. Option B disrupts stability and expertise. Option C erodes auditability. Option D removes structure and oversight.

Q200. Answer: A

Explanation: A benefits realization process ensures IT projects are measured against expected outcomes and aligned with stakeholder value expectations, a key governance function. It provides accountability and continuous refinement. Option B limits adaptability. Option C avoids internal risk management maturity. Option D ignores governance measurement principles.

Question (201-300)

Q201. A financial organization implements behavioral analytics to detect anomalous user activity but does not define baseline behavior profiles for comparison. What is the MOST significant weakness?

(A) Inability to accurately distinguish normal from abnormal behavior
(B) Improved governance
(C) Increased automation
(D) Reduced documentation

Q202. A global enterprise introduces a data retention policy but does not align it with contractual obligations to customers. What is the PRIMARY risk?

(A) Breach of contractual agreements
(B) Improved storage efficiency
(C) Increased flexibility
(D) Reduced documentation

Q203. A company migrates critical applications to a virtualized environment but does not update capacity monitoring thresholds. What is the MOST significant operational concern?

(A) Performance degradation due to inaccurate monitoring
(B) Increased efficiency
(C) Reduced documentation
(D) Improved scalability

Q204. A public agency establishes formal risk acceptance criteria but allows project managers to override them without executive review. What is the PRIMARY governance issue?

(A) Reduced documentation
(B) Weak enforcement of defined risk tolerance
(C) Increased agility
(D) Improved collaboration

Q205. A technology firm implements secure configuration standards for servers but does not validate compliance after deployment. What is the MOST significant limitation?

(A) Improved performance
(B) Lack of assurance that configurations remain secure
(C) Increased documentation
(D) Reduced operational cost

Q206. A healthcare organization allows third party maintenance personnel to access systems without background verification. What is the PRIMARY risk?

(A) Increased efficiency
(B) Reduced documentation
(C) Improved service quality
(D) Elevated insider threat exposure

Q207. A retail enterprise implements encryption for archived customer data but stores encryption keys in plain text configuration files. What is the MOST significant vulnerability?

(A) Increased accessibility
(B) Reduced documentation
(C) Compromise of encryption due to poor key protection
(D) Improved storage management

Q208. A transportation company performs periodic penetration tests but does not include social engineering scenarios. What is the PRIMARY limitation?

(A) Improved automation
(B) Incomplete assessment of human related vulnerabilities

(C) Increased efficiency
(D) Reduced documentation

Q209. A financial institution centralizes log management but does not implement integrity checks on stored logs. What is the MOST significant concern?

(A) Potential alteration of logs without detection
(B) Increased storage
(C) Improved performance
(D) Reduced documentation

Q210. A company introduces automated supplier payments but does not implement exception reporting for unusual transactions. What is the PRIMARY risk?

(A) Improved efficiency
(B) Undetected fraudulent or erroneous payments
(C) Reduced documentation
(D) Increased automation

Q211. A multinational enterprise establishes regional security teams but does not define reporting lines to central governance. What is the MOST significant governance gap?

(A) Improved operational efficiency
(B) Increased flexibility
(C) Lack of coordinated oversight and accountability
(D) Reduced documentation

Q212. A technology company deploys containerized applications but does not monitor inter container communication. What is the PRIMARY exposure?

(A) Increased scalability
(B) Improved automation
(C) Reduced documentation
(D) Unnoticed lateral movement between application components

Q213. A government agency defines mandatory encryption standards but permits legacy systems to operate without compensating controls. What is the MOST significant weakness?

(A) Reduced documentation
(B) Increased efficiency
(C) Improved flexibility
(D) Exposure due to unmitigated security gaps

Q214. A financial services firm automates regulatory reporting but does not perform reconciliation against source systems. What is the PRIMARY audit concern?

(A) Increased speed
(B) Reduced documentation
(C) Inaccurate regulatory submissions
(D) Improved automation

Q215. A corporation outsources software development but does not include security testing requirements in contracts. What is the MOST significant exposure?

(A) Reduced documentation
(B) Delivery of applications with unaddressed vulnerabilities
(C) Improved collaboration
(D) Increased flexibility

Q216. A retail enterprise stores payment information but does not restrict database query capabilities for analysts. What is the PRIMARY concern?

(A) Increased analytical capability
(B) Improved reporting

(C) Unauthorized access to sensitive financial data
(D) Reduced documentation
Q217. A manufacturing company defines system availability targets but does not integrate them into vendor service agreements. What is the MOST significant governance gap?
(A) Misalignment between operational objectives and vendor commitments
(B) Reduced documentation
(C) Increased flexibility
(D) Improved efficiency
Q218. A healthcare organization logs system access but does not protect logs from unauthorized viewing. What is the PRIMARY exposure?
(A) Disclosure of sensitive operational information
(B) Improved automation
(C) Reduced documentation
(D) Increased transparency
Q219. A technology enterprise establishes secure coding guidelines but does not provide automated code analysis tools. What is the MOST significant limitation?
(A) Reduced documentation
(B) Increased manual effort
(C) Reduced effectiveness of detecting coding vulnerabilities
(D) Improved flexibility
Q220. A financial organization performs vendor risk assessments but does not consider subcontractor involvement. What is the PRIMARY risk?
(A) Hidden third party exposure through subcontractors
(B) Reduced documentation
(C) Increased efficiency
(D) Improved governance
Q221. A company establishes system hardening standards but does not disable default accounts on deployed devices. What is the MOST significant vulnerability?
(A) Reduced documentation
(B) Increased accessibility
(C) Improved performance
(D) Exploitation through well known default credentials
Q222. A public institution introduces a whistleblower policy but does not ensure anonymity protections. What is the PRIMARY governance weakness?
(A) Discouragement of reporting due to fear of retaliation
(B) Improved compliance
(C) Reduced documentation
(D) Increased transparency
Q223. A logistics company maintains system redundancy but does not synchronize configuration changes across redundant systems. What is the MOST significant risk?
(A) Increased flexibility
(B) Reduced documentation
(C) Improved scalability
(D) Inconsistent behavior during failover
Q224. A financial services organization defines privacy controls but does not monitor third party marketing partners for compliance. What is the PRIMARY exposure?
(A) Reduced documentation
(B) Increased collaboration

(C) Improved efficiency
(D) Misuse of personal data by external partners

Q225. A technology company formalizes a governance framework but does not define escalation paths for unresolved risk issues. What is the MOST significant governance gap?
(A) Reduced documentation
(B) Increased flexibility
(C) Lack of structured resolution for significant risk concerns
(D) Improved automation

Q226. A large banking institution implements a three lines of defense model for governance. However, operational managers continue to rely solely on the internal audit team to identify and manage risks within their departments. What is the MOST significant control deficiency in this situation?
(A) Excessive independence of internal audit
(B) Failure of operational management to own and manage risk
(C) Over documentation of risk registers
(D) Increased regulatory supervision

Q227. An organization migrates its payroll processing to an external service provider. The contract includes service availability clauses but does not specify data confidentiality requirements. What is the MOST significant risk associated with this omission?
(A) Improved processing time
(B) Increased cost of service
(C) Exposure of sensitive employee information
(D) Reduced operational efficiency

Q228. A manufacturing enterprise implements automated quality control systems on its production line. However, the configuration parameters are modified by engineers without formal approval or documentation. What is the PRIMARY risk in this scenario?
(A) Increased operational flexibility
(B) Improved system responsiveness
(C) Reduced engineering innovation
(D) Lack of traceability and potential production defects

Q229. A health services organization stores patient diagnostic images in a centralized repository accessible by multiple departments. Access is granted based on department rather than individual role. What is the MOST significant concern?
(A) Increased collaboration among medical staff
(B) Improved information sharing
(C) Reduced administrative workload
(D) Violation of least privilege access principles

Q230. A financial regulator mandates periodic stress testing of critical financial systems. A bank conducts the tests but does not involve senior management in reviewing the results. What is the PRIMARY governance weakness?
(A) Improved operational independence
(B) Lack of executive awareness of system resilience
(C) Reduced testing frequency
(D) Increased technical oversight

Q231. A technology startup rapidly deploys new application features directly into the live environment to maintain competitive advantage. No rollback procedures are defined. What is the MOST significant operational risk?
(A) Improved market responsiveness

(B) Reduced documentation
(C) Prolonged service disruption if defects occur
(D) Increased innovation

Q232. A government agency uses a centralized identity management system but does not disable user accounts promptly after employee termination. What is the PRIMARY control weakness?
(A) Continued unauthorized access by former employees
(B) Reduced administrative cost
(C) Increased flexibility
(D) Improved automation

Q233. A multinational corporation implements environmental monitoring sensors in its data center but does not configure automated alerts for threshold breaches. What is the MOST significant limitation?
(A) Improved hardware efficiency
(B) Reduced documentation
(C) Delayed response to environmental hazards
(D) Increased data collection

Q234. A financial institution introduces mandatory job rotation for employees in sensitive accounting roles. What is the PRIMARY objective of this control?
(A) Reduce training cost
(B) Detect and deter fraudulent activities
(C) Improve operational speed
(D) Increase employee satisfaction

Q235. A retail company develops a disaster recovery plan but bases recovery time objectives solely on technical feasibility rather than business impact analysis. What is the MOST significant governance concern?
(A) Increased technical accuracy
(B) Reduced documentation
(C) Improved infrastructure efficiency
(D) Misalignment between recovery priorities and business needs

Q236. A healthcare organization encrypts portable devices but allows automatic login without password after startup. What is the PRIMARY risk?
(A) Reduced documentation
(B) Unauthorized access despite encryption safeguards
(C) Increased convenience
(D) Improved user satisfaction

Q237. A transportation authority integrates ticketing systems with mobile payment platforms but does not validate transaction data integrity between systems. What is the MOST significant operational risk?
(A) Improved transaction speed
(B) Increased customer convenience
(C) Reduced documentation
(D) Financial discrepancies and revenue loss

Q238. A university outsources its online learning platform but does not define incident reporting timelines in the agreement. What is the PRIMARY concern?
(A) Delayed notification of security incidents
(B) Reduced documentation
(C) Improved academic collaboration
(D) Increased vendor flexibility

Q239. A financial services firm conducts quarterly access reviews but excludes privileged accounts from the review scope. What is the MOST significant weakness?
(A) Reduced documentation
(B) Improved governance
(C) Increased efficiency
(D) Higher risk of excessive or inappropriate elevated access
Q240. A manufacturing organization centralizes system monitoring but does not segregate monitoring responsibilities from system administration duties. What is the PRIMARY control concern?
(A) Increased coordination
(B) Conflict of interest reducing independence of monitoring
(C) Reduced documentation
(D) Improved operational speed
Q241. A national utility provider performs annual risk assessments but does not document risk mitigation decisions. What is the MOST significant governance issue?
(A) Reduced documentation
(B) Lack of accountability and audit trail for risk responses
(C) Increased flexibility
(D) Improved efficiency
Q242. A financial institution automates loan approval decisions but does not monitor model performance over time. What is the PRIMARY risk?
(A) Increased automation
(B) Improved efficiency
(C) Degradation of decision accuracy due to changing conditions
(D) Reduced documentation
Q243. A retail organization maintains redundant internet connections but does not test switching between providers. What is the MOST significant operational weakness?
(A) Improved scalability
(B) Reduced documentation
(C) Increased connectivity
(D) Unverified failover capability
Q244. A government department defines information asset ownership but does not assign custodians for technical management. What is the PRIMARY governance gap?
(A) Reduced documentation
(B) Improved efficiency
(C) Increased clarity
(D) Incomplete definition of accountability for data protection
Q245. A healthcare provider logs remote access sessions but does not review session recordings. What is the MOST significant limitation?
(A) Reduced documentation
(B) Improved flexibility
(C) Missed detection of inappropriate remote activity
(D) Increased storage
Q246. A financial organization updates system patches regularly but does not verify patch integrity before installation. What is the PRIMARY risk?
(A) Reduced documentation
(B) Installation of malicious or corrupted updates
(C) Improved performance
(D) Increased automation

Q247. A telecommunications company deploys centralized configuration management tools but does not restrict direct manual changes on devices. What is the MOST significant control weakness?
(A) Increased flexibility
(B) Inconsistent configurations and reduced auditability
(C) Reduced documentation
(D) Improved efficiency
Q248. A multinational retailer stores encryption keys in a single geographic location without backup. What is the PRIMARY operational risk?
(A) Inability to access encrypted data if keys are lost
(B) Improved compliance
(C) Reduced documentation
(D) Increased simplicity
Q249. A public sector organization establishes internal audit reporting directly to operational management rather than to the governing board. What is the MOST significant governance concern?
(A) Reduced documentation
(B) Improved efficiency
(C) Increased collaboration
(D) Reduced independence of the audit function
Q250. A financial enterprise performs scenario analysis for cybersecurity threats but does not integrate findings into strategic planning. What is the PRIMARY limitation?
(A) Lack of alignment between identified risks and business strategy
(B) Increased analytical effort
(C) Reduced documentation
(D) Improved automation
Q251. A financial institution implements a formal enterprise risk management framework aligned with industry guidance. However, risk assessments are conducted independently by each department without a consolidated risk register. What is the MOST significant weakness in this approach?
(A) Increased departmental autonomy
(B) Improved operational speed
(C) Reduced documentation effort
(D) Lack of enterprise wide visibility of aggregated risks
Q252. A healthcare organization performs periodic access reviews but relies solely on automated reports without requiring business owners to validate user privileges. What is the PRIMARY control concern?
(A) Improved compliance posture
(B) Increased automation efficiency
(C) Inadequate confirmation of access appropriateness
(D) Reduced documentation
Q253. A retail company upgrades its point of sale systems and migrates historical transaction data. No reconciliation is performed between old and new systems after migration. What is the MOST significant operational risk?
(A) Improved system integration
(B) Inaccurate financial reporting due to data discrepancies
(C) Increased transaction speed
(D) Reduced documentation
Q254. A public sector agency defines information security roles and responsibilities in policy documents, but employees are unclear about escalation paths for security incidents. What is the PRIMARY governance gap?

(A) Reduced administrative burden
(B) Lack of clear operational communication procedures
(C) Increased documentation
(D) Improved flexibility

Q255. A manufacturing organization conducts vulnerability assessments annually but does not perform them after significant system upgrades. What is the MOST significant risk?
(A) Undetected vulnerabilities introduced by new changes
(B) Reduced documentation
(C) Improved operational control
(D) Increased stability

Q256. A financial services company outsources data processing and receives assurance reports from the provider. However, management does not review the reports in detail. What is the PRIMARY control weakness?
(A) Failure to act upon independent assurance findings
(B) Improved vendor oversight
(C) Increased documentation
(D) Reduced operational cost

Q257. A hospital implements biometric access controls for restricted areas but does not maintain logs of entry attempts. What is the MOST significant limitation?
(A) Increased physical security
(B) Improved user convenience
(C) Lack of audit trail for access activities
(D) Reduced administrative effort

Q258. A technology company establishes formal project management standards but allows projects to proceed without defined success criteria. What is the PRIMARY governance concern?
(A) Inability to measure project performance objectively
(B) Increased innovation
(C) Reduced documentation
(D) Improved flexibility

Q259. A national utility provider centralizes monitoring of operational systems but does not implement network segmentation between administrative and control environments. What is the MOST significant exposure?
(A) Spread of security incidents across critical infrastructure
(B) Increased communication speed
(C) Reduced documentation
(D) Improved integration

Q260. A banking institution requires dual approval for large fund transfers but allows emergency overrides without retrospective review. What is the PRIMARY risk?
(A) Abuse of override privileges without accountability
(B) Increased operational flexibility
(C) Reduced documentation
(D) Improved transaction speed

Q261. A healthcare organization performs periodic risk assessments but does not update mitigation plans after new threats are identified. What is the MOST significant weakness?
(A) Reduced operational cost
(B) Improved compliance
(C) Increased documentation
(D) Failure to adapt controls to evolving risk landscape

Q262. A retail enterprise implements centralized patch management but excludes devices located in remote branches due to connectivity limitations. What is the PRIMARY risk?
(A) Persistent vulnerabilities in remote environments
(B) Improved scalability
(C) Reduced documentation
(D) Increased administrative efficiency
Q263. A financial organization integrates risk management results into quarterly reports but does not include trend analysis over time. What is the MOST significant limitation?
(A) Increased simplicity
(B) Improved reporting speed
(C) Inability to identify patterns and emerging risks
(D) Reduced documentation
Q264. A government department establishes encryption standards for data storage but does not verify compliance during internal audits. What is the PRIMARY governance gap?
(A) Improved flexibility
(B) Lack of assurance that policy requirements are implemented
(C) Increased automation
(D) Reduced documentation
Q265. A manufacturing enterprise conducts disaster recovery exercises but limits participation to information technology personnel only. What is the MOST significant weakness?
(A) Lack of business unit involvement in continuity planning
(B) Reduced documentation
(C) Improved efficiency
(D) Increased technical focus
Q266. A financial services firm implements real time fraud monitoring but does not define escalation thresholds for investigation. What is the PRIMARY risk?
(A) Increased automation
(B) Reduced documentation
(C) Delayed or inconsistent response to suspicious activity
(D) Improved transaction efficiency
Q267. A healthcare provider stores sensitive research data in shared network folders without classification labels. What is the MOST significant exposure?
(A) Inadequate protection of high value information assets
(B) Improved accessibility
(C) Reduced documentation
(D) Increased collaboration
Q268. A telecommunications organization relies on manual approval for configuration changes despite high transaction volume and rapid deployment cycles. What is the PRIMARY operational concern?
(A) Bottlenecks leading to delayed implementation
(B) Reduced flexibility
(C) Improved oversight
(D) Increased documentation
Q269. A financial institution maintains comprehensive audit logs but does not perform periodic independent log reviews. What is the MOST significant control weakness?
(A) Reduced objectivity in monitoring activities
(B) Reduced documentation
(C) Increased storage capacity

(D) Improved system efficiency

Q270. A public utility company defines service level targets for system uptime but does not measure actual performance against these targets. What is the PRIMARY governance limitation?

(A) Improved operational flexibility
(B) Increased simplicity
(C) Reduced documentation
(D) Inability to evaluate service effectiveness

Q271. A retail organization centralizes procurement but does not assess information security risks during vendor selection. What is the MOST significant exposure?

(A) Reduced documentation
(B) Selection of vendors with inadequate security controls
(C) Improved efficiency
(D) Increased negotiation speed

Q272. A healthcare institution implements automated backup solutions but does not encrypt backup media transported offsite. What is the PRIMARY risk?

(A) Increased portability
(B) Improved recovery speed
(C) Unauthorized disclosure during transit
(D) Reduced documentation

Q273. A financial enterprise introduces performance incentives tied to transaction volume without incorporating compliance metrics. What is the MOST significant governance concern?

(A) Encouragement of risky or noncompliant behavior
(B) Improved morale
(C) Increased productivity
(D) Reduced documentation

Q274. A technology company conducts secure system design reviews but does not document identified weaknesses or remediation plans. What is the PRIMARY control weakness?

(A) Increased flexibility
(B) Improved efficiency
(C) Lack of accountability and follow up on design flaws
(D) Reduced documentation

Q275. A government agency defines critical information assets but does not align insurance coverage with identified risks. What is the MOST significant limitation?

(A) Reduced documentation
(B) Financial exposure not mitigated through risk transfer
(C) Increased flexibility
(D) Improved governance

Q276. A financial services organization establishes an information security steering committee composed only of technical personnel. Business executives are not included in the committee. What is the MOST significant governance concern?

(A) Increased technical focus
(B) Improved operational efficiency
(C) Lack of business alignment with security objectives
(D) Reduced documentation

Q277. A manufacturing company introduces automated inventory management but does not reconcile system records with periodic physical counts. What is the PRIMARY operational risk?

(A) Undetected discrepancies between recorded and actual inventory
(B) Reduced documentation

(C) Increased efficiency
(D) Improved scalability

Q278. A healthcare provider grants emergency access to patient records during critical situations but does not review emergency access logs afterward. What is the MOST significant weakness?
(A) Potential misuse of emergency privileges without accountability
(B) Reduced documentation
(C) Increased responsiveness
(D) Improved workflow

Q279. A banking institution develops a comprehensive information asset inventory but does not assign risk ratings to the assets. What is the PRIMARY governance limitation?
(A) Inability to prioritize protection efforts
(B) Improved operational control
(C) Reduced administrative effort
(D) Increased documentation

Q280. A telecommunications provider centralizes system administration functions but does not implement periodic rotation of administrative passwords. What is the MOST significant exposure?
(A) Reduced documentation
(B) Higher likelihood of unauthorized access through compromised credentials
(C) Improved efficiency
(D) Increased convenience

Q281. A public sector organization implements a formal incident response plan but does not conduct simulation exercises. What is the PRIMARY risk?
(A) Reduced compliance
(B) Unpreparedness during actual incidents
(C) Increased documentation
(D) Improved operational focus

Q282. A financial enterprise performs segregation of duties analysis during system implementation but does not reassess conflicts after role changes. What is the MOST significant weakness?
(A) Increased efficiency
(B) Improved flexibility
(C) Emergence of undetected conflicting responsibilities
(D) Reduced documentation

Q283. A healthcare organization stores audit logs for regulatory purposes but does not protect them from alteration by system administrators. What is the PRIMARY concern?
(A) Improved system performance
(B) Compromised integrity of audit evidence
(C) Increased accessibility
(D) Reduced documentation

Q284. A retail company introduces a new customer relationship system without conducting privacy impact analysis. What is the MOST significant risk?
(A) Reduced documentation
(B) Noncompliance with data protection requirements
(C) Improved customer engagement
(D) Increased marketing efficiency

Q285. A manufacturing organization maintains redundant power supplies for critical systems but does not test them under load conditions. What is the PRIMARY operational concern?
(A) Improved scalability
(B) Failure of backup systems during real outages

(C) Reduced documentation
(D) Increased infrastructure cost
Q286. A financial institution implements data loss prevention controls but does not define incident response procedures for detected violations. What is the MOST significant weakness?
(A) Ineffective handling of identified data leakage events
(B) Improved monitoring
(C) Increased automation
(D) Reduced documentation
Q287. A university outsources network management but does not retain internal expertise to evaluate vendor performance. What is the PRIMARY risk?
(A) Inadequate oversight of outsourced technical controls
(B) Reduced documentation
(C) Improved vendor independence
(D) Increased cost savings
Q288. A healthcare facility shares patient billing data with insurance partners without formal data sharing agreements. What is the MOST significant governance issue?
(A) Reduced documentation
(B) Increased efficiency
(C) Absence of defined responsibilities for data protection
(D) Improved collaboration
Q289. A banking organization establishes key performance indicators for information security but does not link them to risk appetite statements. What is the PRIMARY limitation?
(A) Increased simplicity
(B) Improved reporting speed
(C) Reduced documentation
(D) Disconnect between performance measurement and strategic risk tolerance
Q290. A technology company stores development and production data in the same environment without segregation. What is the MOST significant exposure?
(A) Accidental modification of live data during testing
(B) Increased efficiency
(C) Improved collaboration
(D) Reduced documentation
Q291. A government agency defines change management policies but allows emergency changes without documentation if approved verbally. What is the PRIMARY control weakness?
(A) Lack of audit trail for emergency modifications
(B) Increased flexibility
(C) Reduced paperwork
(D) Improved responsiveness
Q292. A financial enterprise implements continuous monitoring tools but does not integrate them with incident management systems. What is the MOST significant limitation?
(A) Delayed coordination of response activities
(B) Reduced documentation
(C) Improved system efficiency
(D) Increased data collection
Q293. A retail company maintains supplier performance metrics but excludes security performance indicators from evaluation criteria. What is the PRIMARY governance concern?
(A) Improved efficiency
(B) Overlooking supplier related security risks

(C) Reduced documentation
(D) Increased simplicity

Q294. A healthcare organization defines data retention policies but does not enforce automated deletion after retention periods expire. What is the MOST significant risk?
(A) Increased data availability
(B) Reduced documentation
(C) Excess accumulation of sensitive information beyond legal requirements
(D) Improved compliance

Q295. A manufacturing enterprise introduces predictive maintenance analytics but does not validate data sources for accuracy. What is the PRIMARY operational concern?
(A) Incorrect maintenance decisions based on inaccurate data
(B) Increased automation
(C) Reduced documentation
(D) Improved efficiency

Q296. A financial institution conducts regular compliance audits but does not track remediation of identified findings. What is the MOST significant weakness?
(A) Reduced efficiency
(B) Increased documentation
(C) Recurrence of previously identified control deficiencies
(D) Improved audit coverage

Q297. A public utility provider implements centralized authentication but allows shared user accounts for operational convenience. What is the PRIMARY risk?
(A) Increased collaboration
(B) Loss of individual accountability for actions
(C) Improved efficiency
(D) Reduced documentation

Q298. A telecommunications company establishes a formal risk acceptance process but does not require executive approval for high impact risks. What is the MOST significant governance gap?
(A) Increased flexibility
(B) Acceptance of significant risks without appropriate authority
(C) Reduced documentation
(D) Improved efficiency

Q299. A healthcare research center encrypts sensitive databases but stores encryption keys on the same server as the data. What is the PRIMARY concern?
(A) Reduced effectiveness of encryption safeguards
(B) Improved performance
(C) Reduced documentation
(D) Increased simplicity

Q300. A global enterprise performs annual strategic planning but does not incorporate information technology risk assessments into the process. What is the MOST significant limitation?
(A) Reduced documentation
(B) Strategic decisions made without understanding technology related risks
(C) Improved flexibility
(D) Increased focus on business growth

Answer Key and Explanation (201-300)

Q201. Answer: A

Explanation: Behavioral analytics relies on established baselines to identify deviations. Without defined normal activity patterns, anomaly detection becomes unreliable. Governance requires structured configuration of monitoring controls. Undefined baselines may result in excessive false alerts or missed threats. Accurate profiling strengthens detection precision. Proper calibration enhances risk identification.

Q202. Answer: A

Explanation: Customer contracts may specify data retention requirements. Misalignment between policy and contract terms can result in violations. Governance frameworks emphasize harmonization of legal and operational obligations. Failure to comply may lead to disputes or penalties. Structured review ensures consistency. Proper alignment strengthens compliance posture.

Q203. Answer: A

Explanation: Virtualized environments change resource allocation dynamics. Monitoring thresholds must reflect new architecture. Governance standards require adjustment following infrastructure changes. Outdated thresholds may fail to detect resource exhaustion. Structured performance review ensures stability. Accurate monitoring supports service reliability.

Q204. Answer: B

Explanation: Risk acceptance criteria define acceptable exposure levels. Overriding them without oversight undermines governance discipline. Executive review ensures accountability and strategic alignment. Governance requires consistent application of tolerance limits. Uncontrolled exceptions increase organizational risk. Structured oversight strengthens risk management maturity.

Q205. Answer: B

Explanation: Secure configuration standards must be verified regularly. Without validation, deviations may occur over time. Governance frameworks emphasize continuous compliance monitoring. Misconfigurations increase vulnerability exposure. Structured audits ensure sustained adherence. Active verification strengthens infrastructure security.

Q206. Answer: D

Explanation: Third party personnel may have access to sensitive environments. Without background checks, risk of malicious behavior increases. Governance standards require due diligence for individuals with privileged access. Vetting enhances trust and accountability. Structured screening reduces insider threat potential. Proper oversight protects sensitive information.

Q207. Answer: C

Explanation: Encryption is only effective when keys are securely managed. Storing keys in plain text exposes them to unauthorized access. Governance frameworks emphasize secure key storage mechanisms. Weak key protection nullifies confidentiality safeguards. Structured key management enhances resilience. Proper handling preserves data security integrity.

Q208. Answer: B

Explanation: Social engineering exploits human behavior rather than technical flaws. Excluding such scenarios leaves significant risks untested. Governance standards encourage comprehensive threat simulation. Human factors represent a common attack vector. Structured testing enhances preparedness. Inclusive assessments strengthen overall security posture.

Q209. Answer: A

Explanation: Log integrity ensures reliability of recorded events. Without integrity checks, unauthorized modification may go unnoticed. Governance frameworks require tamper detection mechanisms. Compromised logs weaken forensic capability. Structured validation preserves evidentiary value. Reliable records support compliance and accountability.

Q210. Answer: B

Explanation: Automated payments increase speed but require oversight. Exception reporting identifies anomalies for review. Governance standards require detective controls in financial processes. Absence of monitoring increases fraud risk. Structured review enhances transparency. Balanced automation strengthens control effectiveness.

Q211. Answer: C

Explanation: Clear reporting lines ensure alignment with enterprise strategy. Without defined governance structure, responsibilities may overlap or be neglected. Governance frameworks emphasize centralized oversight. Structured communication enhances coordination. Ambiguity weakens control consistency. Defined hierarchy strengthens enterprise security management.

Q212. Answer: D

Explanation: Containerized environments introduce new communication pathways. Monitoring internal interactions detects anomalous behavior. Governance standards require security visibility across architecture. Unmonitored communication increases attack surface. Structured oversight strengthens isolation controls. Comprehensive monitoring enhances threat detection.

Q213. Answer: D

Explanation: Legacy systems may lack capability for required encryption. Governance requires compensating measures when standards cannot be met. Operating without mitigation leaves vulnerabilities open. Structured risk assessment guides alternative safeguards. Unprotected systems increase compromise risk. Proper mitigation strengthens enterprise defense.

Q214. Answer: C

Explanation: Automated reporting depends on accurate source data. Reconciliation verifies completeness and correctness. Governance frameworks require independent validation. Inaccurate submissions may result in penalties. Structured review ensures compliance reliability. Effective oversight supports regulatory confidence.

Q215. Answer: B

Explanation: Contractual requirements define expected deliverables. Without security testing clauses, vendors may omit essential controls. Governance standards emphasize secure development expectations. Unverified applications increase exploitation risk. Structured contractual safeguards strengthen accountability. Defined requirements enhance software security quality.

Q216. Answer: C

Explanation: Analysts may not require full access to payment data. Governance frameworks require least privilege enforcement. Broad query access increases confidentiality risk. Structured access controls limit exposure. Proper role design enhances protection. Restricting unnecessary access strengthens compliance.

Q217. Answer: A

Explanation: Vendor agreements should reflect enterprise performance goals. Without integration, vendors may not support required availability. Governance standards emphasize contractual alignment. Misalignment increases service disruption risk. Structured negotiation strengthens accountability. Clear expectations enhance operational continuity.

Q218. Answer: A

Explanation: Logs may contain sensitive system and user details. Unauthorized viewing can reveal security controls or personal data. Governance frameworks require confidentiality of monitoring records. Protecting logs prevents misuse. Structured access control enhances integrity and privacy. Secure storage strengthens overall monitoring effectiveness.

Q219. Answer: C

Explanation: Automated tools enhance detection of common security flaws. Manual review alone may miss complex issues. Governance standards encourage use of supporting technologies. Lack of automation limits scalability. Structured integration improves development security. Effective tooling strengthens application resilience.

Q220. Answer: A

Explanation: Vendors may rely on subcontractors for service delivery. Governance requires visibility into extended supply chains. Ignoring subcontractors leaves blind spots. Risk may propagate through indirect relationships. Structured due diligence enhances oversight. Comprehensive evaluation strengthens third party risk management.

Q221. Answer: D

Explanation: Default accounts often have predictable credentials. Attackers commonly exploit them. Governance standards require secure configuration practices. Disabling unnecessary accounts reduces attack surface. Structured hardening enhances resilience. Eliminating defaults strengthens system protection.

Q222. Answer: A

Explanation: Anonymity encourages reporting of unethical behavior. Without protection, employees may hesitate to disclose concerns. Governance frameworks promote safe reporting mechanisms. Fear of retaliation weakens oversight. Structured safeguards enhance trust. Effective protection strengthens ethical culture.

Q223. Answer: D

Explanation: Redundant systems must remain consistent to ensure seamless operation. Unsynchronized configurations may cause errors during failover. Governance standards require configuration management discipline. Discrepancies reduce reliability. Structured synchronization enhances continuity assurance. Alignment strengthens resilience.

Q224. Answer: D

Explanation: Marketing partners may handle sensitive customer data. Governance requires oversight of external data processors. Without monitoring, misuse may occur undetected. Structured audits enhance accountability. Clear expectations protect privacy rights. Active supervision strengthens compliance management.

Q225. Answer: C

Explanation: Escalation paths ensure unresolved risks receive appropriate attention. Without defined procedures, issues may stagnate. Governance standards emphasize accountability and timely resolution. Structured escalation supports transparency. Clear authority improves decision making. Effective mechanisms strengthen enterprise risk oversight.

Q226. Answer: B

Explanation: In a three lines of defense model, operational management is responsible for identifying and managing risks within their processes. Relying solely on internal audit shifts accountability away from the first line of defense. Internal audit provides independent assurance, not operational risk management. Governance principles emphasize clear ownership of risks at the business level. Without management accountability, risks may not be proactively addressed. This weakens the overall control environment and undermines governance effectiveness.

Q227. Answer: C

Explanation: Payroll data contains highly sensitive personal and financial information. Without contractual confidentiality requirements, the service provider may not implement adequate safeguards. Governance and risk management practices require clear definition of security responsibilities in outsourcing arrangements. Failure to address data protection in contracts increases the likelihood of unauthorized disclosure. Regulatory noncompliance and reputational damage may result from such exposure. Clearly defined confidentiality clauses strengthen third party risk management.

Q228. Answer: D

Explanation: Automated systems rely on defined parameters to maintain consistent output quality. Uncontrolled modifications introduce the risk of undetected defects. Governance requires formal change management procedures to maintain accountability. Without documentation, identifying the source of errors becomes difficult. Traceability supports root cause analysis and corrective action. Proper oversight ensures product quality and operational stability.

Q229. Answer: D

Explanation: Access controls should align with individual job responsibilities. Granting access at the department level may allow unnecessary exposure to sensitive records. Governance frameworks emphasize least privilege to minimize risk. Broad access increases potential for misuse or accidental disclosure. Individual role based permissions strengthen accountability. Proper access management protects patient confidentiality.

Q230. Answer: B

Explanation: Stress testing evaluates the resilience of critical systems under adverse conditions. Senior management must understand results to make informed strategic decisions. Governance standards require executive oversight of significant risk assessments. Without review, corrective actions may not receive appropriate support. Management involvement ensures alignment with risk appetite. Executive engagement strengthens organizational preparedness.

Q231. Answer: C

Explanation: Rapid deployment without rollback capability increases exposure to service failure. If defects are introduced, recovery may be delayed. Governance principles emphasize balancing agility with control. Defined rollback procedures reduce impact of faulty releases. Service continuity is critical to customer trust. Structured deployment practices enhance operational resilience.

Q232. Answer: A

Explanation: Terminated employees should no longer retain system access. Delayed deactivation creates opportunity for misuse. Governance frameworks require timely user lifecycle management. Persistent accounts increase insider threat risk. Automated deprovisioning enhances efficiency and security. Proper controls safeguard sensitive government information.

Q233. Answer: C

Explanation: Monitoring systems must generate alerts to enable timely intervention. Without automated notification, issues may remain unnoticed. Governance standards emphasize proactive risk management. Environmental hazards such as overheating can damage critical infrastructure. Prompt response reduces downtime and loss. Effective alerting strengthens operational continuity.

Q234. Answer: B

Explanation: Job rotation reduces the opportunity for long term concealment of fraud. Changing responsibilities allows fresh review of processes. Governance frameworks recommend rotation as a detective and preventive control. It enhances transparency and accountability. Exposure of irregularities becomes more likely with independent oversight. Structured rotation strengthens internal control integrity.

Q235. Answer: D

Explanation: Recovery objectives should reflect business criticality, not just technical capability. Business impact analysis identifies acceptable downtime thresholds. Governance standards require alignment between continuity planning and strategic priorities. Misaligned objectives may leave critical processes underprotected. Stakeholder involvement ensures realistic targets. Proper alignment enhances resilience and value protection.

Q236. Answer: B

Explanation: Encryption protects stored data but does not prevent unauthorized access if login controls are weak. Automatic login bypasses authentication safeguards. Governance requires layered security measures. Strong authentication complements encryption. Weak access controls undermine overall security posture. Comprehensive configuration enhances data protection.

Q237. Answer: D

Explanation: Integration requires validation to ensure accurate data exchange. Without integrity checks, errors may occur during synchronization. Governance standards emphasize reconciliation between interconnected systems. Financial discrepancies can impact revenue reporting. Structured validation enhances trust and accuracy. Proper controls support reliable financial management.

Q238. Answer: A

Explanation: Incident reporting timelines ensure timely awareness of breaches. Without defined obligations, vendors may delay disclosure. Governance frameworks require clear communication requirements. Prompt reporting supports rapid response and mitigation. Delays increase potential damage. Structured agreements strengthen third party accountability.

Q239. Answer: D

Explanation: Privileged accounts carry higher risk due to extensive permissions. Excluding them undermines effectiveness of access reviews. Governance standards emphasize scrutiny of elevated roles. Regular review ensures privileges remain justified. Unchecked access increases misuse potential. Comprehensive review strengthens control assurance.

Q240. Answer: B

Explanation: Monitoring functions should operate independently from system administration. Combining roles reduces objectivity. Governance frameworks emphasize segregation of duties to prevent concealment of unauthorized actions. Independent monitoring enhances credibility. Conflict of interest weakens oversight. Structured separation strengthens internal control environment.

Q241. Answer: B

Explanation: Documentation of risk decisions ensures transparency and accountability. Without records, management rationale cannot be verified. Governance standards require traceability of risk treatment. Lack of evidence weakens audit assurance. Structured documentation supports continuous improvement. Clear records enhance governance maturity.

Q242. Answer: C

Explanation: Automated decision models may become less accurate as economic conditions change. Continuous monitoring ensures sustained reliability. Governance requires performance validation of automated systems. Unchecked drift increases risk of incorrect approvals or denials. Structured review enhances compliance and fairness. Ongoing evaluation supports responsible automation.

Q243. Answer: D

Explanation: Redundancy is effective only if switching functions correctly. Testing validates readiness during disruption. Governance standards require periodic continuity testing. Untested connections may fail under stress. Structured validation ensures reliable service. Proper testing strengthens resilience.

Q244. Answer: D

Explanation: Asset ownership defines responsibility for business decisions, while custodians manage technical controls. Both roles are necessary for effective governance. Absence of custodians creates ambiguity in operational management. Governance frameworks require clear role differentiation. Structured accountability enhances protection. Proper assignment strengthens data stewardship.

Q245. Answer: C

Explanation: Logging sessions provides evidence but review ensures detection of misuse. Governance standards emphasize active monitoring. Unreviewed logs diminish control effectiveness. Remote access increases exposure risk. Structured oversight enhances accountability. Effective review strengthens security posture.

Q246. Answer: B

Explanation: Patch integrity verification ensures authenticity and completeness. Without validation, compromised updates may introduce malware. Governance frameworks require secure update processes. Trust in update sources is essential. Structured verification enhances reliability. Secure patch management strengthens defense mechanisms.

Q247. Answer: B

Explanation: Centralized management ensures standardized configuration. Allowing manual overrides introduces inconsistency. Governance standards emphasize controlled configuration processes. Inconsistent settings may create vulnerabilities. Structured enforcement improves accountability. Controlled changes strengthen network security.

Q248. Answer: A

Explanation: Encryption keys are critical for data recovery. Loss of keys renders data inaccessible. Governance frameworks require secure backup of cryptographic material. Single location storage increases disaster risk. Structured key management enhances continuity. Proper redundancy protects information availability.

Q249. Answer: D

Explanation: Internal audit must maintain independence to provide objective assurance. Reporting to operational management may create conflict of interest. Governance standards require direct reporting to the board or equivalent oversight body. Independence enhances credibility. Compromised reporting lines weaken assurance effectiveness. Structured governance strengthens accountability.

Q250. Answer: A

Explanation: Scenario analysis identifies potential future risks. Integrating findings into strategy ensures preparedness. Governance frameworks emphasize linking risk assessment with strategic decision making. Ignored insights reduce value of analysis. Structured integration supports resilience planning. Alignment enhances long term organizational stability.

Q251. Answer: D

Explanation: Enterprise risk management requires a consolidated view of risks across the organization. When departments operate independently, interdependencies may be overlooked. Governance principles emphasize centralized oversight and reporting. Without aggregation, senior management cannot prioritize enterprise level risks effectively. Fragmented assessments weaken strategic decision making. A unified risk register enhances transparency and coordinated mitigation efforts.

Q252. Answer: C

Explanation: Automated reports provide data but do not confirm business necessity. Business owners understand role requirements and should validate access rights. Governance frameworks stress accountability at the process level. Without validation, excessive privileges may persist. Independent confirmation reduces risk of unauthorized activity. Proper review strengthens least privilege enforcement.

Q253. Answer: B

Explanation: Data migration processes may introduce errors or omissions. Reconciliation ensures completeness and integrity of transferred records. Governance standards require validation during system transitions. Undetected discrepancies can impact financial statements. Structured verification enhances reporting reliability. Proper controls preserve trust in transactional accuracy.

Q254. Answer: B

Explanation: Clearly defined escalation paths are essential for effective incident management. Policies alone are insufficient without operational clarity. Governance frameworks emphasize structured communication channels. Uncertainty during incidents delays response. Defined procedures ensure timely and coordinated action. Effective communication strengthens organizational resilience.

Q255. Answer: A

Explanation: System upgrades may introduce new configurations and software components. Governance standards require reassessment after major changes. Annual schedules alone may not capture emerging exposures. Failure to reassess increases risk of exploitation. Continuous evaluation supports proactive mitigation. Structured testing enhances system security.

Q256. Answer: A

Explanation: Assurance reports provide insights into service provider control effectiveness. Reviewing them is essential for informed oversight. Governance requires active evaluation of third party performance. Ignoring findings undermines accountability. Detailed review supports risk mitigation. Proper oversight strengthens outsourced operations governance.

Q257. Answer: C

Explanation: Biometric controls prevent unauthorized entry, but logging supports accountability. Without records, investigations become difficult. Governance frameworks emphasize monitoring and traceability. Audit trails provide evidence of compliance. Absence of logs reduces control transparency. Comprehensive oversight strengthens facility security management.

Q258. Answer: A

Explanation: Success criteria provide measurable benchmarks for evaluation. Without them, assessing project outcomes becomes subjective. Governance standards require defined objectives aligned with strategy. Clear metrics support accountability and transparency. Absence of measurable targets reduces effectiveness of oversight. Structured planning enhances project governance.

Q259. Answer: A

Explanation: Segmentation limits the propagation of threats between environments. Without separation, administrative compromises may affect operational systems. Governance frameworks promote layered security architecture. Integrated networks without controls increase systemic risk. Structured isolation enhances resilience. Proper design safeguards essential services.

Q260. Answer: A

Explanation: Dual approval reduces fraud risk through independent verification. Emergency overrides must include retrospective review to maintain control integrity. Governance standards emphasize documentation and follow up. Unreviewed overrides may conceal improper transactions. Structured oversight ensures legitimate use of exceptions. Strong controls protect financial assets.

Q261. Answer: D

Explanation: Risk assessments identify emerging exposures. Mitigation plans must reflect new findings. Governance frameworks emphasize continuous improvement. Static controls may become ineffective over time. Failure to adapt increases vulnerability. Responsive planning strengthens organizational security posture.

Q262. Answer: A

Explanation: Unpatched devices remain susceptible to exploitation. Governance standards require consistent protection across locations. Excluding remote branches creates uneven security posture. Threat actors may target weaker segments. Structured solutions should address connectivity challenges. Comprehensive coverage strengthens enterprise defense.

Q263. Answer: C

Explanation: Trend analysis reveals whether risk exposure is increasing or decreasing. Governance frameworks encourage longitudinal evaluation. Without trends, management lacks strategic insight. Patterns help prioritize resource allocation. Structured analysis enhances predictive capability. Continuous monitoring supports informed decision making.

Q264. Answer: B

Explanation: Policies require validation through audit processes. Without verification, compliance remains uncertain. Governance standards emphasize monitoring and independent review. Assurance confirms effectiveness of implemented controls. Failure to verify weakens accountability. Structured auditing strengthens security governance.

Q265. Answer: A

Explanation: Disaster recovery affects both technical and business operations. Business unit participation ensures realistic response coordination. Governance frameworks emphasize cross functional collaboration. Excluding stakeholders reduces preparedness. Structured exercises improve organizational readiness. Inclusive planning strengthens resilience.

Q266. Answer: C

Explanation: Monitoring requires clear criteria for action. Undefined thresholds lead to inconsistent handling of alerts. Governance standards emphasize documented response procedures. Structured escalation ensures timely investigation. Without guidance, critical events may be overlooked. Clear protocols strengthen fraud detection effectiveness.

Q267. Answer: A

Explanation: Classification labels guide handling and protection requirements. Without them, sensitive data may not receive appropriate safeguards. Governance frameworks stress risk based protection. Shared folders increase exposure if not controlled. Structured classification enhances data governance. Proper labeling supports confidentiality and compliance.

Q268. Answer: A

Explanation: Manual processes may not scale with organizational growth. Delays can impact competitiveness and service quality. Governance requires balance between control and efficiency. Automation with appropriate safeguards may be necessary. Structured review ensures timely yet secure deployment. Optimized processes enhance operational effectiveness.

Q269. Answer: A

Explanation: Independent log review provides unbiased assessment of activities. Self review by system operators may compromise objectivity. Governance standards emphasize separation of monitoring duties. Independent oversight strengthens detection capability. Lack of impartial review weakens assurance. Structured independence enhances accountability.

Q270. Answer: D

Explanation: Service level targets require measurement for accountability. Governance frameworks emphasize performance monitoring. Without measurement, management cannot determine compliance. Data driven evaluation supports improvement. Structured tracking enhances transparency. Monitoring strengthens service management maturity.

Q271. Answer: B

Explanation: Vendor selection should include security due diligence. Governance standards emphasize risk based procurement. Overlooking security may introduce vulnerabilities. Structured assessment ensures alignment with protection requirements. Inadequate evaluation increases third party risk. Comprehensive review strengthens organizational safeguards.

Q272. Answer: C

Explanation: Backup media often contain confidential patient information. Encryption protects against loss or theft. Governance frameworks require safeguards during transport and storage. Unencrypted media increase privacy risk. Structured protection enhances compliance. Proper encryption strengthens confidentiality.

Q273. Answer: A

Explanation: Incentives influence employee behavior. Excluding compliance metrics may motivate excessive risk taking. Governance standards emphasize balanced performance evaluation. Ethical considerations should align with financial objectives. Structured incentive design reduces misconduct risk. Proper alignment supports sustainable performance.

Q274. Answer: C

Explanation: Documentation ensures traceability of identified issues. Without records, remediation may not occur. Governance frameworks require formal tracking of weaknesses. Accountability depends on transparent reporting. Structured documentation supports continuous improvement. Effective follow up strengthens system security.

Q275. Answer: B

Explanation: Insurance can serve as a risk transfer mechanism for identified exposures. Governance requires aligning risk management strategies with asset criticality. Failure to adjust coverage leaves financial gaps. Structured evaluation ensures appropriate protection. Risk transfer complements preventive controls. Proper alignment enhances overall resilience.

Q276. Answer: C

Explanation: Information security governance requires alignment with business strategy and risk appetite. Excluding business executives limits strategic oversight and decision making authority. Governance frameworks emphasize cross functional participation. Without executive involvement, security initiatives may not reflect organizational priorities. This separation weakens accountability at the highest level. Inclusive governance structures strengthen enterprise wide risk management.

Q277. Answer: A

Explanation: Automated systems may produce errors due to configuration or data input issues. Physical reconciliation verifies system accuracy. Governance standards require validation of automated controls. Failure to reconcile increases risk of financial misstatement and theft. Periodic verification supports reliability of records. Proper oversight enhances asset management integrity.

Q278. Answer: A

Explanation: Emergency access is necessary in urgent circumstances but carries higher risk. Post event review ensures access was appropriate and justified. Governance principles require monitoring of exception based privileges. Without review, misuse may go undetected. Accountability supports trust and compliance. Structured follow up strengthens control effectiveness.

Q279. Answer: A

Explanation: Asset inventories provide visibility, but risk ratings guide prioritization. Governance frameworks emphasize risk based resource allocation. Without classification of criticality, protection efforts may be misdirected. Structured evaluation supports effective control implementation. Risk ratings enhance decision making clarity. Prioritization strengthens overall security posture.

Q280. Answer: B

Explanation: Administrative credentials grant extensive privileges. Regular password rotation reduces risk of prolonged compromise. Governance standards recommend periodic credential updates. Static passwords increase vulnerability to unauthorized use. Structured credential management enhances security. Proactive control reduces potential insider and external threats.

Q281. Answer: B

Explanation: Simulation exercises validate the effectiveness of incident response plans. Governance frameworks emphasize testing to ensure readiness. Without practice, roles and procedures may be unclear during crises. Delayed or ineffective responses increase impact. Structured drills enhance coordination and awareness. Testing strengthens organizational resilience.

Q282. Answer: C

Explanation: Role changes may introduce new conflicts of interest. Governance standards require continuous monitoring of segregation controls. Initial assessment alone is insufficient. Unaddressed conflicts increase fraud risk. Structured reassessment maintains control integrity. Ongoing review strengthens internal control effectiveness.

Q283. Answer: B

Explanation: Audit logs serve as evidence during investigations and compliance reviews. If administrators can alter them, integrity is undermined. Governance frameworks emphasize secure log storage and restricted access. Tampered logs reduce reliability of forensic analysis. Structured protection enhances trustworthiness. Preserving integrity strengthens compliance assurance.

Q284. Answer: B

Explanation: Privacy impact analysis identifies risks related to personal information processing. Governance standards require evaluation before deploying systems that handle sensitive data. Failure to assess may result in regulatory violations. Structured analysis ensures appropriate safeguards are implemented. Proactive review supports lawful data handling. Compliance enhances organizational reputation.

Q285. Answer: B

Explanation: Redundant components must be tested to ensure reliability. Governance frameworks emphasize validation of continuity mechanisms. Untested systems may fail unexpectedly. Load testing simulates real conditions. Structured evaluation confirms operational readiness. Reliable backups strengthen service continuity.

Q286. Answer: A

Explanation: Detection alone does not mitigate risk. Governance standards require defined response procedures. Without action plans, identified incidents may escalate. Structured response ensures containment and remediation. Clear guidance enhances accountability. Effective coordination strengthens data protection measures.

Q287. Answer: A

Explanation: Even when outsourcing, accountability remains with the organization. Governance frameworks require sufficient internal knowledge for oversight. Lack of expertise reduces ability to assess performance. Structured evaluation ensures compliance with contractual obligations. Effective monitoring strengthens vendor governance. Retained capability supports informed decision making.

Q288. Answer: C

Explanation: Formal agreements clarify obligations and security requirements. Governance standards emphasize documented arrangements for information exchange. Without agreements, liability and accountability remain unclear. Structured contracts reduce legal and compliance risk. Clear terms ensure consistent protection. Defined responsibilities strengthen trust among parties.

Q289. Answer: D

Explanation: Key performance indicators should reflect organizational risk tolerance. Governance frameworks emphasize alignment between metrics and risk appetite. Without linkage, performance may not support strategic objectives. Structured integration enhances decision making clarity. Relevant metrics guide resource allocation. Alignment strengthens governance effectiveness.

Q290. Answer: A

Explanation: Separation of environments reduces risk of unintended impact. Governance standards require distinct development and production systems. Mixing environments increases likelihood of errors. Structured segregation protects operational stability. Controlled testing prevents disruption. Clear boundaries enhance data integrity.

Q291. Answer: A

Explanation: Emergency changes must be documented to maintain accountability. Governance frameworks require retrospective review and formal recording. Verbal approval alone is insufficient. Without documentation, tracking becomes difficult. Structured procedures ensure transparency. Proper records strengthen control reliability.

Q292. Answer: A

Explanation: Monitoring tools generate alerts that require coordinated action. Integration with incident management ensures structured response. Governance standards emphasize process alignment. Without integration, response may be fragmented. Structured workflows enhance accountability. Effective linkage strengthens operational readiness.

Q293. Answer: B
Explanation: Supplier performance should include security considerations. Governance frameworks emphasize holistic evaluation of vendor risk. Ignoring security metrics increases exposure. Structured assessment ensures comprehensive oversight. Security indicators guide corrective actions. Balanced evaluation strengthens supply chain resilience.
Q294. Answer: C
Explanation: Retaining data longer than necessary increases exposure. Governance standards require adherence to defined retention periods. Automated enforcement ensures consistency. Excess data increases legal and breach impact risk. Structured lifecycle management enhances privacy compliance. Controlled deletion supports responsible data governance.
Q295. Answer: A
Explanation: Predictive analytics rely on accurate input data. Governance frameworks require data quality assurance. Inaccurate data may lead to premature or delayed maintenance. Structured validation supports reliable outcomes. Data integrity underpins effective analytics. Proper oversight strengthens operational decision making.
Q296. Answer: C
Explanation: Tracking remediation ensures issues are resolved. Governance standards emphasize follow up on audit findings. Without monitoring, deficiencies may persist. Structured tracking enhances accountability. Continuous oversight strengthens compliance posture. Effective remediation reduces risk exposure.
Q297. Answer: B
Explanation: Shared accounts prevent attribution of actions to individuals. Governance frameworks require unique identification for accountability. Lack of traceability complicates investigations. Structured identity management strengthens oversight. Individual credentials support responsibility. Proper control reduces insider threat risk.
Q298. Answer: B
Explanation: High impact risks should be approved by senior leadership. Governance standards define authority levels for risk acceptance. Without executive oversight, exposure may exceed tolerance. Structured approval ensures alignment with strategy. Documented authorization strengthens accountability. Proper governance balances risk and opportunity.
Q299. Answer: A
Explanation: Encryption is effective only if keys are protected separately. Storing keys with data increases compromise risk. Governance frameworks require secure key management. Separation reduces likelihood of unauthorized access. Structured protection enhances confidentiality. Strong cryptographic practices support regulatory compliance.
Q300. Answer: B
Explanation: Information technology risks can significantly impact organizational objectives. Governance standards emphasize integration of risk assessment into strategic planning. Without inclusion, decisions may overlook vulnerabilities. Structured alignment ensures informed choices. Risk awareness supports sustainable growth. Comprehensive planning strengthens enterprise resilience.

Question (301-400)

Q301. Auditor reviewing IT governance notes that IT strategy is not formally aligned with enterprise business objectives; what should be the auditor's PRIMARY recommendation?
(A) Increase IT budget allocation
(B) Implement additional security controls
(C) Establish a formal IT steering committee
(D) Develop and approve an IT strategic plan aligned with business goals
Q302. During risk-based audit planning, which factor MOST influences audit priority?
(A) Age of the system
(B) Auditor experience level
(C) Number of users
(D) Inherent risk and business impact
Q303. An IS auditor finds that user access reviews are performed but not documented; what is the GREATEST concern?
(A) Users may resist reviews
(B) Absence of audit trail evidence
(C) Excessive system downtime
(D) Lack of segregation of duties
Q304. Which control BEST ensures completeness of batch data processing?
(A) Checksum totals
(B) Firewall configuration
(C) Encryption
(D) Biometric authentication
Q305. When evaluating third-party service providers, what is the auditor's PRIMARY focus?
(A) Vendor marketing reputation
(B) Vendor office location
(C) Length of vendor existence
(D) Contract alignment with business and control requirements
Q306. In system development life cycle reviews, the MOST critical control during requirements phase is:
(A) Patch management
(B) Code review
(C) Formal requirement approval
(D) User acceptance testing
Q307. What is the PRIMARY objective of a business impact analysis?
(A) Determine recovery time objectives
(B) Install backup software
(C) Identify hackers
(D) Reduce insurance premiums
Q308. During audit testing, substantive testing is performed to:
(A) Evaluate policy documentation
(B) Verify effectiveness of controls directly
(C) Assess financial statement balances and transaction accuracy
(D) Approve project budgets
Q309. The MOST effective method to detect unauthorized network intrusion is:
(A) Strong password policy
(B) Segregation of duties

(C) Intrusion detection system monitoring
(D) Data classification policy
Q310. Which metric BEST measures IT service performance?
(A) System uptime percentage
(B) Number of IT staff
(C) Office floor size
(D) Vendor profit margin
Q311. The PRIMARY purpose of segregation of duties is to:
(A) Reduce hardware costs
(B) Prevent and detect fraud
(C) Simplify management hierarchy
(D) Improve system speed
Q312. A key risk of inadequate patch management is:
(A) Reduced employee morale
(B) Excessive encryption strength
(C) Increased hardware depreciation
(D) Exposure to known vulnerabilities
Q313. When using CAATs, the auditor should FIRST:
(A) Install antivirus
(B) Verify data integrity and completeness
(C) Inform external regulators
(D) Rewrite system code
Q314. What is the PRIMARY benefit of encryption?
(A) Faster data transmission
(B) Increasing storage capacity
(C) Simplifying password resets
(D) Ensuring confidentiality of data
Q315. A disaster recovery test involving actual shutdown of production systems is called:
(A) Checklist review
(B) Parallel test
(C) Full interruption test
(D) Tabletop exercise
Q316. The MOST significant advantage of preventive controls is that they:
(A) Eliminate audit requirements
(B) Guarantee profit growth
(C) Identify fraud after occurrence
(D) Reduce likelihood of control failures
Q317. What is the PRIMARY concern if audit independence is compromised?
(A) Increased documentation
(B) Faster reporting
(C) Reduced staffing
(D) Biased audit conclusions
Q318. Which component MOST directly supports non-repudiation?
(A) Antivirus software
(B) Firewall
(C) Digital signature
(D) Backup tape
Q319. Capacity management primarily ensures:

(A) Systems operate within performance thresholds
(B) Higher salaries for IT staff
(C) Complete elimination of downtime
(D) Unlimited storage

Q320. The MOST important element of an audit report is:
(A) Page numbering format
(B) Font style consistency
(C) Auditor biography
(D) Clear statement of findings and impact

Q321. The absence of an approved audit charter would MOST likely result in:
(A) Reduced hardware performance
(B) Increased system encryption
(C) Lack of formal authority and scope clarity
(D) Faster audit reporting

Q322. During audit evidence collection, which type of evidence is considered MOST reliable?
(A) Verbal confirmation from staff
(B) Informal email communication
(C) Copies of system generated logs obtained directly by the auditor
(D) Unsigned management notes

Q323. The PRIMARY objective of change management is to:
(A) Reduce audit documentation
(B) Increase number of system upgrades
(C) Eliminate project management processes
(D) Ensure controlled and authorized modifications to systems

Q324. In risk assessment, residual risk refers to:
(A) Risk eliminated entirely
(B) Risk transferred to insurance
(C) Risk remaining after controls are applied
(D) Risk identified but not documented

Q325. A business continuity plan should be reviewed and updated:
(A) Only after a disaster occurs
(B) Regularly and after significant organizational changes
(C) Once every ten years
(D) When required by vendors

Q326. Which control BEST prevents unauthorized logical access?
(A) Role based access controls
(B) Insurance coverage
(C) Background checks
(D) Environmental monitoring systems

Q327. The PRIMARY purpose of a post implementation review is to:
(A) Replace project managers
(B) Increase system complexity
(C) Approve new vendor contracts
(D) Assess whether project objectives and controls were achieved

Q328. In sampling methodology, sampling risk is defined as:
(A) Risk that sample results differ from population conclusions
(B) Risk of hardware malfunction
(C) Risk of selecting too many records

(D) Risk of auditor resignation

Q329. The PRIMARY objective of information asset classification is to:

(A) Assign protection levels based on sensitivity and value
(B) Reduce printing costs
(C) Increase data duplication
(D) Simplify database indexing

Q330. Which recovery metric defines acceptable data loss measured in time?

(A) Service delivery objective
(B) Recovery time objective
(C) Recovery point objective
(D) Performance threshold

Q331. A key responsibility of an audit committee is to:

(A) Approve daily transactions
(B) Provide oversight of audit activities
(C) Perform system coding
(D) Configure firewalls

Q332. When evaluating database controls, the auditor should FIRST verify:

(A) Office furniture layout
(B) Employee salary levels
(C) Graphic interface design
(D) Access restrictions and user privileges

Q333. The MOST effective way to ensure integrity of transmitted data is:

(A) Increasing bandwidth
(B) Data compression
(C) Archiving files
(D) Hashing mechanisms

Q334. An auditor reviewing outsourcing arrangements should ensure service level agreements include:

(A) Internal office procedures
(B) Vendor vacation policies
(C) Measurable performance metrics and security obligations
(D) Marketing campaign details

Q335. The PRIMARY objective of quality assurance in the audit process is to:

(A) Increase number of findings
(B) Reduce report length
(C) Ensure audit standards and methodologies are consistently applied
(D) Eliminate regulatory oversight

Q336. In system migration, phased changeover reduces risk by:

(A) Eliminating testing requirements
(B) Increasing immediate downtime
(C) Avoiding documentation
(D) Gradually implementing components over time

Q337. The PRIMARY reason for performing vulnerability assessments is to:

(A) Replace firewall devices
(B) Increase system complexity
(C) Identify weaknesses before exploitation
(D) Shorten audit duration

Q338. An effective incident response plan should include:

(A) Employee vacation scheduling
(B) Advertising strategies
(C) Sales performance metrics
(D) Defined roles, communication procedures, and escalation paths

Q339. The PRIMARY objective of operational log management is to:
(A) Provide traceability and support investigations
(B) Increase disk usage
(C) Simplify payroll processing
(D) Replace backup systems

Q340. When evaluating enterprise risk management, the auditor should verify that:
(A) Technology risks are ignored
(B) Only financial risks are considered
(C) Risks are systematically identified, assessed, and monitored
(D) Risk identification is informal and undocumented

Q341. The PRIMARY benefit of conducting user acceptance testing is to:
(A) Increase number of developers
(B) Avoid documentation
(C) Confirm system meets business requirements before deployment
(D) Reduce hardware cost

Q342. The MOST effective control to prevent duplicate transaction processing is:
(A) Encryption keys
(B) Sequence numbering with validation checks
(C) Antivirus scanning
(D) Firewall filtering

Q343. A strong information security policy should be approved by:
(A) Entry level employees
(B) Temporary contractors
(C) Senior management or governing body
(D) External customers

Q344. The PRIMARY objective of capacity planning is to:
(A) Ensure resources meet future demand efficiently
(B) Over purchase hardware
(C) Increase employee workload
(D) Eliminate system documentation

Q345. In evaluating encryption key management, the auditor should confirm:
(A) Keys are stored in plain text
(B) All employees know master keys
(C) Keys never change
(D) Keys are securely generated, distributed, stored, and revoked

Q346. A primary objective of compliance testing is to:
(A) Eliminate documentation
(B) Evaluate effectiveness of internal controls
(C) Increase server speed
(D) Assess marketing strategies

Q347. The MOST critical factor in disaster recovery site selection is:
(A) Office decoration
(B) Parking availability
(C) Geographic distance and risk separation

(D) Staff cafeteria quality

Q348. A preventive control example in application systems is:

(A) Forensic investigation

(B) Input validation checks

(C) Log review after transaction

(D) Incident reporting

Q349. An effective segregation of duties review should be conducted:

(A) Only at system installation

(B) Once every decade

(C) Periodically and after role changes

(D) By external vendors only

Q350. The PRIMARY objective of security awareness training is to:

(A) Eliminate technical controls

(B) Promote employee understanding of security responsibilities

(C) Reduce audit frequency

(D) Increase network bandwidth

Q351. When reviewing system documentation, the auditor should ensure it is:

(A) Optional

(B) Restricted to executives only

(C) Current, accurate, and accessible

(D) Informal and verbal

Q352. The PRIMARY benefit of continuous monitoring is to:

(A) Provide real time oversight of control effectiveness

(B) Reduce storage capacity

(C) Eliminate audit committees

(D) Delay incident detection

Q353. A key objective of data retention policies is to:

(A) Keep all data indefinitely

(B) Delete records immediately

(C) Avoid compliance

(D) Retain information according to legal and business requirements

Q354. The MOST effective way to validate backup restoration capability is to:

(A) Perform periodic restoration tests

(B) Review backup schedule only

(C) Increase storage capacity

(D) Encrypt backups

Q355. The PRIMARY purpose of configuration management is to:

(A) Increase emergency changes

(B) Randomize system settings

(C) Remove documentation

(D) Maintain integrity and consistency of system configurations

Q356. In evaluating privacy programs, the auditor should confirm that personal data is:

(A) Shared publicly

(B) Stored without restriction

(C) Ignored in risk assessment

(D) Collected, processed, and protected in accordance with policy and regulation

Q357. The PRIMARY advantage of parallel testing during implementation is:

(A) Comparison of outputs between old and new systems

(B) Elimination of documentation
(C) Immediate shutdown of old system
(D) Increased downtime

Q358. A strong risk management process includes:
(A) Identification, assessment, treatment, and monitoring
(B) Ignoring low probability risks
(C) No documentation
(D) Single annual meeting

Q359. The PRIMARY purpose of logical access review is to:
(A) Increase data redundancy
(B) Improve office layout
(C) Ensure access rights remain appropriate and authorized
(D) Reduce encryption strength

Q360. An effective internal audit function should report functionally to:
(A) Information technology manager
(B) Governing board or audit committee
(C) Human resources department
(D) Chief financial officer only

Q361. An auditor reviewing project governance should verify that project risks are:
(A) Ignored until project completion
(B) Documented only in financial statements
(C) Formally identified, assessed, and tracked throughout the project lifecycle
(D) Transferred automatically to vendors

Q362. The PRIMARY objective of input controls in application systems is to:
(A) Accelerate processing speed
(B) Replace database administrators
(C) Ensure data accuracy and completeness before processing
(D) Eliminate encryption needs

Q363. When assessing information security governance, the auditor should confirm that security strategy is:
(A) Aligned with organizational goals and risk appetite
(B) Focused only on physical security
(C) Developed independently of enterprise objectives
(D) Managed solely by technical staff

Q364. The MOST reliable method to verify existence of backup media is to:
(A) Examine vendor brochures
(B) Review backup policy document
(C) Physically inspect and reconcile backup inventory
(D) Interview system operators

Q365. The PRIMARY purpose of an information security incident log is to:
(A) Replace firewall controls
(B) Maintain record of events for analysis and reporting
(C) Increase storage costs
(D) Advertise security achievements

Q366. During system acquisition, the MOST important factor in vendor selection is:
(A) Lowest purchase price
(B) Advertising reputation
(C) Vendor office size

(D) Ability to meet defined functional and control requirements
Q367. The PRIMARY objective of environmental controls in a data center is to:
(A) Protect equipment from damage due to heat, humidity, or power issues
(B) Enhance network bandwidth
(C) Improve employee comfort
(D) Replace logical security controls
Q368. A key indicator of ineffective segregation of duties is when:
(A) Access reviews are conducted periodically
(B) Documentation is well maintained
(C) One individual can initiate, approve, and record transactions
(D) Multiple employees share tasks appropriately
Q369. The PRIMARY goal of penetration testing is to:
(A) Improve graphic interface design
(B) Simulate attacks to identify exploitable weaknesses
(C) Replace audit processes
(D) Increase system load
Q370. In evaluating data integrity controls, the auditor should focus on:
(A) Controls ensuring data remains accurate and unaltered throughout processing
(B) Marketing objectives
(C) Office policies only
(D) Hardware warranty details
Q371. The PRIMARY objective of job rotation in sensitive positions is to:
(A) Increase vacation time
(B) Reduce risk of long term fraud or concealed irregularities
(C) Eliminate need for audits
(D) Improve system speed
Q372. An auditor reviewing cloud service arrangements should ensure that:
(A) Internal policies are discontinued
(B) All responsibilities are transferred entirely to the provider
(C) Monitoring is unnecessary
(D) Roles and security responsibilities are clearly defined in contracts
Q373. The PRIMARY purpose of reconciliation controls is to:
(A) Increase database size
(B) Replace encryption methods
(C) Compare data sets to identify discrepancies
(D) Simplify user interfaces
Q374. An effective information classification scheme should be based on:
(A) Sensitivity, criticality, and regulatory requirements
(B) Employee preference
(C) Office location
(D) Storage device type
Q375. The PRIMARY risk of inadequate logging is:
(A) Inability to detect and investigate security incidents
(B) Improved performance
(C) Reduced storage
(D) Excessive documentation
Q376. When reviewing strategic information technology planning, the auditor should confirm that:
(A) Only technical staff contribute

(B) Objectives are measurable and aligned with enterprise direction
(C) Technology initiatives are random
(D) Plans are informal and undocumented

Q377. The PRIMARY objective of access provisioning procedures is to:
(A) Ensure access is authorized, approved, and appropriate to role
(B) Reduce password length
(C) Eliminate authentication
(D) Grant unlimited privileges

Q378. The MOST effective method to ensure completeness of transaction processing is:
(A) Graphic interface testing
(B) Control totals and record counts
(C) File encryption
(D) Hardware replacement

Q379. The PRIMARY purpose of an information security awareness program is to:
(A) Replace firewalls
(B) Increase network speed
(C) Eliminate governance structures
(D) Educate users about threats and secure behavior

Q380. An effective disaster recovery plan should prioritize systems based on:
(A) Employee preference
(B) Hardware age
(C) Vendor recommendation only
(D) Results of business impact analysis

Q381. The PRIMARY control to prevent unauthorized physical access to servers is:
(A) Password complexity
(B) Software patching
(C) Data compression
(D) Biometric access controls and restricted entry

Q382. The MOST important characteristic of audit evidence is that it is:
(A) Informal
(B) Lengthy
(C) Color coded
(D) Relevant, reliable, and sufficient

Q383. The PRIMARY objective of system monitoring tools is to:
(A) Detect performance issues and security events proactively
(B) Reduce governance oversight
(C) Replace documentation
(D) Increase downtime

Q384. When evaluating enterprise architecture, the auditor should verify that it:
(A) Eliminates documentation
(B) Exists only verbally
(C) Focuses solely on hardware
(D) Supports strategic objectives and standardization

Q385. The PRIMARY purpose of a data loss prevention mechanism is to:
(A) Increase printing
(B) Prevent unauthorized transmission of sensitive information
(C) Replace backups
(D) Improve processor speed

Q386. An auditor assessing maturity of internal controls should consider:
(A) Office layout
(B) Informal practices only
(C) Marketing performance
(D) Documentation, consistency, monitoring, and continuous improvement
Q387. The PRIMARY objective of database encryption at rest is to:
(A) Simplify user training
(B) Replace fire suppression systems
(C) Protect stored data from unauthorized access
(D) Accelerate processing
Q388. When reviewing information technology service management processes, the auditor should verify that incidents are:
(A) Logged, categorized, prioritized, and resolved in timely manner
(B) Ignored
(C) Handled informally
(D) Deleted immediately
Q389. The PRIMARY purpose of system hardening is to:
(A) Remove updates
(B) Simplify passwords
(C) Reduce attack surface by disabling unnecessary services
(D) Increase default settings
Q390. An effective control self assessment program enables:
(A) External regulators to manage systems
(B) Management to evaluate and improve internal controls
(C) Removal of documentation
(D) Elimination of audits
Q391. The PRIMARY objective of identity verification procedures is to:
(A) Increase system downtime
(B) Replace encryption
(C) Reduce hardware cost
(D) Ensure users are who they claim to be
Q392. The MOST critical component of an effective audit follow up process is:
(A) Increasing report length
(B) Eliminating deadlines
(C) Ignoring previous findings
(D) Tracking remediation actions until closure
Q393. When evaluating system interfaces, the auditor should verify:
(A) Data transfer controls ensure accuracy and completeness
(B) Hardware color consistency
(C) Marketing alignment
(D) Interfaces are undocumented
Q394. The PRIMARY purpose of a privacy impact assessment is to:
(A) Eliminate data classification
(B) Replace encryption
(C) Identify and mitigate privacy risks in projects or systems
(D) Increase marketing outreach
Q395. An effective configuration baseline should be:
(A) Informal and undocumented

(B) Approved, documented, and protected from unauthorized change
(C) Frequently ignored
(D) Accessible to all users for modification

Q396. The PRIMARY objective of audit documentation is to:
(A) Replace governance
(B) Provide evidence supporting audit conclusions
(C) Reduce independence
(D) Increase storage needs

Q397. When assessing mobile device security, the auditor should verify:
(A) Policies enforce authentication, encryption, and remote wipe capability
(B) Devices are unmanaged
(C) All applications are unrestricted
(D) Devices lack encryption

Q398. The PRIMARY objective of vulnerability remediation is to:
(A) Ignore scan results
(B) Document weaknesses only
(C) Increase network complexity
(D) Eliminate or reduce identified security exposures

Q399. The MOST important factor when evaluating audit risk is:
(A) Vendor popularity
(B) Office layout
(C) Auditor preference
(D) Materiality and likelihood of misstatement

Q400. The PRIMARY responsibility of senior management in information security governance is to:
(A) Perform daily log reviews
(B) Configure firewalls personally
(C) Establish policies, allocate resources, and oversee risk management
(D) Ignore audit findings

Answer Key and Explanation (301-400)

Q301. Answer: D

Explanation: An IT strategic plan ensures that technology initiatives directly support enterprise objectives and long-term vision. Alignment between IT and business strategy is a core governance requirement and reduces risk of misdirected investments. A documented and approved strategy provides measurable goals and accountability. Governance structures and budgets are important but secondary to formal strategic alignment. Without a clear strategic plan, committees and controls lack direction. Strategic integration strengthens value delivery and resource optimization.

Q302. Answer: D

Explanation: Risk-based audit planning prioritizes areas with the highest inherent risk combined with significant business impact. Systems affecting critical processes or financial reporting require more immediate attention. Risk assessment ensures efficient use of audit resources. Other operational attributes may contribute context but do not determine priority alone. Impact and likelihood drive risk magnitude. Audits must focus where potential losses or disruptions would be greatest.

Q303. Answer: B

Explanation: Documentation provides evidence that control activities were performed effectively and consistently. Without records, management cannot demonstrate compliance or accountability. Audit trails support traceability and regulatory requirements. Controls lacking documentation are considered ineffective from an assurance perspective. Even if reviews occur, absence of proof undermines reliability. Proper documentation strengthens governance and monitoring processes.

Q304. Answer: A

Explanation: Checksum totals validate that all data within a batch has been processed without omission. They compare calculated totals before and after processing to confirm integrity and completeness. This technique detects missing or altered records. It is widely used in financial and transaction systems. Authentication and encryption address security but not completeness validation. Batch controls are essential for reliable transaction processing.

Q305. Answer: D

Explanation: Contracts must clearly define security, compliance, service-level, and control obligations aligned with enterprise needs. Properly structured agreements reduce operational and legal risks. Auditors assess whether responsibilities and performance expectations are enforceable. Governance over outsourcing depends on contractual clarity. Reputation and longevity are helpful but not sufficient assurance. Risk transfer and accountability must be formally documented.

Q306. Answer: C

Explanation: Formal approval of requirements ensures business needs are accurately defined before design and development begin. Errors at this stage propagate throughout the project lifecycle. Clear documentation reduces scope creep and misinterpretation. Governance oversight at requirements phase lowers rework costs. Testing and coding occur later in the cycle. Early validation improves project success probability.

Q307. Answer: A

Explanation: A business impact analysis identifies critical processes and defines acceptable downtime thresholds. It establishes recovery time and recovery point objectives for systems and data. These metrics guide disaster recovery planning and resource allocation. BIA quantifies financial and operational consequences of disruptions. It forms the foundation of business continuity strategies. Without BIA, recovery priorities may be misaligned.

Q308. Answer: C

Explanation: Substantive testing validates the accuracy and integrity of transactions and balances directly. It provides assurance beyond control reliance. This approach is often used when control effectiveness is uncertain. It examines actual data for misstatements or anomalies. Compliance testing focuses on control adherence, whereas substantive testing verifies outcomes. Both methods complement each other in audit engagements.

Q309. Answer: C

Explanation: Intrusion detection systems monitor network traffic and alert on suspicious activity patterns. They provide real-time detection of unauthorized access attempts. Continuous monitoring enhances early response capability. Preventive policies reduce risk but do not actively detect breaches. Detection controls complement preventive mechanisms. Monitoring logs and alerts strengthen incident response readiness.

Q310. Answer: A

Explanation: System uptime percentage directly reflects service availability and reliability. Availability is a core service-level metric in IT operations. Measuring uptime enables comparison against defined service-level agreements. Performance metrics must align with operational objectives. Staffing and facilities do not indicate service effectiveness. Quantifiable indicators support governance and reporting.

Q311. Answer: B

Explanation: Segregation of duties reduces risk of fraud by dividing critical tasks among multiple individuals. It prevents any single person from completing incompatible functions. This control limits opportunity for unauthorized actions. Effective segregation enhances accountability and oversight. It is a foundational internal control principle. Operational efficiency is secondary to risk mitigation.

Q312. Answer: D

Explanation: Patch management addresses known security vulnerabilities in software and systems. Failure to apply updates leaves systems exposed to exploitation. Many cyber incidents exploit unpatched weaknesses. Regular updates reduce likelihood of compromise. Operational stability must be balanced with timely patching. Security governance requires structured patch processes.

Q313. Answer: B

Explanation: Ensuring data integrity and completeness is critical before analysis. CAAT results are only reliable if input data is accurate and complete. Verification prevents misleading conclusions. Proper validation supports audit credibility. Analytical tools depend on quality source data. Controls over data extraction must be reviewed first.

Q314. Answer: D

Explanation: Encryption transforms readable data into unreadable format to protect confidentiality. It prevents unauthorized disclosure during storage or transmission. Cryptographic techniques are fundamental to information security frameworks. Encryption supports regulatory compliance requirements. Integrity and authentication may also be supported depending on implementation. Confidentiality remains the principal objective.

Q315. Answer: C

Explanation: A full interruption test requires complete shutdown of live systems to validate recovery capability. It provides the highest assurance of disaster readiness. This method demonstrates real operational resilience. However, it involves significant risk and coordination. It is typically conducted in mature environments. Comprehensive validation ensures recovery procedures function as intended.

Q316. Answer: D

Explanation: Preventive controls stop undesirable events before they occur. They reduce the probability of errors or fraud. Early risk mitigation lowers potential losses. Preventive measures are generally more cost-effective than corrective actions. Effective design minimizes reliance on detection. Strong preventive frameworks enhance overall control environment.

Q317. Answer: D

Explanation: Audit independence ensures objective evaluation and unbiased reporting. Compromised independence undermines credibility and stakeholder trust. Objectivity is fundamental to assurance engagements. Biased findings may conceal risks or misrepresent conditions. Ethical standards emphasize independence as core principle. Reliable audits depend on impartial judgment.

Q318. Answer: C

Explanation: Digital signatures provide proof of origin and integrity of electronic messages. They ensure that a sender cannot deny sending a message. Cryptographic validation supports authenticity verification. Non-repudiation is essential in electronic transactions and contracts. It enhances legal enforceability. Strong key management underpins effectiveness.

Q319. Answer: A

Explanation: Capacity management aligns IT resources with current and projected workload demands. It prevents performance degradation due to resource shortages. Monitoring trends supports proactive scaling decisions. Effective planning optimizes cost and performance balance. It contributes to service-level achievement. Continuous review ensures adaptability to growth.

Q320. Answer: D

Explanation: An audit report must clearly communicate findings, associated risks, and business impact. Clarity enables management to take corrective action. Well-articulated recommendations support remediation. Transparency strengthens governance accountability. Reports serve as formal documentation of assurance activities. Effective communication is central to audit value delivery.

Q321. Answer: C

Explanation: An audit charter formally defines the purpose, authority, and responsibility of the audit function. Without it, auditors may lack clear organizational mandate and independence. This can lead to scope disputes and restricted access to information. Governance bodies rely on the charter to support audit activities. It also clarifies reporting lines and accountability. Absence of this document weakens the foundation of the audit function.

Q322. Answer: C

Explanation: Evidence obtained directly by the auditor from independent system sources provides higher reliability. System generated logs reduce risk of manipulation compared to verbal or informal sources. Reliability increases when evidence is objective and verifiable. Direct access strengthens credibility of conclusions. Documentary evidence is superior to testimonial evidence. Proper chain of custody enhances integrity of collected data.

Q323. Answer: D

Explanation: Change management ensures that modifications to systems are reviewed, approved, tested, and documented before implementation. It minimizes unintended disruptions and security weaknesses. Structured processes reduce operational risk. Proper authorization maintains accountability. Testing prior to deployment prevents production failures. Effective change governance preserves system integrity and availability.

Q324. Answer: C

Explanation: Residual risk represents the level of risk that remains after implementing mitigating controls. No control environment eliminates risk completely. Management must decide whether residual exposure is acceptable. Evaluation of remaining risk supports informed decision making. Continuous monitoring ensures it stays within tolerance levels. Proper documentation enhances governance transparency.

Q325. Answer: B

Explanation: Regular review ensures the plan reflects current organizational structure, technology, and risk environment. Significant changes such as mergers or system upgrades may alter recovery priorities. Testing and maintenance maintain effectiveness. Outdated plans may fail during real disruptions. Continuous improvement strengthens resilience. Governance requires periodic reassessment.

Q326. Answer: A

Explanation: Role based access controls restrict system permissions according to job responsibilities. This enforces the principle of least privilege. Logical access controls directly protect digital resources. Proper configuration reduces risk of misuse. Regular review maintains effectiveness. Administrative controls complement but do not replace logical restrictions.

Q327. Answer: D

Explanation: A post implementation review evaluates whether the system meets business requirements and control expectations. It identifies lessons learned for future improvements. This review confirms that risks were addressed appropriately. Cost, schedule, and quality outcomes are analyzed. Governance accountability requires validation after deployment. Continuous improvement depends on structured feedback.

Q328. Answer: A

Explanation: Sampling risk arises when conclusions drawn from a sample differ from those that would be reached from the entire population. It is inherent in statistical and nonstatistical sampling. Proper sample size reduces this risk. Understanding sampling limitations strengthens audit reliability. Risk evaluation ensures confidence in findings. Documentation supports defensible conclusions.

Q329. Answer: A

Explanation: Classification categorizes information according to sensitivity, criticality, and regulatory requirements. Appropriate safeguards are applied based on classification level. This ensures efficient allocation of security resources. It supports compliance with privacy and protection standards. Clear labeling enhances user awareness. Governance policies depend on structured classification frameworks.

Q330. Answer: C

Explanation: Recovery point objective specifies the maximum tolerable period of data loss measured backward from disruption. It determines backup frequency requirements. This metric guides replication and storage strategies. It directly influences disaster recovery design. Alignment with business needs is essential. Proper definition prevents excessive data loss exposure.

Q331. Answer: B

Explanation: The audit committee provides governance oversight and ensures independence of the audit function. It reviews audit plans and findings. Oversight strengthens accountability and transparency. It supports effective communication between auditors and board members. Governance frameworks emphasize this supervisory role. Proper oversight enhances control environment maturity.

Q332. Answer: D

Explanation: Access restrictions ensure only authorized individuals can modify or view database content. Logical security is fundamental to protecting data integrity and confidentiality. Reviewing privileges helps identify excessive rights. Proper segregation reduces fraud risk. Database security forms core of information asset protection. Continuous monitoring reinforces compliance.

Q333. Answer: D

Explanation: Hashing generates unique values that detect alteration of data during transmission. Any modification changes the hash output. This mechanism ensures integrity verification. It is widely used in secure communications. Integrity complements confidentiality protections. Strong cryptographic functions enhance reliability.

Q334. Answer: C

Explanation: Service level agreements must define measurable service expectations and security responsibilities. Clear metrics enable performance monitoring. Defined obligations reduce disputes. Governance over outsourced services depends on enforceable terms. Security clauses ensure compliance with enterprise policies. Regular review strengthens accountability.

Q335. Answer: C

Explanation: Quality assurance verifies that audits adhere to professional standards and internal methodologies. Consistency improves reliability of results. Periodic review identifies improvement opportunities. Strong quality processes enhance stakeholder confidence. Governance demands structured evaluation. Continuous education supports competency development.

Q336. Answer: D

Explanation: Phased changeover introduces new systems incrementally. This allows issues to be identified and corrected before full deployment. Gradual implementation reduces operational disruption. It provides opportunity for user adaptation. Risk exposure is minimized compared to abrupt transitions. Proper planning ensures smoother migration.

Q337. Answer: C

Explanation: Vulnerability assessments detect security weaknesses proactively. Early identification reduces likelihood of successful attacks. Remediation strengthens defensive posture. Continuous scanning supports compliance requirements. Governance frameworks emphasize preventive risk management. Addressing weaknesses protects confidentiality, integrity, and availability.

Q338. Answer: D

Explanation: Clear roles and responsibilities ensure coordinated response during incidents. Communication procedures facilitate timely notification. Escalation paths support decision making. Structured planning reduces confusion under pressure. Documentation ensures accountability. Preparedness minimizes operational and reputational impact.

Q339. Answer: A

Explanation: Logs record system activities and user actions. They enable detection of anomalies and support forensic analysis. Proper retention preserves evidence. Centralized monitoring enhances security oversight. Log review strengthens compliance posture. Controlled access protects log integrity.

Q340. Answer: C

Explanation: Enterprise risk management requires structured processes for identifying and evaluating risks. Documentation ensures transparency. Continuous monitoring tracks mitigation effectiveness. Inclusion of operational, strategic, and technological risks strengthens resilience. Governance maturity depends on systematic approach. Comprehensive assessment supports informed leadership decisions.

Q341. Answer: C

Explanation: User acceptance testing validates that the developed system satisfies business needs. It provides final verification before production release. Engagement of users reduces post implementation defects. Early validation lowers rework expenses. Governance requires confirmation of requirements fulfillment. Acceptance sign off formalizes accountability.

Q342. Answer: B

Explanation: Sequence numbering ensures transactions are processed in proper order and prevents duplicates. Validation checks detect missing or repeated entries. This strengthens transaction integrity. Batch processing environments rely on such controls. Preventive mechanisms reduce financial misstatements. Monitoring improves data reliability.

Q343. Answer: C

Explanation: Approval by senior leadership demonstrates commitment and accountability. Governance endorsement ensures authority and enforcement capability. Policies must align with enterprise objectives. Top level support strengthens compliance culture. Formal approval provides legitimacy. Clear communication ensures organizational adherence.

Q344. Answer: A

Explanation: Capacity planning forecasts resource requirements based on projected growth. It balances performance and cost considerations. Proactive management prevents bottlenecks. Monitoring usage trends supports informed decisions. Governance requires optimization of investments. Strategic planning reduces risk of outages.

Q345. Answer: D

Explanation: Effective key management ensures confidentiality and integrity of encrypted data. Secure generation prevents predictability. Controlled distribution limits exposure. Proper storage protects against compromise. Revocation procedures address termination or compromise events. Lifecycle management maintains security strength.

Q346. Answer: B

Explanation: Compliance testing determines whether established controls are operating as intended. It verifies adherence to policies and procedures. Results influence extent of substantive testing. Proper evaluation strengthens reliance on control environment. Documentation supports defensible conclusions. Effective compliance testing reduces audit risk.

Q347. Answer: C

Explanation: Geographic separation reduces likelihood that both primary and recovery sites are affected by same event. Risk diversification enhances resilience. Site selection considers natural and man made threats. Proximity must balance accessibility and risk exposure. Infrastructure reliability is essential. Proper evaluation supports continuity objectives.

Q348. Answer: B

Explanation: Input validation checks prevent incorrect or unauthorized data entry. They stop errors at source before processing. Preventive design reduces downstream corrections. Application controls ensure data accuracy. Early validation enhances reliability. Proper configuration minimizes operational disruption.

Q349. Answer: C

Explanation: Organizational changes may create conflicting responsibilities. Periodic review identifies emerging risks. Ongoing monitoring maintains control effectiveness. Documentation ensures accountability. Governance requires proactive assessment. Adjustments reduce fraud exposure.

Q350. Answer: B

Explanation: Awareness training educates employees about risks and expected behaviors. Human error is a major source of security incidents. Training strengthens organizational defense. Regular sessions reinforce policy adherence. Knowledgeable staff reduce vulnerability. Governance depends on informed participation.

Q351. Answer: C

Explanation: Updated documentation supports maintenance and control review. Accuracy ensures reliable system understanding. Accessibility allows effective oversight. Proper documentation aids continuity planning. Governance frameworks emphasize record retention. Outdated materials increase operational risk.

Q352. Answer: A

Explanation: Continuous monitoring enables early detection of control failures. Real time insights improve responsiveness. Automation enhances efficiency. Ongoing assessment strengthens risk management. Governance maturity depends on proactive oversight. Timely information supports decision making.

Q353. Answer: D

Explanation: Retention policies ensure information is preserved for required duration while minimizing unnecessary storage. Legal and regulatory mandates influence timelines. Proper disposal reduces privacy risk. Governance requires structured management of records. Clear guidelines prevent litigation exposure. Periodic review ensures alignment.

Q354. Answer: A

Explanation: Restoration testing confirms backups are usable and complete. Without testing, recovery success is uncertain. Periodic drills identify configuration issues. Validation ensures alignment with recovery objectives. Testing strengthens confidence in continuity planning. Documentation supports audit assurance.

Q355. Answer: D
Explanation: Configuration management tracks and controls system settings throughout lifecycle. Consistency reduces errors and vulnerabilities. Proper documentation supports change tracking. Controlled configuration prevents unauthorized modifications. Governance emphasizes integrity of baseline settings. Continuous review ensures compliance.
Q356. Answer: D
Explanation: Privacy programs ensure lawful and ethical handling of personal information. Policies must align with regulatory requirements. Safeguards protect confidentiality and integrity. Transparency builds stakeholder trust. Governance frameworks emphasize accountability. Periodic assessment strengthens compliance posture.
Q357. Answer: A
Explanation: Parallel testing runs old and new systems simultaneously. Output comparison validates accuracy before full transition. This reduces operational risk. Discrepancies can be resolved early. Controlled approach improves confidence. Proper planning ensures resource readiness.
Q358. Answer: A
Explanation: Comprehensive risk management follows structured stages from identification to monitoring. Documentation ensures traceability. Treatment decisions align with tolerance levels. Continuous monitoring tracks changes. Governance maturity requires systematic approach. Integration with enterprise objectives enhances resilience.
Q359. Answer: C
Explanation: Logical access reviews validate that permissions correspond to job roles. Changes in employment status may create excessive privileges. Periodic review prevents misuse. Documentation supports compliance evidence. Governance standards require oversight. Proper review enhances confidentiality and integrity.
Q360. Answer: B
Explanation: Functional reporting to the governing board or audit committee preserves independence. Direct oversight prevents management interference. This structure enhances objectivity. Governance frameworks recommend board level reporting. Independence strengthens credibility of findings. Clear reporting lines support accountability.
Q361. Answer: C
Explanation: Effective project governance requires structured risk management from initiation through closure. Risks must be identified early and reassessed as conditions change. Continuous tracking ensures mitigation actions remain effective. Documentation provides transparency and accountability to stakeholders. Without ongoing monitoring, emerging threats may disrupt objectives. Integrating risk management into governance increases project success rates.
Q362. Answer: C
Explanation: Input controls validate data at the point of entry to prevent errors from entering the system. Accuracy and completeness at this stage reduce downstream correction costs. Validation rules such as format checks and limit checks are essential. Preventing incorrect input strengthens overall data integrity. Reliable processing depends on valid initial data. Effective controls enhance operational efficiency and reliability.
Q363. Answer: A
Explanation: Security governance must align with enterprise strategy to ensure risk management supports business priorities. Alignment ensures resources are allocated effectively. Risk appetite defines acceptable exposure levels. Senior leadership involvement reinforces accountability. Integrated strategy strengthens resilience and compliance. Governance maturity depends on coordinated planning.
Q364. Answer: C

Explanation: Physical inspection provides direct evidence that backup media exists and is properly stored. Reconciliation with inventory records confirms completeness. Documentation alone does not guarantee existence. Observation strengthens audit assurance. Secure storage conditions should also be evaluated. Direct verification reduces risk of false assurance.

Q365. Answer: B

Explanation: Incident logs provide structured documentation of security events and responses. They support trend analysis and root cause investigation. Accurate logging enables regulatory reporting where required. Historical records improve future prevention strategies. Documentation enhances accountability and transparency. Continuous review strengthens security posture.

Q366. Answer: D

Explanation: Vendor solutions must satisfy business and control requirements identified during planning. Functional alignment ensures operational effectiveness. Security and compliance considerations are equally critical. Cost is important but should not compromise control standards. Structured evaluation criteria support objective decision making. Proper due diligence reduces implementation risk.

Q367. Answer: A

Explanation: Environmental controls maintain optimal conditions for hardware operation. Excessive heat or humidity can cause equipment failure. Stable power supply prevents data corruption and downtime. These safeguards protect availability of critical systems. Physical protection complements logical controls. Reliable infrastructure underpins business continuity.

Q368. Answer: C

Explanation: When a single person controls incompatible functions, the risk of fraud or error increases significantly. Proper segregation distributes responsibilities to reduce opportunity for misuse. Concentrated authority undermines internal control frameworks. Oversight mechanisms may fail without separation. Regular review identifies such conflicts. Balanced role assignment enhances accountability.

Q369. Answer: B

Explanation: Penetration testing evaluates security by simulating real-world attack techniques. It identifies vulnerabilities that could be exploited by malicious actors. Results guide remediation efforts. Controlled testing enhances defensive preparedness. Regular assessments strengthen security maturity. Ethical testing reduces likelihood of successful breaches.

Q370. Answer: A

Explanation: Data integrity controls ensure information is not improperly modified during transmission or storage. Accuracy and consistency are fundamental to reliable reporting. Validation checks and reconciliation procedures are essential. Monitoring safeguards prevent unauthorized changes. Strong integrity measures support trust in information systems. Governance depends on reliable data.

Q371. Answer: B

Explanation: Rotating personnel in sensitive roles limits opportunity for sustained misconduct. Fresh oversight may uncover hidden issues. It enhances transparency and control effectiveness. Job rotation complements segregation of duties. Governance frameworks recommend this practice in high risk areas. Regular rotation reduces dependency on single individuals.

Q372. Answer: D

Explanation: Clear delineation of responsibilities prevents gaps in security and compliance. Contracts must specify obligations for data protection and incident response. Shared responsibility models require active governance. Internal oversight remains essential even with outsourcing. Proper agreement reduces legal and operational risk. Continuous monitoring validates adherence.

Q373. Answer: C

Explanation: Reconciliation verifies consistency between independent data sources. Discrepancies highlight errors or unauthorized changes. Regular comparison strengthens financial and operational accuracy. Documentation supports audit verification. Timely detection prevents material misstatements. Reliable reconciliation enhances control effectiveness.

Q374. Answer: A

Explanation: Classification reflects the value and sensitivity of information assets. Regulatory obligations influence required safeguards. Critical data demands stronger protection. Structured criteria ensure consistent labeling. Governance relies on risk based protection measures. Clear classification guides access and handling procedures.

Q375. Answer: A

Explanation: Without adequate logs, suspicious activities may go unnoticed. Investigations require reliable historical records. Logging supports accountability and forensic analysis. Insufficient records weaken compliance posture. Monitoring relies on comprehensive data capture. Strong logging enhances transparency and response capability.

Q376. Answer: B

Explanation: Strategic planning must define measurable objectives supporting organizational goals. Alignment ensures technology investments deliver value. Documentation enhances accountability. Cross functional participation strengthens planning quality. Governance frameworks emphasize measurable outcomes. Continuous evaluation supports adaptability.

Q377. Answer: A

Explanation: Access provisioning ensures that users receive permissions consistent with job responsibilities. Approval processes prevent unauthorized privilege escalation. Proper documentation provides audit evidence. Role alignment supports least privilege principle. Periodic review confirms continued necessity. Structured provisioning strengthens logical security.

Q378. Answer: B

Explanation: Control totals and record counts verify that all expected transactions are processed. Discrepancies indicate missing or duplicate entries. Batch reconciliation strengthens data reliability. Such controls are fundamental in financial systems. Verification prevents unnoticed processing failures. Continuous monitoring enhances assurance.

Q379. Answer: D

Explanation: Awareness programs address human factors in security. Educated users are less likely to fall victim to social engineering. Regular training reinforces policy compliance. Human vigilance complements technical safeguards. Governance maturity requires organization wide participation. Ongoing education reduces overall risk exposure.

Q380. Answer: D

Explanation: Business impact analysis identifies critical processes and acceptable downtime. Recovery priorities must reflect operational and financial impact. Structured evaluation ensures resource allocation aligns with importance. Recovery objectives guide sequencing decisions. Governance demands risk based prioritization. Proper planning minimizes disruption.

Q381. Answer: D

Explanation: Physical access controls restrict entry to authorized personnel. Biometric mechanisms enhance identification accuracy. Securing server rooms prevents tampering and theft. Physical protection complements logical safeguards. Unauthorized access can compromise entire systems. Strong environmental security supports overall resilience.

Q382. Answer: D

Explanation: Audit conclusions depend on quality of evidence gathered. Relevance ensures evidence supports objectives. Reliability increases credibility. Sufficiency provides adequate basis for opinion. Professional standards emphasize these attributes. Strong evidence underpins defensible reporting.

Q383. Answer: A
Explanation: Monitoring tools provide continuous visibility into system health and security posture. Early detection prevents escalation of issues. Alerts enable timely response. Performance metrics support capacity planning. Security monitoring identifies anomalies. Proactive oversight strengthens operational stability.
Q384. Answer: D
Explanation: Enterprise architecture provides structured blueprint aligning technology with strategy. Standardization reduces complexity and cost. Documentation supports informed decision making. Alignment enhances efficiency and scalability. Governance frameworks recommend integrated architecture planning. Proper oversight ensures sustainability.
Q385. Answer: B
Explanation: Data loss prevention solutions monitor and restrict movement of sensitive data. They reduce risk of accidental or intentional leakage. Policies define acceptable use parameters. Monitoring supports compliance obligations. Protection of confidential information is central objective. Effective configuration enhances security maturity.
Q386. Answer: D
Explanation: Mature controls are documented and consistently applied. Monitoring ensures ongoing effectiveness. Continuous improvement reflects adaptive governance. Informal controls lack reliability. Structured evaluation identifies gaps. Comprehensive assessment supports risk reduction.
Q387. Answer: C
Explanation: Encryption at rest secures data stored on disks or storage media. It prevents unauthorized disclosure if devices are compromised. Cryptographic safeguards protect confidentiality. Regulatory requirements often mandate such protection. Secure key management is essential. Stored data remains protected even if physical access occurs.
Q388. Answer: A
Explanation: Structured incident management ensures consistent handling of operational issues. Logging creates accountability and tracking capability. Categorization and prioritization allocate resources effectively. Timely resolution minimizes business impact. Documentation supports performance analysis. Mature processes enhance service reliability.
Q389. Answer: C
Explanation: Hardening removes or disables unnecessary features and services. Reducing attack surface limits potential exploitation points. Secure configuration strengthens defense in depth. Baseline standards guide implementation. Continuous review maintains effectiveness. Strong configuration reduces vulnerability exposure.
Q390. Answer: B
Explanation: Control self assessment empowers management to review effectiveness of controls proactively. It encourages ownership of risk management. Structured evaluation identifies weaknesses early. Documentation supports transparency. Complementary to independent audits, it strengthens governance. Continuous assessment fosters accountability.
Q391. Answer: D
Explanation: Identity verification confirms authenticity of users before granting access. Strong authentication reduces unauthorized access risk. Multi factor approaches enhance assurance. Reliable identification protects confidentiality and integrity. Governance requires consistent verification processes. Proper controls strengthen overall security framework.
Q392. Answer: D
Explanation: Follow up ensures that identified weaknesses are addressed promptly. Tracking mechanisms monitor progress. Management accountability is reinforced through status reporting.

Closure verification confirms risk reduction. Unresolved issues may persist without oversight. Continuous monitoring strengthens governance outcomes.

Q393. Answer: A

Explanation: Interfaces connect systems and require reliable transfer controls. Validation ensures information is not lost or altered. Error handling procedures must be defined. Documentation supports maintenance and review. Reliable integration prevents reconciliation issues. Strong controls enhance overall data integrity.

Q394. Answer: C

Explanation: Privacy impact assessments evaluate how personal information is collected and processed. They identify potential risks to individuals. Mitigation strategies are recommended before implementation. Regulatory compliance often requires such assessments. Transparency enhances stakeholder trust. Proactive evaluation reduces legal exposure.

Q395. Answer: B

Explanation: A configuration baseline defines approved system settings. Documentation ensures clarity and consistency. Protection prevents unauthorized modification. Periodic review maintains alignment with security standards. Baselines support change management processes. Controlled configurations enhance stability and security.

Q396. Answer: B

Explanation: Audit documentation records procedures performed and evidence obtained. It supports conclusions and opinions issued. Proper records enable quality review. Documentation demonstrates compliance with professional standards. Clear records strengthen transparency. Reliable documentation ensures defensibility.

Q397. Answer: A

Explanation: Mobile devices pose risk of data exposure if lost or stolen. Authentication prevents unauthorized use. Encryption protects stored information. Remote wipe capability enables quick response to compromise. Policy enforcement ensures consistency. Strong controls mitigate mobility related risks.

Q398. Answer: D

Explanation: Remediation addresses vulnerabilities identified through assessment. Timely correction reduces likelihood of exploitation. Prioritization aligns with risk severity. Documentation tracks resolution progress. Continuous improvement strengthens defensive posture. Effective remediation lowers overall threat exposure.

Q399. Answer: D

Explanation: Audit risk reflects probability that significant misstatements remain undetected. Materiality determines impact on stakeholders. Likelihood assesses probability of occurrence. Combined evaluation guides audit scope and testing depth. Professional judgment supports assessment. Structured risk evaluation enhances audit effectiveness.

Q400. Answer: C

Explanation: Senior management sets direction and accountability for security governance. Policy approval establishes organizational standards. Resource allocation enables implementation of controls. Oversight ensures risks remain within tolerance levels. Leadership commitment drives security culture. Effective governance requires active executive involvement.

Question (401-500)

Q401. A financial institution is implementing a new core banking application, and management decides to bypass formal requirement documentation to accelerate delivery. As an information systems auditor, what would be the MOST significant risk associated with this decision?

(A) Increased hardware procurement cost
(B) Reduced employee training time
(C) Excessive network bandwidth usage
(D) Inability to demonstrate alignment between system capabilities and business needs

Q402. A manufacturing company experiences repeated system outages due to unexpected server overload during peak production periods. Which control process would MOST effectively prevent recurrence of this issue?

(A) Structured capacity planning with trend analysis
(B) Enhanced password policy enforcement
(C) Reduction of audit documentation
(D) Implementation of social media monitoring

Q403. During a review of logical access controls, an auditor discovers that terminated employees retain remote access credentials for several weeks. What is the MOST appropriate recommendation?

(A) Implement automated deprovisioning linked to human resource records
(B) Increase employee salaries
(C) Expand physical security measures
(D) Disable system monitoring

Q404. An organization stores confidential customer data in an external cloud environment. The service contract lacks clear language regarding data ownership and breach notification timelines. What should the auditor identify as the PRIMARY concern?

(A) Cloud provider office location
(B) Overly detailed training manuals
(C) Undefined legal and security accountability
(D) Excessive data encryption strength

Q405. A healthcare organization conducts a business impact analysis and identifies that patient record systems must be restored within two hours of disruption. Which recovery metric has been defined in this scenario?

(A) Data encryption key length
(B) Acceptable variance threshold
(C) Recovery time objective
(D) Service desk response time

Q406. During an audit of application development practices, it is noted that developers have direct access to modify production code. What risk does this situation MOST directly introduce?

(A) Increased risk of unauthorized or untested changes
(B) Improved system performance
(C) Lower hardware expenses
(D) Reduced training cost

Q407. A retail enterprise implements data classification but fails to label documents according to sensitivity levels. What is the MOST likely outcome of this weakness?

(A) Faster document printing
(B) Reduced need for encryption
(C) Increased employee productivity
(D) Inconsistent application of security controls

Q408. An organization performs regular vulnerability assessments but does not track remediation status. Which governance weakness does this indicate?
(A) Effective cost reduction strategy
(B) Lack of follow up and risk monitoring
(C) Strong preventive control culture
(D) Excessive compliance
Q409. A newly implemented enterprise resource planning system is running concurrently with the legacy system for comparison of outputs. What implementation strategy is being used?
(A) Phased migration
(B) Pilot deployment
(C) Parallel changeover
(D) Direct conversion
Q410. A data center is located in a flood prone region without secondary site arrangements. From a resilience perspective, what is the MOST critical deficiency?
(A) Insufficient employee parking
(B) Lack of modern furniture
(C) Absence of geographic risk diversification
(D) Overuse of encryption
Q411. A project sponsor insists on deploying a system despite incomplete user acceptance testing results. What is the auditor's PRIMARY concern?
(A) Reduced vendor marketing
(B) System may not meet business or control requirements
(C) Excessive documentation
(D) Increased electricity consumption
Q412. An enterprise implements encryption for stored financial records but stores cryptographic keys in an unsecured shared folder. What is the MOST significant risk?
(A) Compromise of encrypted data through key exposure
(B) Improved processing speed
(C) Reduced storage cost
(D) Excessive documentation
Q413. An auditor notes that system logs are retained for only three days despite regulatory requirements mandating ninety day retention. What is the PRIMARY implication?
(A) Noncompliance and limited investigation capability
(B) Improved system performance
(C) Increased bandwidth
(D) Reduced storage needs
Q414. A technology steering committee meets quarterly to review progress of strategic initiatives and risk reports. Which governance objective does this practice MOST directly support?
(A) Oversight and alignment of information technology initiatives
(B) Reduction of server capacity
(C) Avoidance of training programs
(D) Elimination of project documentation
Q415. A bank introduces multi factor authentication for remote access to internal systems. What primary risk is being mitigated?
(A) Increased audit workload
(B) Hardware depreciation
(C) Reduced storage efficiency
(D) Unauthorized access through credential compromise

Q416. An auditor reviewing procurement processes finds that technical specifications for new systems are drafted solely by vendors. What is the MOST significant control weakness?
(A) Faster system deployment
(B) Reduced documentation effort
(C) Improved vendor satisfaction
(D) Potential misalignment with internal control and business requirements
Q417. A company relies entirely on manual monitoring of network activity without automated alerting mechanisms. What is the PRIMARY limitation of this approach?
(A) Delayed detection of suspicious activity
(B) Increased electricity usage
(C) Reduced documentation
(D) Enhanced performance
Q418. After a major outage, management updates the disaster recovery plan but does not conduct any testing. What is the MOST important next step?
(A) Increase marketing efforts
(B) Archive previous plan versions
(C) Replace hardware unnecessarily
(D) Perform structured recovery testing to validate effectiveness
Q419. An organization introduces job rotation in its financial systems department. What control objective is primarily supported by this action?
(A) Detection and prevention of long term fraudulent activity
(B) Increased software licensing
(C) Faster system upgrades
(D) Reduction of encryption usage
Q420. A company's strategic plan includes measurable objectives for digital transformation initiatives. From an audit perspective, why are measurable objectives important?
(A) They eliminate risk assessment
(B) They replace internal controls
(C) They enable evaluation of performance and accountability
(D) They reduce documentation requirements
Q421. An organization has implemented an enterprise risk management framework, but risk assessments are performed inconsistently across departments. What is the MOST significant impact of this weakness?
(A) Increased employee satisfaction
(B) Improved system performance
(C) Reduced printing expenses
(D) Inaccurate enterprise level risk reporting and prioritization
Q422. A software development team deploys application updates directly to production after informal peer discussion without documented approval. What control deficiency does this represent?
(A) Excessive hardware redundancy
(B) Strong preventive monitoring
(C) Effective configuration baseline
(D) Weak change authorization and documentation process
Q423. A multinational company stores employee personal records in multiple regional databases without consistent privacy controls. What is the PRIMARY risk associated with this situation?
(A) Faster data retrieval
(B) Noncompliance with varying legal and regulatory requirements
(C) Increased server capacity

(D) Reduced documentation workload

Q424. During a review of disaster recovery preparedness, the auditor finds that backup copies are stored in the same building as the primary data center. What is the MOST critical risk?

(A) Single point of failure during a physical disaster

(B) Reduced transportation cost

(C) Improved retrieval speed

(D) Increased encryption strength

Q425. An enterprise introduces a formal information asset inventory process. What is the PRIMARY governance benefit of maintaining such an inventory?

(A) Reduced need for encryption

(B) Elimination of risk assessment

(C) Improved visibility and accountability over critical assets

(D) Increased office space

Q426. A financial services organization performs user access reviews annually, although systems process high value transactions daily. What is the MOST appropriate improvement?

(A) Increase review frequency based on risk level

(B) Reduce monitoring controls

(C) Outsource password management only

(D) Eliminate access reviews

Q427. A project team completes system testing successfully but fails to update operating procedures and training materials before launch. What is the PRIMARY operational risk?

(A) Improved documentation quality

(B) Users may operate the system incorrectly or inefficiently

(C) Reduced audit scope

(D) Increased hardware reliability

Q428. An organization implements continuous monitoring tools that generate frequent alerts, but no defined escalation process exists. What is the MOST significant weakness?

(A) Lack of structured incident response and accountability

(B) Reduced documentation requirements

(C) Increased system uptime

(D) Excessive automation

Q429. A technology department relies heavily on one senior administrator who possesses exclusive knowledge of critical systems. Which control should be implemented to reduce associated risk?

(A) Eliminate monitoring tools

(B) Implement knowledge transfer and documentation procedures

(C) Remove access restrictions

(D) Increase salary incentives

Q430. A public sector agency conducts procurement for a new information system without performing a formal risk assessment. What is the PRIMARY concern?

(A) Reduced documentation

(B) Faster acquisition timeline

(C) Inadequate identification of security and compliance requirements

(D) Increased vendor marketing

Q431. A company encrypts data in transit but transmits it over an unsecured wireless network accessible to the public. What additional control would MOST effectively enhance security?

(A) Disable password complexity

(B) Implement secure network authentication and segmentation

(C) Reduce encryption key size

(D) Eliminate monitoring logs

Q432. A business continuity exercise reveals confusion among employees regarding their responsibilities during a disruption. What is the MOST appropriate corrective action?

(A) Remove continuity planning
(B) Eliminate documentation
(C) Increase hardware investment only
(D) Clarify roles and conduct regular awareness training

Q433. An organization permits privileged system access through shared administrator accounts. What is the PRIMARY audit concern?

(A) Faster troubleshooting
(B) Lack of individual accountability and traceability
(C) Increased password length
(D) Reduced storage consumption

Q434. A large enterprise integrates multiple systems without standardized interface controls. What is the MOST likely operational risk?

(A) Reduced documentation
(B) Enhanced system performance
(C) Data inconsistency and processing errors between systems
(D) Improved marketing analytics

Q435. An organization conducts a post implementation review six months after deploying a major system. What is the PRIMARY objective of this review?

(A) Increase system cost
(B) Reduce documentation requirements
(C) Evaluate whether benefits and control objectives have been realized
(D) Eliminate governance oversight

Q436. A company stores archival records indefinitely without a defined retention schedule. What risk does this practice MOST directly introduce?

(A) Improved compliance
(B) Increased legal exposure and storage management challenges
(C) Reduced privacy risk
(D) Faster retrieval speed

Q437. An auditor reviewing physical security observes that visitor access logs are maintained but not periodically reviewed. What is the PRIMARY weakness?

(A) Excessive documentation
(B) Reduced training needs
(C) Lack of monitoring and oversight of physical access activity
(D) Improved operational efficiency

Q438. A global corporation establishes key performance indicators for information technology services but does not link them to strategic objectives. What governance gap does this represent?

(A) Lack of measurable oversight
(B) Misalignment between operational metrics and enterprise strategy
(C) Strong alignment
(D) Reduced monitoring

Q439. An organization introduces automated configuration management tools but does not define a baseline standard. What is the MOST critical deficiency?

(A) Increased automation
(B) Reduced network monitoring
(C) Absence of approved configuration reference point

(D) Excessive documentation

Q440. A chief executive delegates all information security responsibilities to technical staff without periodic review or reporting. From a governance perspective, what is the PRIMARY concern?

(A) Increased training frequency
(B) Reduced documentation workload
(C) Lack of executive oversight and accountability
(D) Improved operational efficiency

Q441. A technology organization has established policies for information security, but employees are unaware of their existence and no acknowledgment process is in place. What is the MOST significant governance weakness in this situation?

(A) Excessive documentation
(B) Reduced network segmentation
(C) Increased hardware cost
(D) Lack of communication and enforcement of policies

Q442. A company performs a risk assessment for a new online service and identifies potential threats but does not evaluate their likelihood or impact. What is the PRIMARY limitation of this assessment?

(A) It prevents prioritization of risks for mitigation
(B) It reduces system performance
(C) It eliminates documentation requirements
(D) It increases audit scope

Q443. A regional office maintains its own independent backup procedures that differ from enterprise standards. What is the MOST significant risk of this practice?

(A) Improved flexibility
(B) Reduced storage cost
(C) Inconsistent recovery capability and potential noncompliance
(D) Faster data processing

Q444. During a review of access controls, an auditor observes that system administrators are able to modify audit logs without oversight. What is the PRIMARY concern?

(A) Reduced documentation effort
(B) Potential concealment of unauthorized activities
(C) Increased storage capacity
(D) Improved troubleshooting

Q445. An enterprise introduces a formal process for evaluating third party service providers annually. What is the PRIMARY objective of this evaluation?

(A) Improve office layout
(B) Assess continued compliance with contractual and security obligations
(C) Increase vendor advertising
(D) Reduce documentation

Q446. A development team implements input validation to restrict invalid data entries in a financial application. What control objective is MOST directly supported by this measure?

(A) Reduced audit cost
(B) Preservation of data integrity and accuracy
(C) Enhanced marketing analytics
(D) Improved hardware lifespan

Q447. An organization performs penetration testing once but never repeats the exercise despite system upgrades and new threats. What is the PRIMARY deficiency?

(A) Excessive monitoring
(B) Increased training programs

(C) Reduced encryption strength
(D) Lack of continuous security assessment

Q448. A company implements a configuration management database but does not assign ownership for updating records. What risk does this create?

(A) Reduced storage usage
(B) Outdated or inaccurate configuration information
(C) Improved system uptime
(D) Increased automation

Q449. A financial institution requires dual authorization for high value electronic fund transfers. What is the PRIMARY control objective achieved?

(A) Lower network bandwidth
(B) Faster transaction processing
(C) Increased storage capacity
(D) Reduction of fraud risk through segregation of duties

Q450. An auditor reviewing strategic planning observes that information technology initiatives are funded without documented cost benefit analysis. What is the MOST significant governance concern?

(A) Improved system speed
(B) Increased documentation
(C) Lack of justification and value assessment for investments
(D) Reduced training requirements

Q451. A company conducts awareness training annually, but new employees receive no training until the following year. What is the PRIMARY risk?

(A) Reduced documentation
(B) Employees may engage in insecure practices due to lack of timely education
(C) Increased hardware cost
(D) Improved operational efficiency

Q452. A data center has fire suppression equipment installed but it has not been inspected for several years. What is the MOST significant control weakness?

(A) Lack of maintenance and testing of critical environmental safeguards
(B) Reduced energy consumption
(C) Increased audit frequency
(D) Improved system availability

Q453. An organization defines recovery objectives but does not align them with available infrastructure capacity. What is the PRIMARY risk?

(A) Increased documentation
(B) Excessive encryption
(C) Reduced compliance
(D) Inability to meet recovery commitments during disruption

Q454. A manager requests temporary privileged access for an urgent project, and the access remains active long after project completion. What is the MOST effective control to prevent recurrence?

(A) Implement automated expiration and periodic review of elevated privileges
(B) Remove monitoring logs
(C) Increase server capacity
(D) Eliminate temporary access

Q455. An enterprise implements a centralized logging solution but does not protect the log repository from unauthorized modification. What is the PRIMARY concern?

(A) Increased storage use
(B) Reduced monitoring capability

(C) Compromise of evidence integrity during investigations
(D) Improved processing speed

Q456. A public utility provider integrates operational technology systems with corporate information systems without conducting a security assessment. What is the MOST significant risk?
(A) Increased training efficiency
(B) Reduced documentation
(C) Improved network speed
(D) Introduction of new vulnerabilities across interconnected environments

Q457. A chief information officer receives quarterly security reports but does not share them with the governing board. What governance gap does this indicate?
(A) Strong transparency
(B) Improved performance metrics
(C) Limited oversight and insufficient risk visibility at highest level
(D) Reduced reporting requirements

Q458. A company introduces automated deployment tools that bypass formal testing environments. What is the PRIMARY control risk?
(A) Deployment of untested or unstable changes into production
(B) Reduced documentation
(C) Faster release cycles
(D) Increased encryption strength

Q459. An auditor evaluating data governance finds that no data owner has been assigned for critical databases. What is the MOST important recommendation?
(A) Reduce monitoring frequency
(B) Increase storage capacity
(C) Establish clear data ownership and accountability
(D) Eliminate classification procedures

Q460. A technology enterprise conducts regular internal audits but fails to track whether corrective actions are implemented. What is the PRIMARY impact of this deficiency?
(A) Improved governance
(B) Reduced audit independence
(C) Persistent control weaknesses due to lack of follow up
(D) Increased documentation

Q461. A global organization allows each regional office to define its own password standards without oversight from central governance. What is the MOST significant risk of this approach?
(A) Improved flexibility in local operations
(B) Increased hardware procurement
(C) Inconsistent security posture across the enterprise
(D) Reduced documentation effort

Q462. An auditor observes that system changes are properly approved but emergency changes are not reviewed after implementation. What control weakness does this represent?
(A) Excessive preventive controls
(B) Lack of post implementation validation for high risk changes
(C) Improved operational efficiency
(D) Reduced documentation

Q463. A financial reporting application relies on automated calculations, but no independent reconciliation is performed. What is the PRIMARY audit concern?
(A) Undetected errors in automated computations
(B) Reduced system storage

(C) Faster processing speed
(D) Improved audit independence

Q464. A company performs regular backups but stores encryption keys on the same server as the encrypted backup files. What is the MOST significant vulnerability?
(A) Reduced documentation
(B) Increased storage capacity
(C) Improved restoration speed
(D) Exposure of backup data if the server is compromised

Q465. An enterprise introduces a new customer relationship management system without involving the internal audit function during planning. What is the PRIMARY risk?
(A) Increased marketing outreach
(B) Improved independence
(C) Missed opportunity to identify control gaps early
(D) Reduced documentation

Q466. A technology team grants developers access to live customer data for testing purposes. What is the MOST significant concern?
(A) Improved troubleshooting capability
(B) Reduced infrastructure cost
(C) Violation of privacy and confidentiality principles
(D) Faster development cycles

Q467. A company defines key performance indicators for incident response but does not measure actual performance against them. What governance weakness does this demonstrate?
(A) Ineffective performance monitoring and oversight
(B) Increased operational efficiency
(C) Strong accountability
(D) Reduced compliance requirements

Q468. An organization centralizes procurement decisions but does not include information security requirements in vendor contracts. What is the PRIMARY risk?
(A) Insufficient protection of organizational information assets
(B) Reduced documentation
(C) Increased employee satisfaction
(D) Faster contract approval

Q469. A system generates exception reports highlighting unusual transactions, but management does not review them regularly. What is the MOST critical issue?
(A) Reduced audit workload
(B) Improved operational speed
(C) Failure to act on detective control outputs
(D) Excessive documentation

Q470. A company expands into a new market but does not update its information security risk assessment to reflect regional threats. What is the PRIMARY impact?
(A) Incomplete understanding of new risk exposure
(B) Improved strategic planning
(C) Increased hardware costs
(D) Reduced documentation

Q471. An enterprise maintains detailed disaster recovery procedures but key personnel have never participated in recovery drills. What is the MOST significant concern?
(A) Lack of practical readiness during an actual disruption
(B) Reduced operational risk

(C) Improved documentation quality
(D) Increased system uptime

Q472. A bank implements transaction monitoring software but does not calibrate alert thresholds according to risk levels. What is the PRIMARY risk?

(A) Increased storage use
(B) Reduced network efficiency
(C) Ineffective detection due to inappropriate alert sensitivity
(D) Excessive documentation

Q473. An organization outsources payroll processing but does not obtain independent assurance reports from the service provider. What is the MOST important audit recommendation?

(A) Eliminate internal audits
(B) Increase employee salaries
(C) Reduce documentation requirements
(D) Obtain independent control assurance over outsourced services

Q474. A company implements network segmentation to separate sensitive systems from general user networks. What is the PRIMARY objective of this control?

(A) Reduce employee training
(B) Limit spread of potential security breaches
(C) Increase storage capacity
(D) Improve printing efficiency

Q475. An information systems auditor discovers that risk acceptance decisions are made verbally without formal documentation. What is the MOST significant governance deficiency?

(A) Improved operational speed
(B) Increased flexibility
(C) Lack of accountability and traceability in risk management
(D) Reduced documentation

Q476. A large retailer upgrades its inventory system but does not conduct reconciliation between old and new system records. What is the PRIMARY risk?

(A) Reduced storage usage
(B) Data discrepancies leading to inaccurate reporting
(C) Increased documentation
(D) Improved efficiency

Q477. A company relies solely on perimeter security controls without implementing internal monitoring mechanisms. What is the MOST significant weakness?

(A) Inability to detect internal or lateral threats
(B) Increased documentation
(C) Improved compliance
(D) Reduced hardware costs

Q478. An enterprise defines data ownership but does not empower owners with authority to enforce controls. What governance gap does this create?

(A) Increased automation
(B) Ineffective stewardship due to lack of authority
(C) Strong accountability
(D) Reduced documentation

Q479. A company introduces automated user provisioning but fails to periodically review access rights. What is the PRIMARY control weakness?

(A) Accumulation of excessive or outdated privileges
(B) Improved governance

(C) Increased efficiency
(D) Reduced monitoring

Q480. A telecommunications provider conducts a risk assessment for new infrastructure but excludes operational staff from the evaluation process. What is the MOST likely consequence?
(A) Reduced compliance requirements
(B) Improved documentation
(C) Incomplete identification of practical operational risks
(D) Increased automation

Q481. An enterprise maintains incident response procedures but does not define communication protocols with external stakeholders. What is the PRIMARY concern?
(A) Improved compliance
(B) Faster recovery
(C) Ineffective coordination during public incidents
(D) Reduced documentation

Q482. A company measures system availability but ignores user satisfaction metrics. What governance limitation does this represent?
(A) Improved risk management
(B) Reduced documentation
(C) Comprehensive oversight
(D) Narrow performance evaluation lacking service quality perspective

Q483. An organization conducts internal audits annually but does not update the audit plan to reflect emerging technologies. What is the MOST significant risk?
(A) Failure to address new and evolving risk areas
(B) Reduced documentation
(C) Increased automation
(D) Improved efficiency

Q484. A government agency integrates identity management systems but does not enforce strong authentication for privileged users. What is the PRIMARY exposure?
(A) Improved performance
(B) Reduced compliance
(C) Elevated risk of unauthorized administrative access
(D) Increased documentation

Q485. A corporation establishes a data governance committee but does not define measurable objectives or reporting requirements. What is the MOST significant governance weakness?
(A) Reduced documentation
(B) Improved flexibility
(C) Increased automation
(D) Lack of accountability and performance evaluation

Q486. A financial institution implements automated reconciliation between subsidiary ledgers and the general ledger but does not investigate reconciling differences. What is the MOST significant control weakness?
(A) Improved system availability
(B) Increased processing speed
(C) Reduced documentation
(D) Failure to resolve identified discrepancies

Q487. An organization adopts a formal information security framework but does not allocate sufficient budget for implementation. What is the PRIMARY risk?
(A) Improved compliance

(B) Increased system uptime
(C) Reduced documentation
(D) Inability to effectively implement required controls

Q488. A company maintains a detailed asset inventory but does not classify assets according to criticality. What is the MOST likely consequence?
(A) Reduced documentation
(B) Inefficient allocation of security controls
(C) Increased storage capacity
(D) Faster procurement

Q489. A project manager modifies system requirements after approval without updating project documentation. What is the PRIMARY control concern?
(A) Increased flexibility
(B) Reduced training cost
(C) Loss of traceability and potential scope creep
(D) Improved vendor relations

Q490. An organization uses strong authentication for external access but allows unrestricted internal network access. What is the MOST significant security weakness?
(A) Faster data transfer
(B) Reduced documentation
(C) Improved internal collaboration
(D) Increased risk from insider threats

Q491. A company conducts risk assessments annually but does not reassess risks after major system changes. What is the PRIMARY impact?
(A) Improved governance maturity
(B) Reduced audit workload
(C) Failure to identify newly introduced vulnerabilities
(D) Increased documentation

Q492. A development environment shares the same database server as the production environment. What is the MOST critical risk?
(A) Accidental or unauthorized impact on live data
(B) Reduced infrastructure cost
(C) Increased performance
(D) Improved documentation

Q493. An organization performs background checks on new employees but does not conduct periodic reviews for long term staff in sensitive roles. What control gap does this create?
(A) Improved employee morale
(B) Increased risk of undetected long term misconduct
(C) Faster hiring process
(D) Reduced documentation

Q494. A bank implements transaction limits but allows overrides without secondary approval. What is the PRIMARY concern?
(A) Reduced documentation
(B) Weak enforcement of control thresholds
(C) Improved operational speed
(D) Increased customer satisfaction

Q495. An enterprise updates its privacy policy but fails to notify customers of significant changes. What is the MOST significant compliance issue?
(A) Reduced documentation

(B) Improved transparency
(C) Failure to meet legal and ethical disclosure obligations
(D) Increased storage cost

Q496. A company implements automated log analysis tools but does not retain raw log data. What is the PRIMARY risk?
(A) Increased storage cost
(B) Improved performance
(C) Reduced documentation
(D) Inability to perform detailed forensic investigation

Q497. A project steering committee rarely meets and does not review project risk reports. What governance weakness does this demonstrate?
(A) Increased automation
(B) Improved efficiency
(C) Reduced documentation
(D) Insufficient executive oversight of project risks

Q498. An organization allows vendors remote maintenance access without time restrictions. What is the MOST significant exposure?
(A) Improved support response
(B) Reduced documentation
(C) Increased risk of unauthorized or prolonged external access
(D) Increased storage efficiency

Q499. A company migrates sensitive records to a new storage system but does not verify data completeness after transfer. What is the PRIMARY risk?
(A) Increased automation
(B) Improved performance
(C) Loss or corruption of critical information
(D) Reduced documentation

Q500. An enterprise maintains documented security procedures but does not monitor adherence to them. What is the MOST significant weakness?
(A) Increased documentation
(B) Improved flexibility
(C) Ineffective enforcement and control monitoring
(D) Reduced operational cost

Answer Key and Explanation (401-500)

Q401. Answer: D

Explanation: Formal requirement documentation ensures that system functionality aligns with business objectives and regulatory expectations. Without documented requirements, it becomes difficult to validate whether the implemented solution fulfills stakeholder needs. Lack of traceability increases the risk of scope creep and unmet expectations. Auditability is weakened because there is no baseline for comparison during testing. This also affects accountability among project stakeholders. Structured requirement management is essential for effective governance and long term system reliability.

Q402. Answer: A

Explanation: Capacity planning anticipates resource demand based on historical usage and projected growth. Trend analysis identifies peak utilization patterns that may require infrastructure scaling. Proactive resource allocation prevents performance degradation and downtime. Without structured forecasting, systems remain vulnerable to overload. Monitoring metrics supports informed investment decisions. Effective capacity management ensures consistent operational availability.

Q403. Answer: A

Explanation: Automated deprovisioning ensures timely removal of access rights upon employment termination. Integration with human resource systems reduces manual errors and delays. Prompt revocation limits risk of unauthorized access or malicious activity. Manual processes often lead to oversight and inconsistent enforcement. Strong access lifecycle management supports confidentiality and accountability. Automation enhances reliability and control efficiency.

Q404. Answer: C

Explanation: Contracts must clearly define ownership, responsibilities, and incident notification requirements. Ambiguity creates legal and operational exposure in case of breach. Governance over outsourced services depends on enforceable terms. Without defined accountability, risk management becomes ineffective. Clear contractual clauses protect organizational interests and regulatory compliance. Structured agreements strengthen trust and oversight.

Q405. Answer: C

Explanation: Recovery time objective defines the maximum tolerable downtime for a system following disruption. It is derived from business impact analysis findings. This metric guides disaster recovery infrastructure design and testing frequency. Meeting defined timelines ensures continuity of critical services. Failure to meet this objective may result in financial and reputational damage. Proper documentation aligns recovery capability with business expectations.

Q406. Answer: A

Explanation: Direct access to production environments bypasses formal change management controls. This increases likelihood of untested or malicious modifications. Separation between development and production environments is fundamental to control integrity. Without segregation, accountability is compromised. Proper authorization and testing protect operational stability. Structured governance prevents unauthorized alterations.

Q407. Answer: D

Explanation: Classification systems rely on clear labeling to guide handling procedures. Without labels, employees may not apply appropriate safeguards. Sensitive information could be exposed inadvertently. Consistent protection depends on visible identification. Governance frameworks require structured implementation. Effective classification reduces confidentiality breaches.

Q408. Answer: B

Explanation: Identification of vulnerabilities is only effective if remediation is tracked to completion. Without monitoring, weaknesses may persist unaddressed. Governance requires accountability and measurable progress. Failure to follow up undermines risk reduction efforts. Documentation of corrective actions supports transparency. Continuous oversight ensures sustained security improvement.

Q409. Answer: C

Explanation: Parallel changeover involves simultaneous operation of old and new systems. Output comparison validates accuracy before full transition. This approach reduces operational risk. Discrepancies can be identified and corrected early. Although resource intensive, it enhances reliability. Careful monitoring ensures successful implementation.

Q410. Answer: C

Explanation: Geographic concentration increases likelihood that a single disaster affects operations. Resilience planning requires separation from region specific risks. Secondary site arrangements mitigate environmental threats. Without diversification, continuity capability is severely limited. Risk assessment should guide site selection. Structured planning strengthens disaster preparedness.

Q411. Answer: B

Explanation: User acceptance testing validates that system functionality aligns with defined requirements. Incomplete testing increases probability of defects and unmet expectations. Early deployment may lead to operational disruption. Governance standards require formal acceptance before release. Risk exposure rises when testing evidence is insufficient. Thorough validation protects organizational objectives.

Q412. Answer: A

Explanation: Encryption is only effective if key management is secure. Unprotected keys allow unauthorized parties to decrypt sensitive data. Secure generation, storage, and rotation are essential. Weak key handling undermines confidentiality objectives. Governance policies must address lifecycle management. Strong controls ensure cryptographic effectiveness.

Q413. Answer: A

Explanation: Regulatory requirements establish minimum retention periods for accountability. Insufficient log retention hampers forensic analysis and compliance reporting. Investigations may lack necessary historical evidence. Governance frameworks emphasize adherence to legal obligations. Failure to comply may result in penalties. Structured retention policies mitigate such risks.

Q414. Answer: A

Explanation: Steering committees provide executive oversight of technology investments. Regular review ensures alignment with enterprise strategy. Monitoring progress enables timely corrective actions. Governance structures enhance accountability. Risk reporting supports informed decision making. Structured oversight strengthens value delivery.

Q415. Answer: D

Explanation: Multi factor authentication strengthens identity verification by requiring additional proof beyond passwords. This reduces risk of access through stolen or guessed credentials. Enhanced authentication protects sensitive systems. Strong access controls support confidentiality and integrity. Governance policies encourage layered defense mechanisms. Implementation reduces exposure to cyber threats.

Q416. Answer: D

Explanation: Internal stakeholders must define requirements to ensure systems meet business and control needs. Vendor driven specifications may prioritize commercial interests. Lack of independent requirement definition weakens governance oversight. Structured procurement ensures accountability. Clear criteria support objective evaluation. Effective involvement reduces implementation risk.

Q417. Answer: A

Explanation: Manual monitoring may not provide real time awareness of threats. Automated alerting enables immediate response to anomalies. Delays increase potential damage from incidents.

Governance requires proactive detection capability. Technology tools enhance monitoring efficiency. Strong oversight reduces operational and security risk.

Q418. Answer: D

Explanation: Updated plans must be tested to ensure practical effectiveness. Testing reveals gaps not apparent in documentation. Structured exercises validate recovery objectives. Without validation, preparedness remains uncertain. Governance standards require periodic testing. Continuous improvement strengthens resilience capability.

Q419. Answer: A

Explanation: Job rotation limits opportunity for individuals to conceal misconduct. Changing responsibilities introduces independent oversight. Long term fraud schemes become harder to sustain. This practice enhances transparency and accountability. Governance frameworks recommend rotation in sensitive roles. Combined with segregation of duties, it strengthens internal control.

Q420. Answer: C

Explanation: Measurable objectives allow progress tracking against defined targets. Accountability depends on quantifiable outcomes. Clear metrics support governance reporting. Without measurement, performance cannot be objectively assessed. Structured evaluation enhances transparency. Defined indicators improve strategic oversight and value realization.

Q421. Answer: D

Explanation: Inconsistent risk assessments lead to unreliable aggregation of risk data at the enterprise level. Without standardized methodology, comparing and prioritizing risks becomes difficult. Management decisions may be based on incomplete or distorted information. Governance effectiveness depends on uniform risk evaluation criteria. Lack of consistency undermines accountability across departments. Structured and standardized assessments enhance transparency and decision quality.

Q422. Answer: D

Explanation: Formal approval and documentation are essential elements of change management. Informal discussions do not provide sufficient audit trail or accountability. Without proper authorization, unauthorized or risky changes may occur. Documentation supports traceability and rollback if necessary. Governance frameworks require structured review before production deployment. Weak authorization processes increase operational risk.

Q423. Answer: B

Explanation: Different jurisdictions impose distinct privacy and data protection requirements. Inconsistent controls may result in violations of applicable laws. Regulatory penalties and reputational damage could follow. Governance of personal data requires harmonized standards and oversight. Standardized privacy frameworks reduce compliance gaps. Proper alignment ensures lawful and ethical data handling.

Q424. Answer: A

Explanation: Storing backups at the same physical location exposes them to identical environmental risks. A fire, flood, or other disaster could destroy both primary and backup data. Effective resilience requires geographic separation. Diversification reduces probability of simultaneous loss. Governance practices emphasize off site storage for critical assets. Physical separation enhances continuity capability.

Q425. Answer: C

Explanation: An asset inventory identifies and tracks systems and data critical to operations. Visibility supports effective risk assessment and control allocation. Without inventory, assets may remain unprotected or unmanaged. Accountability ensures responsible ownership. Governance frameworks require asset identification as foundational step. Comprehensive inventory enhances security and compliance management.

Q426. Answer: A

Explanation: High risk systems require more frequent access reviews to prevent privilege misuse. Risk based frequency aligns control effort with exposure level. Annual reviews may be insufficient for sensitive environments. Regular validation ensures permissions remain appropriate. Governance maturity involves proportional control application. Increased frequency strengthens access integrity.

Q427. Answer: B

Explanation: Updated procedures and training ensure users understand new system functionalities. Lack of documentation may lead to errors and inconsistent usage. Operational inefficiencies can arise from misunderstanding. Governance requires preparation before deployment. Proper training supports effective control implementation. Accurate documentation strengthens continuity and compliance.

Q428. Answer: A

Explanation: Monitoring is effective only when alerts trigger appropriate actions. Without defined escalation, issues may remain unresolved. Structured response ensures timely mitigation. Governance standards require clear roles and communication paths. Accountability supports corrective measures. Effective oversight depends on coordinated response mechanisms.

Q429. Answer: B

Explanation: Concentration of knowledge creates dependency and continuity risk. Documentation ensures organizational memory is preserved. Knowledge transfer reduces disruption in case of absence. Governance emphasizes redundancy in critical roles. Structured procedures support sustainable operations. Shared expertise strengthens resilience.

Q430. Answer: C

Explanation: Risk assessment identifies potential threats and control requirements before acquisition. Without it, critical security considerations may be overlooked. Procurement decisions may not address regulatory obligations. Governance frameworks require risk informed planning. Structured evaluation reduces implementation surprises. Proper assessment supports sustainable and secure solutions.

Q431. Answer: B

Explanation: Even when encryption is used, network level protections add defense in depth. Secure authentication prevents unauthorized network access. Segmentation isolates sensitive traffic from public exposure. Layered security reduces likelihood of compromise. Governance promotes multiple control layers. Comprehensive safeguards strengthen overall protection.

Q432. Answer: D

Explanation: Clearly defined roles ensure coordinated response during incidents. Training reinforces understanding of assigned duties. Exercises identify gaps in preparedness. Governance requires periodic awareness programs. Structured communication enhances resilience. Continuous practice improves readiness and confidence.

Q433. Answer: B

Explanation: Shared accounts prevent attribution of actions to specific individuals. Accountability is essential for monitoring and investigation. Individual identification supports deterrence of misuse. Governance standards discourage shared privileged credentials. Unique accounts strengthen traceability. Proper oversight enhances security posture.

Q434. Answer: C

Explanation: Standardized interface controls ensure accurate and complete data exchange. Lack of uniform validation may result in mismatched records. Processing errors can propagate across integrated systems. Governance requires structured data reconciliation. Reliable integration supports business reporting accuracy. Consistency safeguards operational integrity.

Q435. Answer: C

Explanation: Post implementation review assesses whether projected benefits were achieved. It evaluates effectiveness of implemented controls. Lessons learned guide future initiatives. Governance emphasizes accountability for investment outcomes. Continuous improvement depends on structured feedback. Objective evaluation supports strategic alignment.

Q436. Answer: B

Explanation: Retaining data beyond required periods may violate privacy regulations. Excessive storage increases management complexity. Unnecessary retention expands exposure in case of breach. Governance frameworks define retention based on legal and business needs. Structured schedules balance compliance and efficiency. Proper disposal reduces long term risk.

Q437. Answer: C

Explanation: Maintaining logs without review does not provide effective control. Monitoring identifies unusual access patterns. Oversight ensures compliance with visitor policies. Governance requires active evaluation, not passive record keeping. Regular review supports security enforcement. Proactive monitoring enhances protection.

Q438. Answer: B

Explanation: Performance indicators must reflect strategic priorities to provide meaningful insight. Metrics without alignment fail to demonstrate value contribution. Governance requires integration between operations and strategy. Clear linkage supports accountability. Decision makers rely on relevant performance data. Alignment enhances effective oversight.

Q439. Answer: C

Explanation: A baseline defines approved system settings for comparison and control. Without it, automation lacks direction and control reference. Deviations cannot be effectively identified. Governance requires documented standards. Structured baseline management enhances integrity. Clear reference points support consistent security posture.

Q440. Answer: C

Explanation: Senior leadership retains ultimate accountability for information security governance. Delegation without oversight weakens control environment. Regular reporting ensures risk visibility at executive level. Governance frameworks emphasize tone at the top. Absence of oversight may lead to unmanaged risk exposure. Active involvement strengthens organizational resilience.

Q441. Answer: D

Explanation: Policies are effective only when communicated and understood by employees. Without awareness and formal acknowledgment, compliance cannot be assured. Governance requires both documentation and dissemination. Employees may unintentionally violate requirements due to lack of knowledge. Formal acknowledgment establishes accountability. Effective communication strengthens organizational control culture.

Q442. Answer: A

Explanation: Risk assessment requires evaluation of both likelihood and impact to determine severity. Without quantification, management cannot prioritize mitigation efforts. Identification alone does not support informed decision making. Governance frameworks emphasize structured evaluation. Risk ranking guides resource allocation. Comprehensive analysis enhances strategic oversight.

Q443. Answer: C

Explanation: Deviating from enterprise standards creates inconsistent recovery readiness. Local practices may not meet defined recovery objectives. Governance requires centralized oversight to ensure uniform protection. Nonstandard procedures increase risk of failure during disaster. Alignment with corporate policy ensures accountability. Standardization strengthens resilience.

Q444. Answer: B

Explanation: Audit logs provide evidence of system activity and security events. If administrators can alter logs without monitoring, accountability is compromised. Unauthorized actions could be hidden. Governance requires protection and independent review of logs. Segregation of duties enhances reliability. Strong controls preserve integrity of audit evidence.

Q445. Answer: B
Explanation: Periodic evaluation ensures vendors continue to meet defined performance and security standards. Risk profiles may change over time. Ongoing oversight supports contractual compliance. Governance requires monitoring of outsourced activities. Regular assessment reduces exposure to service disruption. Structured review strengthens accountability.
Q446. Answer: B
Explanation: Input validation ensures only accurate and properly formatted data enters the system. Preventing invalid entries reduces downstream errors. Data integrity is foundational to reliable reporting. Governance emphasizes accuracy in financial systems. Preventive controls reduce correction effort. Structured validation enhances trustworthiness of information.
Q447. Answer: D
Explanation: Security environments evolve with new vulnerabilities and threat actors. Single testing events do not provide ongoing assurance. Regular assessment identifies newly introduced weaknesses. Governance frameworks require periodic evaluation. Continuous improvement strengthens protection posture. Recurrent testing supports proactive risk management.
Q448. Answer: B
Explanation: Configuration data must be maintained to remain useful. Without assigned responsibility, records may become obsolete. Inaccurate information undermines change management and incident response. Governance requires accountability for data accuracy. Updated records support operational efficiency. Clear ownership strengthens reliability of configuration controls.
Q449. Answer: D
Explanation: Dual authorization ensures that no single individual can complete sensitive transactions independently. This reduces risk of unauthorized or fraudulent transfers. Segregation of duties is a fundamental internal control principle. Governance structures emphasize shared responsibility. Independent review enhances transaction legitimacy. Strong approval processes protect financial assets.
Q450. Answer: C
Explanation: Cost benefit analysis supports informed investment decisions. Without justification, projects may not deliver expected value. Governance requires evaluation of economic feasibility. Structured analysis enhances transparency. Resource allocation should align with strategic priorities. Proper assessment strengthens accountability and performance measurement.
Q451. Answer: B
Explanation: New employees may be unaware of security expectations without immediate training. Delayed education increases risk of policy violations. Governance frameworks emphasize onboarding awareness. Early instruction supports consistent compliance culture. Continuous reinforcement strengthens control environment. Timely training reduces human error exposure.
Q452. Answer: A
Explanation: Environmental controls require periodic inspection to ensure functionality. Neglected maintenance may lead to failure during emergencies. Governance requires ongoing validation of safeguards. Testing confirms operational readiness. Reliable environmental protection supports business continuity. Structured maintenance reduces catastrophic risk.
Q453. Answer: D
Explanation: Recovery objectives must be supported by adequate technical capability. Misalignment leads to unrealistic expectations. Governance requires feasibility assessment. Infrastructure planning should match defined timelines. Testing verifies practical effectiveness. Alignment ensures reliable continuity performance.
Q454. Answer: A
Explanation: Temporary access should include predefined expiration dates. Automated revocation prevents prolonged exposure. Periodic review confirms necessity of privileges. Governance emphasizes

least privilege principle. Monitoring ensures accountability. Structured lifecycle management strengthens logical access controls.

Q455. Answer: C

Explanation: Logs must be protected to maintain evidentiary value. Unauthorized modification undermines trustworthiness. Governance requires safeguarding critical records. Access controls and integrity checks enhance protection. Reliable logs support incident response and compliance. Preservation of integrity is fundamental to accountability.

Q456. Answer: D

Explanation: Integration expands attack surface and may introduce new threats. Without assessment, vulnerabilities remain unidentified. Governance requires evaluation before major architectural changes. Cross environment connectivity increases exposure. Structured analysis supports risk mitigation. Proper planning enhances operational security.

Q457. Answer: C

Explanation: Governing boards require visibility into significant risk exposures. Withholding reports limits informed oversight. Governance frameworks emphasize accountability and transparency. Executive reporting supports strategic decision making. Regular communication strengthens organizational alignment. Effective oversight requires timely information sharing.

Q458. Answer: A

Explanation: Testing environments validate changes before production release. Bypassing this stage increases risk of defects and disruption. Governance requires structured testing procedures. Automation must integrate with control checkpoints. Controlled deployment protects system stability. Proper review ensures reliable operations.

Q459. Answer: C

Explanation: Data ownership defines responsibility for accuracy and protection. Without assigned owners, accountability is unclear. Governance frameworks require defined stewardship. Owners ensure compliance with policies. Structured accountability strengthens data integrity. Clear roles enhance risk management.

Q460. Answer: C

Explanation: Audit effectiveness depends on remediation of identified issues. Without follow up, weaknesses may continue unchecked. Governance requires monitoring of corrective actions. Tracking ensures accountability. Closure verification confirms risk reduction. Continuous improvement strengthens internal control maturity.

Q461. Answer: C

Explanation: Allowing independent password standards may create uneven levels of protection. Some regions may adopt weaker requirements, increasing vulnerability. Governance frameworks emphasize centralized oversight for critical security controls. Consistency ensures minimum security baselines are maintained. Without alignment, attackers may target weaker regions. Standardized policies strengthen overall enterprise resilience.

Q462. Answer: B

Explanation: Emergency changes often bypass normal procedures due to urgency. However, governance requires retrospective review to ensure appropriateness. Without validation, unauthorized or harmful modifications may persist. Documentation and approval after the fact support accountability. Structured follow up reduces operational risk. Post implementation assessment ensures compliance with change standards.

Q463. Answer: A

Explanation: Automated calculations can contain logic errors if not validated. Independent reconciliation verifies accuracy of results. Without oversight, incorrect outputs may remain unnoticed.

Governance requires monitoring of critical financial processes. Control validation enhances reliability of reporting. Structured checks strengthen trust in automated systems.

Q464. Answer: D

Explanation: Encryption protects data only when keys are securely separated. Storing keys with encrypted files defeats confidentiality objectives. If attackers access the server, both data and keys may be obtained. Governance practices require secure key management. Separation of duties strengthens protection. Proper handling preserves integrity of backup security.

Q465. Answer: C

Explanation: Early involvement of internal audit helps identify control weaknesses during system design. Proactive review reduces costly corrections later. Governance encourages collaboration while maintaining independence. Without input, control deficiencies may be embedded in implementation. Early risk identification enhances assurance. Preventive oversight strengthens project outcomes.

Q466. Answer: C

Explanation: Live customer data often contains sensitive information requiring protection. Using it in testing environments increases risk of exposure. Governance standards recommend anonymized or masked data for development. Confidentiality obligations must be maintained at all stages. Unauthorized access can lead to legal and reputational damage. Controlled testing practices reduce privacy risk.

Q467. Answer: A

Explanation: Defining indicators without measurement provides no practical oversight. Governance requires monitoring and comparison against targets. Performance gaps cannot be identified without evaluation. Structured reporting supports improvement. Accountability depends on measurable outcomes. Continuous assessment strengthens response capability.

Q468. Answer: A

Explanation: Contracts define obligations for safeguarding sensitive information. Without security clauses, vendors may not implement adequate controls. Governance requires clear expectations and accountability. Third party risk management depends on contractual safeguards. Lack of requirements increases exposure to breaches. Structured agreements enhance protective measures.

Q469. Answer: C

Explanation: Exception reports are detective controls designed to identify anomalies. Without review, the control becomes ineffective. Governance requires active monitoring of identified issues. Timely review allows corrective action. Ignored reports may permit fraud or errors to continue. Proper oversight ensures control effectiveness.

Q470. Answer: A

Explanation: Entering new markets introduces different legal, environmental, and threat conditions. Risk assessments must reflect changing environments. Governance frameworks require periodic reassessment. Failure to update may leave new vulnerabilities unaddressed. Accurate understanding supports informed mitigation. Continuous evaluation strengthens resilience.

Q471. Answer: A

Explanation: Practical exercises validate both procedures and personnel readiness. Documentation alone does not ensure effective response. Without drills, confusion may occur during emergencies. Governance standards emphasize regular testing. Training builds confidence and competence. Preparedness requires both planning and practice.

Q472. Answer: C

Explanation: Alert thresholds must reflect risk tolerance and transaction patterns. Improper calibration may generate too many false positives or miss genuine threats. Governance requires tuning controls to operational realities. Effective monitoring depends on balanced sensitivity. Regular review enhances detection quality. Proper configuration supports reliable oversight.

Q473. Answer: D
Explanation: Independent assurance reports provide insight into effectiveness of service provider controls. Outsourcing does not transfer accountability. Governance requires oversight of third party operations. Without assurance, risks may remain unidentified. Regular review enhances confidence in service reliability. Structured oversight mitigates external dependency risk.
Q474. Answer: B
Explanation: Segmentation isolates critical systems to reduce attack propagation. If one segment is compromised, others remain protected. Governance promotes layered security architecture. Isolation reduces exposure to unauthorized access. Structured network design enhances resilience. Preventive containment strengthens defensive strategy.
Q475. Answer: C
Explanation: Formal documentation records rationale for accepting risk. Without it, accountability is unclear. Governance frameworks require evidence of informed decision making. Traceability supports transparency and review. Verbal agreements may be forgotten or disputed. Structured documentation enhances oversight and compliance.
Q476. Answer: B
Explanation: System upgrades may introduce data migration errors. Reconciliation verifies completeness and accuracy. Without comparison, discrepancies may remain undetected. Governance standards require validation during transitions. Accurate reporting depends on reliable migration. Structured verification prevents operational disruption.
Q477. Answer: A
Explanation: Perimeter controls protect against external threats but not internal misuse. Internal monitoring detects anomalous behavior within the network. Governance promotes defense in depth strategies. Sole reliance on perimeter creates blind spots. Comprehensive monitoring enhances detection capability. Balanced security architecture reduces exposure.
Q478. Answer: B
Explanation: Ownership must include both responsibility and authority. Without enforcement power, owners cannot ensure compliance. Governance frameworks require clear role definition. Effective stewardship depends on decision making capability. Authority enables corrective action. Proper empowerment strengthens data governance maturity.
Q479. Answer: A
Explanation: Automated provisioning improves consistency but does not eliminate need for review. Over time, roles and responsibilities change. Without periodic validation, users may retain unnecessary access. Governance standards require ongoing oversight. Excess privileges increase risk of misuse. Structured reviews maintain least privilege principle.
Q480. Answer: C
Explanation: Operational staff possess practical knowledge of system behavior and vulnerabilities. Excluding them may result in overlooked risks. Governance encourages cross functional participation. Comprehensive assessment improves mitigation planning. Diverse input enhances risk accuracy. Collaboration strengthens decision making.
Q481. Answer: C
Explanation: External communication is critical during significant incidents. Undefined protocols may cause delays or inconsistent messaging. Governance frameworks emphasize clear communication strategies. Stakeholder trust depends on transparency. Structured planning reduces reputational impact. Coordinated communication enhances crisis management effectiveness.
Q482. Answer: D
Explanation: Availability metrics reflect technical uptime but not user experience. Governance requires holistic performance measurement. Satisfaction indicators provide insight into service effectiveness.

Balanced evaluation supports strategic improvement. Ignoring qualitative factors limits oversight. Comprehensive metrics enhance service management maturity.

Q483. Answer: A

Explanation: Emerging technologies introduce new vulnerabilities and compliance requirements. Static audit plans may overlook critical developments. Governance standards require risk based planning. Continuous reassessment ensures relevance. Adaptive audit strategy enhances assurance effectiveness. Proactive evaluation supports organizational resilience.

Q484. Answer: C

Explanation: Privileged accounts possess extensive system control. Weak authentication increases likelihood of compromise. Governance frameworks emphasize stronger safeguards for elevated access. Enhanced authentication reduces attack success probability. Proper controls protect critical systems. Structured security measures support confidentiality and integrity.

Q485. Answer: D

Explanation: Committees require clear objectives to guide activities. Without measurable targets, effectiveness cannot be assessed. Governance depends on transparency and reporting. Defined metrics enable oversight and improvement. Accountability ensures alignment with strategic goals. Structured evaluation strengthens governance maturity.

Q486. Answer: D

Explanation: Reconciliation identifies differences between independent records, but unresolved discrepancies undermine the purpose of the control. Without investigation, errors or fraudulent transactions may persist. Governance requires timely review and corrective action. Automated detection alone does not ensure integrity. Effective oversight depends on resolution procedures. Structured follow up strengthens financial reliability.

Q487. Answer: D

Explanation: Framework adoption requires resources for training, tools, and monitoring. Without adequate funding, policies remain theoretical. Governance effectiveness depends on practical execution. Resource allocation demonstrates leadership commitment. Insufficient support weakens control maturity. Sustainable security requires aligned budgeting.

Q488. Answer: B

Explanation: Asset criticality determines appropriate level of protection. Without classification, resources may be misdirected. High value systems could remain underprotected. Governance emphasizes risk based prioritization. Structured classification supports strategic decision making. Proper alignment enhances operational resilience.

Q489. Answer: C

Explanation: Approved requirements serve as baseline for design and testing. Uncontrolled modifications weaken governance oversight. Traceability ensures alignment with business objectives. Scope creep can increase cost and risk. Documentation updates maintain accountability. Structured change control supports project integrity.

Q490. Answer: D

Explanation: Insider threats represent substantial security risk. Unrestricted internal access may allow lateral movement and misuse. Governance promotes defense in depth within networks. Segmentation and monitoring enhance internal protection. Balanced controls address both external and internal risks. Comprehensive strategy strengthens overall security posture.

Q491. Answer: C

Explanation: Major system changes may alter threat landscape and exposure levels. Governance requires reassessment when significant modifications occur. Static risk evaluations overlook emerging issues. Continuous evaluation enhances responsiveness. Updated assessments support informed mitigation. Proactive review strengthens resilience.

Q492. Answer: A
Explanation: Separation of environments protects production integrity. Shared infrastructure increases possibility of unintended changes. Testing activities may affect operational systems. Governance requires logical and physical segregation. Controlled environments reduce operational disruption. Structured separation safeguards data accuracy.
Q493. Answer: B
Explanation: Circumstances may change over time, affecting employee risk profiles. Periodic review enhances monitoring in sensitive roles. Governance frameworks encourage ongoing oversight. Long term access without review may increase exposure. Structured revalidation strengthens trustworthiness. Continuous evaluation supports internal control effectiveness.
Q494. Answer: B
Explanation: Transaction limits mitigate risk by capping exposure. Overrides without oversight negate control purpose. Governance requires dual review for high risk exceptions. Structured authorization ensures accountability. Without supervision, abuse may occur. Effective enforcement strengthens financial safeguards.
Q495. Answer: C
Explanation: Privacy regulations often require notification of material policy changes. Transparency builds stakeholder trust. Failure to inform customers may result in regulatory penalties. Governance requires communication of policy updates. Ethical practices support organizational reputation. Proper disclosure strengthens compliance posture.
Q496. Answer: D
Explanation: Summarized analysis cannot replace original log evidence. Raw data supports comprehensive investigation when needed. Governance frameworks require sufficient retention. Without original records, detailed review may be impossible. Preservation enhances accountability. Structured retention strengthens investigative capability.
Q497. Answer: D
Explanation: Steering committees provide oversight and strategic direction. Regular meetings ensure timely identification of issues. Ignoring risk reports reduces accountability. Governance standards require active engagement. Effective oversight supports project success. Structured review enhances transparency.
Q498. Answer: C
Explanation: Remote access should be limited to defined timeframes and monitored. Unrestricted access increases potential misuse. Governance emphasizes least privilege and controlled connectivity. Logging and time based controls enhance oversight. Structured vendor management reduces third party risk. Defined boundaries strengthen security posture.
Q499. Answer: C
Explanation: Data migration may introduce errors or omissions. Verification ensures completeness and accuracy. Governance requires reconciliation during transitions. Unchecked transfers may compromise reporting integrity. Structured validation reduces operational disruption. Accurate migration supports continuity and compliance.
Q500. Answer: C
Explanation: Policies require monitoring to ensure compliance. Without oversight, procedures may not be followed. Governance depends on verification mechanisms. Structured audits and reviews reinforce accountability. Lack of monitoring weakens control environment. Active supervision strengthens security maturity.

Question (501-600)

Q501. A financial services organization performs penetration testing internally without independent review of results. What is the PRIMARY concern?

(A) Potential bias and incomplete identification of weaknesses
(B) Increased transparency
(C) Reduced documentation
(D) Improved operational efficiency

Q502. A company implements multifactor authentication but does not enforce strong password complexity. What is the MOST significant implication?

(A) Reduced documentation
(B) Increased storage
(C) Improved governance
(D) Weak first factor reducing overall authentication strength

Q503. An organization conducts regular system backups but does not document restoration procedures. What is the PRIMARY risk?

(A) Reduced storage cost
(B) Delayed or ineffective recovery during disruption
(C) Improved efficiency
(D) Increased automation

Q504. A retail company integrates payment processing systems with inventory management without conducting interface testing. What is the MOST significant operational risk?

(A) Increased automation
(B) Improved sales tracking
(C) Transaction errors affecting financial accuracy
(D) Reduced documentation

Q505. A government agency establishes risk tolerance levels but does not communicate them to management teams. What is the PRIMARY governance weakness?

(A) Reduced documentation
(B) Lack of alignment between risk decisions and defined tolerance
(C) Increased flexibility
(D) Improved oversight

Q506. A corporation centralizes user account management but does not require periodic certification by business owners. What is the MOST critical deficiency?

(A) Reduced documentation
(B) Increased automation
(C) Lack of validation that access remains appropriate
(D) Improved efficiency

Q507. A company upgrades its network infrastructure but fails to update network diagrams and documentation. What is the PRIMARY risk?

(A) Reduced compliance requirements
(B) Increased automation
(C) Reduced effectiveness of troubleshooting and security management
(D) Improved flexibility

Q508. An organization conducts periodic vulnerability scans but ignores findings categorized as medium risk. What is the MOST significant issue?

(A) Increased automation
(B) Reduced documentation

(C) Improved efficiency
(D) Accumulation of exploitable weaknesses over time

Q509. A company stores sensitive employee information in spreadsheets shared across departments without access restrictions. What is the PRIMARY control weakness?

(A) Improved efficiency
(B) Increased collaboration
(C) Lack of confidentiality safeguards
(D) Reduced documentation

Q510. A large enterprise establishes an information technology governance framework but does not measure its effectiveness periodically. What is the MOST significant governance gap?

(A) Absence of performance evaluation and continuous improvement
(B) Improved automation
(C) Increased documentation
(D) Reduced compliance

Q511. A multinational organization stores customer data in multiple jurisdictions but does not evaluate cross border data transfer restrictions. What is the MOST significant risk?

(A) Reduced documentation
(B) Improved operational flexibility
(C) Increased system availability
(D) Noncompliance with regional data protection laws

Q512. A company implements role based access controls but allows managers to assign roles without documented approval. What is the PRIMARY control weakness?

(A) Improved governance maturity
(B) Lack of accountability in role assignment
(C) Increased efficiency
(D) Reduced documentation

Q513. An organization conducts a business impact analysis but does not update it after introducing new critical services. What is the MOST likely consequence?

(A) Reduced documentation
(B) Increased storage cost
(C) Improved planning efficiency
(D) Outdated recovery priorities and objectives

Q514. A development team deploys code directly to production without maintaining version control records. What is the PRIMARY audit concern?

(A) Loss of traceability and accountability for system changes
(B) Improved system speed
(C) Increased flexibility
(D) Reduced documentation

Q515. A healthcare provider stores backup media in an unlocked cabinet within the primary facility. What is the MOST significant vulnerability?

(A) Reduced documentation
(B) Improved accessibility
(C) Increased recovery speed
(D) Physical compromise of sensitive information

Q516. An enterprise establishes security metrics but does not align them with strategic objectives. What governance limitation does this create?

(A) Reduced documentation
(B) Improved compliance

(C) Metrics that fail to measure meaningful performance outcomes
(D) Increased automation

Q517. A company uses automated account lockout after multiple failed login attempts but does not monitor repeated lockout events. What is the PRIMARY risk?

(A) Improved governance
(B) Undetected brute force attack attempts
(C) Reduced documentation
(D) Increased system performance

Q518. A financial services firm migrates applications to a cloud environment but does not update its incident response procedures. What is the MOST significant issue?

(A) Reduced documentation
(B) Improved availability
(C) Increased flexibility
(D) Inadequate response planning for new operational model

Q519. A manufacturing company performs periodic risk assessments but excludes supply chain dependencies from evaluation. What is the PRIMARY consequence?

(A) Increased automation
(B) Reduced documentation
(C) Improved efficiency
(D) Incomplete understanding of operational risk exposure

Q520. A public sector organization defines segregation of duties policies but does not configure systems to enforce them. What is the MOST significant weakness?

(A) Improved performance
(B) Increased flexibility
(C) Reduced documentation
(D) Policies not translated into effective technical controls

Q521. A company retains system logs for only a short duration despite regulatory requirements for longer retention. What is the PRIMARY risk?

(A) Increased storage efficiency
(B) Improved system speed
(C) Noncompliance and inability to support investigations
(D) Reduced documentation

Q522. An enterprise introduces artificial intelligence driven analytics without assessing ethical implications. What is the MOST significant governance concern?

(A) Reduced documentation
(B) Improved operational efficiency
(C) Potential bias and reputational damage
(D) Increased automation

Q523. A technology organization implements data masking in testing environments but allows administrators unrestricted access to original data. What is the PRIMARY exposure?

(A) Increased storage capacity
(B) Reduced documentation
(C) Improved troubleshooting
(D) Confidential information accessible beyond necessity

Q524. A company establishes a security awareness program but does not evaluate its effectiveness. What is the MOST significant weakness?

(A) Reduced operational cost
(B) Improved governance

(C) Increased documentation
(D) Inability to measure behavioral improvement and risk reduction

Q525. A retail enterprise introduces centralized monitoring tools but does not define escalation procedures for identified incidents. What is the PRIMARY risk?
(A) Delayed response to detected security events
(B) Reduced documentation
(C) Increased efficiency
(D) Improved automation

Q526. A financial organization permits shared user accounts for convenience in certain departments. What is the MOST critical control weakness?
(A) Reduced documentation
(B) Loss of individual accountability and audit trail integrity
(C) Increased efficiency
(D) Improved collaboration

Q527. A company performs regular capacity planning but does not consider peak seasonal demand. What is the PRIMARY operational risk?
(A) Increased automation
(B) Improved governance
(C) System performance degradation during high demand periods
(D) Reduced documentation

Q528. A university maintains sensitive research data but does not restrict portable storage device usage. What is the MOST significant exposure?
(A) Improved data mobility
(B) Reduced documentation
(C) Increased collaboration
(D) Risk of unauthorized data exfiltration

Q529. A company integrates security requirements into procurement but does not verify vendor compliance after contract signing. What is the PRIMARY weakness?
(A) Lack of ongoing assurance over third party controls
(B) Increased documentation
(C) Improved governance
(D) Reduced operational cost

Q530. A transportation organization deploys surveillance systems but does not restrict access to recorded footage. What is the MOST significant risk?
(A) Reduced documentation
(B) Increased storage efficiency
(C) Breach of privacy and misuse of surveillance data
(D) Improved monitoring

Q531. A corporation defines acceptable use policies but does not enforce sanctions for violations. What governance issue does this represent?
(A) Weak enforcement reducing policy effectiveness
(B) Increased flexibility
(C) Improved employee morale
(D) Reduced documentation

Q532. A company relies on manual monitoring of security alerts despite rapid growth in system complexity. What is the PRIMARY risk?
(A) Reduced documentation
(B) Inability to detect and respond to threats in a timely manner

(C) Improved governance
(D) Increased employment

Q533. A firm updates encryption standards but does not replace outdated certificates in deployed systems. What is the MOST significant exposure?

(A) Improved performance
(B) Continued reliance on weak cryptographic implementations
(C) Reduced documentation
(D) Increased automation

Q534. A company conducts social engineering testing but does not share results with employees. What is the PRIMARY limitation?

(A) Missed opportunity for awareness improvement
(B) Reduced documentation
(C) Improved governance
(D) Increased confidentiality

Q535. A technology enterprise defines service level agreements with internal departments but does not measure compliance against them. What is the MOST significant governance gap?

(A) Improved automation
(B) Increased flexibility
(C) Lack of performance accountability and oversight
(D) Reduced documentation

Q536. A global enterprise defines a formal change management policy but allows senior executives to bypass it without documentation. What is the MOST significant governance risk?

(A) Increased operational flexibility
(B) Reduced documentation requirements
(C) Undermining of control consistency and accountability
(D) Improved project speed

Q537. A company deploys a new enterprise resource planning system but does not perform user acceptance testing before going live. What is the PRIMARY risk?

(A) Deployment of a system that fails to meet business requirements
(B) Reduced documentation
(C) Improved system performance
(D) Increased automation

Q538. A financial organization encrypts sensitive databases but does not restrict administrator access to decryption keys. What is the MOST significant exposure?

(A) Increased storage capacity
(B) Excessive privileged access to confidential information
(C) Improved efficiency
(D) Reduced documentation

Q539. A company performs internal vulnerability scanning but does not remediate findings due to budget constraints. What is the PRIMARY audit concern?

(A) Reduced documentation
(B) Increased cost savings
(C) Known weaknesses left unaddressed
(D) Improved risk tolerance

Q540. A telecommunications provider maintains redundant network connections but does not test failover capabilities. What is the MOST significant weakness?

(A) Reduced documentation
(B) Increased automation

(C) Unverified continuity during actual network disruption
(D) Improved performance
Q541. A corporation introduces data classification guidelines but does not provide tools to enforce labeling. What is the PRIMARY limitation?
(A) Increased awareness
(B) Inconsistent implementation of classification requirements
(C) Improved automation
(D) Reduced documentation
Q542. A bank relies on a single supplier for critical infrastructure components without contingency planning. What is the MOST significant operational risk?
(A) Disruption due to supplier failure or unavailability
(B) Improved supplier relationship
(C) Reduced documentation
(D) Increased efficiency
Q543. A company allows remote work but does not require secure configuration standards for personal devices. What is the PRIMARY exposure?
(A) Improved governance
(B) Reduced documentation
(C) Increased employee satisfaction
(D) Introduction of unmanaged security vulnerabilities
Q544. A public agency defines incident severity levels but does not align response resources accordingly. What governance gap does this reveal?
(A) Ineffective prioritization of response efforts
(B) Reduced documentation
(C) Improved compliance
(D) Increased flexibility
Q545. A retail organization implements encryption for data in transit but leaves internal data transmissions unprotected. What is the MOST significant concern?
(A) Increased performance
(B) Improved automation
(C) Reduced documentation
(D) Exposure of sensitive information within internal networks
Q546. A company establishes a risk committee but does not include representation from business units. What is the PRIMARY consequence?
(A) Increased efficiency
(B) Improved governance
(C) Limited understanding of operational risks
(D) Reduced documentation
Q547. An organization conducts system audits but does not communicate findings to system owners. What is the MOST significant weakness?
(A) Lack of corrective action and accountability
(B) Reduced documentation
(C) Increased confidentiality
(D) Improved operational efficiency
Q548. A financial institution stores archived records but does not define retention schedules. What is the PRIMARY compliance risk?
(A) Improved governance
(B) Reduced documentation

(C) Over retention or premature disposal of records
(D) Increased storage capacity

Q549. A company uses automated patch management but excludes legacy systems from updates. What is the MOST significant exposure?
(A) Increased performance
(B) Reduced documentation
(C) Persistent vulnerabilities in unsupported systems
(D) Improved automation

Q550. A transportation firm introduces monitoring dashboards but does not verify data accuracy feeding into them. What is the PRIMARY risk?
(A) Increased transparency
(B) Reduced documentation
(C) Improved governance
(D) Decisions based on inaccurate information

Q551. A technology organization develops mobile applications but does not conduct code review for security vulnerabilities. What is the MOST critical risk?
(A) Increased development speed
(B) Introduction of exploitable weaknesses into production
(C) Improved automation
(D) Reduced documentation

Q552. A company permits unrestricted use of public wireless networks for accessing corporate systems without secure connection requirements. What is the PRIMARY exposure?
(A) Reduced documentation
(B) Interception of sensitive communications
(C) Increased mobility
(D) Improved flexibility

Q553. A manufacturing enterprise defines environmental controls for its data center but does not monitor temperature fluctuations continuously. What is the MOST significant operational risk?
(A) Improved governance
(B) Equipment damage due to undetected overheating
(C) Reduced documentation
(D) Increased automation

Q554. A company establishes key risk indicators but does not integrate them into management reporting. What governance limitation does this create?
(A) Limited visibility of emerging risks
(B) Increased flexibility
(C) Improved automation
(D) Reduced documentation

Q555. A financial institution performs regular reconciliation of accounts but does not segregate duties between transaction processing and reconciliation. What is the PRIMARY control weakness?
(A) Improved governance
(B) Reduced documentation
(C) Increased efficiency
(D) Elevated risk of fraud due to conflicting responsibilities

Q556. A company migrates to a centralized identity management system but does not decommission legacy authentication databases. What is the MOST significant exposure?
(A) Improved efficiency
(B) Increased flexibility

(C) Reduced documentation
(D) Multiple active credential repositories increasing attack surface

Q557. An organization defines recovery time objectives but does not test whether systems meet them. What is the PRIMARY risk?
(A) Reduced operational cost
(B) Failure to achieve expected recovery performance
(C) Increased documentation
(D) Improved governance

Q558. A retail enterprise implements inventory access controls but allows temporary contractors unrestricted access. What is the MOST significant weakness?
(A) Inconsistent enforcement of access restrictions
(B) Increased staffing flexibility
(C) Reduced documentation
(D) Improved efficiency

Q559. A company develops an information security strategy but does not align it with corporate objectives. What is the PRIMARY governance issue?
(A) Improved automation
(B) Reduced documentation
(C) Increased flexibility
(D) Misalignment between security initiatives and business priorities

Q560. A global enterprise performs annual compliance audits but does not track regulatory changes throughout the year. What is the MOST significant risk?
(A) Failure to adapt to new legal requirements promptly
(B) Reduced documentation
(C) Improved governance
(D) Increased automation

Q561. A financial services organization introduces automated credit approval but does not periodically validate the decision algorithms against current lending policies. What is the MOST significant risk?
(A) Reduced documentation
(B) Decisions that no longer comply with updated regulatory or policy requirements
(C) Improved automation maturity
(D) Increased operational efficiency

Q562. A healthcare organization restricts access to patient records but does not monitor access logs for unusual activity. What is the PRIMARY control weakness?
(A) Reduced documentation
(B) Improved governance
(C) Ineffective detection of unauthorized access attempts
(D) Increased confidentiality

Q563. A company establishes an information classification policy but does not train employees on how to apply it. What is the MOST likely outcome?
(A) Improved compliance
(B) Reduced documentation
(C) Inconsistent classification and handling of information
(D) Increased automation

Q564. A government department conducts system penetration testing but fails to remediate identified critical vulnerabilities promptly. What is the PRIMARY risk?
(A) Reduced documentation

(B) Increased transparency
(C) Exploitation of known weaknesses by threat actors
(D) Improved governance maturity

Q565. A manufacturing firm allows system administrators to both request and approve access privileges for employees. What is the MOST significant internal control concern?
(A) Increased efficiency
(B) Improved governance
(C) Reduced documentation
(D) Violation of segregation of duties principles

Q566. A company performs daily data backups but does not test restoration procedures for several years. What is the PRIMARY operational risk?
(A) Increased storage capacity
(B) Inability to restore data effectively during an emergency
(C) Improved system performance
(D) Reduced documentation

Q567. A financial institution introduces real time transaction monitoring but sets alert thresholds too high to reduce workload. What is the MOST significant exposure?
(A) Reduced documentation
(B) Improved automation
(C) Increased efficiency
(D) Failure to detect fraudulent or suspicious transactions

Q568. A retail organization migrates its customer database to a new platform without conducting a privacy impact assessment. What is the PRIMARY compliance risk?
(A) Improved scalability
(B) Reduced documentation
(C) Increased performance
(D) Violation of data protection obligations

Q569. A company maintains multiple overlapping security policies that contain conflicting requirements. What is the MOST significant governance issue?
(A) Reduced documentation
(B) Increased flexibility
(C) Improved automation
(D) Confusion leading to inconsistent control implementation

Q570. A telecommunications firm outsources network monitoring but does not define service performance metrics in the contract. What is the PRIMARY risk?
(A) Reduced documentation
(B) Inability to measure and enforce service quality
(C) Improved efficiency
(D) Increased vendor flexibility

Q571. A company conducts annual information security awareness training but does not update content to address emerging threats. What is the MOST significant limitation?
(A) Outdated knowledge among employees
(B) Reduced documentation
(C) Improved governance
(D) Increased automation

Q572. A bank establishes transaction reconciliation procedures but does not investigate reconciling items older than ninety days. What is the PRIMARY risk?
(A) Increased efficiency

(B) Reduced documentation
(C) Improved automation
(D) Accumulation of unresolved discrepancies

Q573. A technology company permits employees to install unauthorized software on corporate devices. What is the MOST significant exposure?
(A) Increased flexibility
(B) Improved innovation
(C) Reduced documentation
(D) Introduction of malware or unsupported applications

Q574. A public organization maintains a documented incident response plan but does not assign specific roles and responsibilities. What is the PRIMARY weakness?
(A) Improved governance
(B) Lack of accountability during incident handling
(C) Increased flexibility
(D) Reduced documentation

Q575. A corporation implements encryption for stored data but uses weak cryptographic keys. What is the MOST significant risk?
(A) Improved compliance
(B) Increased performance
(C) Reduced documentation
(D) Compromise of encrypted information

Q576. A company integrates financial systems with external partners but does not validate data received from those partners. What is the PRIMARY concern?
(A) Reduced documentation
(B) Improved governance
(C) Increased efficiency
(D) Acceptance of inaccurate or malicious data

Q577. A healthcare provider conducts periodic risk assessments but does not involve senior management in reviewing results. What is the MOST significant governance gap?
(A) Reduced documentation
(B) Increased operational independence
(C) Limited strategic oversight of risk exposure
(D) Improved automation

Q578. A company deploys endpoint protection tools but disables automatic updates to reduce bandwidth usage. What is the PRIMARY risk?
(A) Reduced documentation
(B) Outdated protection against evolving threats
(C) Increased performance
(D) Improved governance

Q579. A logistics organization maintains redundant power supplies but does not monitor battery health. What is the MOST significant operational risk?
(A) Increased efficiency
(B) Reduced documentation
(C) Improved governance
(D) Failure of backup power during outage

Q580. A company establishes data sharing agreements with partners but does not monitor compliance with those agreements. What is the PRIMARY weakness?
(A) Lack of assurance that partners follow agreed controls

(B) Improved automation
(C) Reduced documentation
(D) Increased collaboration

Q581. A financial institution uses automated fraud detection but does not document the rationale for rule configuration. What is the MOST significant governance issue?
(A) Lack of transparency and traceability in control design
(B) Reduced documentation
(C) Increased efficiency
(D) Improved automation

Q582. A company retains privileged access rights for employees after role changes. What is the PRIMARY risk?
(A) Accumulation of excessive access privileges
(B) Increased flexibility
(C) Reduced documentation
(D) Improved governance

Q583. A retail organization conducts vendor risk assessments during onboarding but not thereafter. What is the MOST significant exposure?
(A) Increased efficiency
(B) Improved compliance
(C) Reduced documentation
(D) Failure to detect changes in vendor risk profile

Q584. A technology firm introduces secure coding standards but does not enforce compliance through review processes. What is the PRIMARY weakness?
(A) Improved automation
(B) Reduced documentation
(C) Increased flexibility
(D) Policies not translated into practical development controls

Q585. A public sector organization implements centralized logging but does not synchronize system clocks across devices. What is the MOST significant limitation?
(A) Difficulty correlating events accurately during investigations
(B) Reduced documentation
(C) Improved governance
(D) Increased storage usage

Q586. A multinational corporation centralizes data storage but does not implement data residency controls based on geographic requirements. What is the MOST significant compliance risk?
(A) Violation of jurisdictional data localization laws
(B) Improved system scalability
(C) Reduced documentation
(D) Increased operational efficiency

Q587. A financial institution implements automated account provisioning but does not require independent approval for privileged roles. What is the PRIMARY control weakness?
(A) Improved automation maturity
(B) Increased efficiency
(C) Reduced documentation
(D) Lack of segregation in granting elevated access

Q588. A healthcare provider deploys a new electronic records system but does not perform a post implementation review. What is the MOST significant governance gap?
(A) Reduced documentation

(B) Improved operational efficiency
(C) Failure to evaluate whether objectives and controls are effective
(D) Increased automation

Q589. A retail company allows database administrators to modify production data directly without logging changes. What is the PRIMARY risk?
(A) Reduced documentation
(B) Increased flexibility
(C) Loss of audit trail and data integrity assurance
(D) Improved troubleshooting

Q590. A transportation authority maintains a disaster recovery site but does not ensure data replication occurs in real time. What is the MOST significant operational risk?
(A) Reduced documentation
(B) Data loss exceeding acceptable recovery objectives
(C) Improved governance
(D) Increased cost efficiency

Q591. A technology enterprise defines security architecture standards but permits project teams to deviate without risk assessment. What is the PRIMARY governance concern?
(A) Improved efficiency
(B) Increased innovation
(C) Reduced documentation
(D) Unmanaged architectural inconsistencies introducing vulnerabilities

Q592. A financial organization implements monitoring controls but assigns responsibility for reviewing alerts to staff without adequate training. What is the MOST significant weakness?
(A) Improved governance
(B) Reduced documentation
(C) Ineffective detection due to lack of reviewer competence
(D) Increased staffing

Q593. A company establishes formal vendor termination procedures but does not revoke system access for departing vendors. What is the PRIMARY exposure?
(A) Improved collaboration
(B) Increased flexibility
(C) Continued unauthorized external access
(D) Reduced documentation

Q594. A public institution stores confidential records on portable devices without encryption. What is the MOST significant risk?
(A) Increased portability
(B) Reduced documentation
(C) Improved efficiency
(D) Exposure of sensitive information if devices are lost or stolen

Q595. A company defines recovery time objectives for critical systems but does not allocate sufficient infrastructure resources to meet them. What is the PRIMARY consequence?
(A) Failure to restore operations within acceptable timeframes
(B) Improved governance
(C) Increased automation
(D) Reduced documentation

Q596. A financial services firm conducts compliance training but does not track employee participation. What is the MOST significant governance weakness?
(A) Improved operational efficiency

(B) Increased flexibility
(C) Reduced documentation
(D) Lack of evidence that mandatory training requirements are met

Q597. A manufacturing organization integrates operational control systems with corporate networks but does not implement network segmentation. What is the PRIMARY risk?
(A) Spread of cyber incidents between environments
(B) Reduced documentation
(C) Improved efficiency
(D) Increased communication speed

Q598. A retail enterprise conducts periodic internal audits but does not adjust audit frequency based on risk levels. What is the MOST significant limitation?
(A) Inefficient allocation of audit resources
(B) Improved governance
(C) Increased documentation
(D) Reduced compliance

Q599. A technology company retains system administrator credentials in shared documentation repositories accessible to multiple employees. What is the PRIMARY security concern?
(A) Improved efficiency
(B) Reduced documentation
(C) Compromise of privileged credentials
(D) Increased collaboration

Q600. A global enterprise establishes an information security governance framework but does not perform independent assessments of its effectiveness. What is the MOST significant governance gap?
(A) Improved automation
(B) Reduced documentation
(C) Increased flexibility
(D) Absence of objective assurance over control performance

Answer Key and Explanation (501-600)

Q501. Answer: A

Explanation: Independent review enhances objectivity in security testing. Internal teams may overlook familiar weaknesses. Governance frameworks encourage impartial assessment. External validation increases credibility. Comprehensive evaluation strengthens defense mechanisms. Balanced oversight reduces blind spots.

Q502. Answer: D

Explanation: Authentication strength depends on robustness of each factor. Weak passwords undermine layered protection. Governance requires comprehensive configuration of controls. Balanced security reduces likelihood of compromise. Strong credential standards complement additional factors. Holistic implementation enhances protection.

Q503. Answer: B

Explanation: Backup creation alone does not ensure recovery capability. Documented restoration procedures guide response during emergencies. Governance requires clarity and preparedness. Without guidance, confusion may delay operations. Structured documentation supports timely restoration. Preparedness strengthens business continuity.

Q504. Answer: C

Explanation: Interface testing verifies accurate data exchange between systems. Without validation, discrepancies may arise. Governance requires controlled integration processes. Financial records depend on reliable synchronization. Structured testing prevents revenue misstatements. Accurate integration supports operational integrity.

Q505. Answer: B

Explanation: Risk tolerance guides management decision making. Without communication, teams may exceed acceptable exposure. Governance requires shared understanding of limits. Alignment ensures consistent risk management practices. Structured communication strengthens accountability. Clear guidance enhances enterprise risk discipline.

Q506. Answer: C

Explanation: Business owners understand functional necessity of access. Periodic certification confirms continued appropriateness. Governance standards require regular review. Centralization alone does not guarantee correctness. Structured validation prevents privilege accumulation. Ongoing oversight strengthens logical access control.

Q507. Answer: C

Explanation: Accurate documentation supports maintenance and incident response. Outdated diagrams hinder problem resolution. Governance emphasizes record accuracy. Security monitoring depends on understanding network architecture. Structured updates enhance operational awareness. Reliable documentation strengthens control environment.

Q508. Answer: D

Explanation: Medium risk vulnerabilities may still be exploited. Over time, combined weaknesses increase exposure. Governance requires risk based remediation. Ignoring findings undermines proactive defense. Structured prioritization supports balanced mitigation. Comprehensive remediation strengthens security posture.

Q509. Answer: C

Explanation: Sensitive employee data requires restricted access. Shared spreadsheets without controls expose information to unauthorized viewing. Governance standards emphasize confidentiality and need to know principles. Structured access management reduces privacy risk. Controlled sharing strengthens compliance. Effective safeguards protect personal information.

Q510. Answer: A

Explanation: Governance frameworks require ongoing assessment to remain effective. Without measurement, deficiencies may persist unnoticed. Performance indicators support accountability. Continuous improvement enhances maturity. Structured evaluation ensures alignment with strategic objectives. Active monitoring strengthens overall governance effectiveness.

Q511. Answer: D

Explanation: Many jurisdictions impose restrictions on transferring personal data across borders. Failure to assess these requirements can result in regulatory penalties. Governance requires awareness of legal obligations in each region of operation. Cross border transfers must include adequate safeguards. Ignoring such obligations may damage organizational reputation. Structured compliance management reduces legal exposure.

Q512. Answer: B

Explanation: Role based access improves consistency but requires formal approval mechanisms. Without documentation, inappropriate privileges may be granted. Governance frameworks emphasize traceability of access decisions. Proper authorization ensures alignment with job responsibilities. Informal assignment increases risk of misuse. Structured approval strengthens access governance.

Q513. Answer: D

Explanation: Business impact analysis identifies critical processes and recovery needs. Adding new services may change priorities and recovery time objectives. Governance requires periodic updates to reflect operational changes. Outdated analysis weakens continuity planning. Accurate prioritization ensures effective resource allocation. Continuous review enhances resilience.

Q514. Answer: A

Explanation: Version control maintains history of modifications and supports rollback if needed. Without records, identifying responsible parties becomes difficult. Governance standards require documented change management. Traceability supports testing and compliance verification. Uncontrolled deployment increases operational risk. Structured documentation enhances system integrity.

Q515. Answer: D

Explanation: Backup media often contain sensitive and regulated information. Physical security controls are essential to prevent theft or tampering. Governance frameworks emphasize layered protection including environmental safeguards. Unlocked storage increases risk of unauthorized access. Secure offsite storage enhances resilience. Proper handling protects confidentiality and compliance.

Q516. Answer: C

Explanation: Metrics should reflect organizational goals and risk appetite. Misaligned measures may not support decision making. Governance requires strategic alignment of performance indicators. Meaningful metrics guide resource allocation. Without alignment, reporting lacks value. Structured measurement strengthens oversight and accountability.

Q517. Answer: B

Explanation: Account lockout prevents immediate compromise but does not eliminate attack attempts. Monitoring repeated events identifies potential malicious activity. Governance frameworks emphasize proactive threat detection. Ignored alerts reduce effectiveness of preventive controls. Structured analysis enhances security awareness. Continuous monitoring strengthens defense posture.

Q518. Answer: D

Explanation: Cloud environments introduce different responsibilities and response requirements. Incident procedures must reflect new roles and escalation paths. Governance requires alignment between operational changes and policies. Outdated plans may delay containment. Updated procedures enhance coordination. Structured adaptation strengthens resilience.

Q519. Answer: D

Explanation: Supply chain disruptions can significantly impact operations. Excluding dependencies leaves major risks unidentified. Governance emphasizes comprehensive enterprise risk management. External partners influence continuity and security posture. Holistic assessment improves mitigation strategies. Structured evaluation enhances strategic preparedness.

Q520. Answer: D

Explanation: Segregation of duties must be supported by system configuration. Policies alone do not prevent conflicting access. Governance requires implementation and monitoring of controls. Technical enforcement reduces opportunity for fraud. Structured configuration ensures practical compliance. Effective controls strengthen integrity of operations.

Q521. Answer: C

Explanation: Regulatory standards often mandate specific log retention periods. Short retention may violate legal requirements. Governance requires alignment with compliance obligations. Logs support investigations and audit trails. Premature deletion limits evidence availability. Structured retention policies strengthen accountability.

Q522. Answer: C

Explanation: Artificial intelligence systems may inadvertently introduce bias. Ethical assessment ensures fairness and transparency. Governance frameworks increasingly emphasize responsible innovation. Failure to evaluate implications can harm reputation. Structured oversight supports trust. Ethical alignment strengthens stakeholder confidence.

Q523. Answer: D

Explanation: Data masking protects sensitive information in nonproduction environments. Allowing unrestricted administrator access undermines this safeguard. Governance requires least privilege even for privileged roles. Oversight and logging enhance accountability. Excessive access increases misuse risk. Structured control reduces confidentiality exposure.

Q524. Answer: D

Explanation: Training effectiveness must be assessed through metrics such as testing or simulated exercises. Without evaluation, impact remains unknown. Governance requires measurable outcomes. Continuous improvement depends on feedback. Structured assessment strengthens cultural maturity. Monitoring enhances risk awareness.

Q525. Answer: A

Explanation: Detection must be accompanied by response protocols. Without escalation paths, incidents may remain unresolved. Governance frameworks require clear accountability. Defined procedures ensure timely containment. Structured communication enhances coordination. Effective escalation strengthens incident management capability.

Q526. Answer: B

Explanation: Shared accounts prevent identification of specific users. Accountability depends on traceable individual access. Governance standards discourage shared credentials. Audit trails lose evidentiary value when identities are unclear. Structured access management supports transparency. Eliminating shared accounts strengthens internal control.

Q527. Answer: C

Explanation: Capacity planning must account for fluctuations in usage. Ignoring peak demand may cause outages or slow response times. Governance requires realistic forecasting. Adequate resources ensure service continuity. Structured analysis supports customer satisfaction. Comprehensive planning enhances operational stability.

Q528. Answer: D

Explanation: Portable storage devices can facilitate unauthorized copying of data. Sensitive research information requires strict handling controls. Governance frameworks emphasize data loss prevention.

Without restrictions, confidentiality may be compromised. Monitoring and technical safeguards reduce risk. Structured policy enforcement strengthens protection.

Q529. Answer: A

Explanation: Security clauses must be supported by continuous monitoring. Vendors may change practices over time. Governance requires periodic verification. Without oversight, compliance cannot be assured. Structured assessments enhance accountability. Ongoing review strengthens third party risk management.

Q530. Answer: C

Explanation: Surveillance footage often contains sensitive personal information. Unrestricted access increases potential for abuse. Governance standards require defined access controls. Logging and monitoring enhance accountability. Privacy regulations mandate protective measures. Structured safeguards preserve confidentiality.

Q531. Answer: A

Explanation: Policies require consistent enforcement to remain credible. Lack of sanctions diminishes deterrence. Governance frameworks emphasize accountability. Employees may ignore rules without consequences. Structured disciplinary processes strengthen compliance culture. Effective enforcement supports risk mitigation.

Q532. Answer: B

Explanation: Growing environments generate large volumes of alerts. Manual monitoring may become inefficient and error prone. Governance requires scalable controls. Automation enhances detection accuracy. Delayed response increases potential damage. Structured monitoring strengthens operational security.

Q533. Answer: B

Explanation: Updating standards must include practical implementation. Outdated certificates may contain vulnerabilities. Governance requires comprehensive transition planning. Incomplete updates weaken protection. Structured review ensures consistency. Proper implementation enhances confidentiality and integrity.

Q534. Answer: A

Explanation: Social engineering tests highlight behavioral vulnerabilities. Sharing findings educates employees and strengthens defenses. Governance encourages feedback and improvement. Without communication, awareness gaps persist. Structured training enhances resilience. Transparent reporting supports cultural growth.

Q535. Answer: C

Explanation: Service level agreements establish expectations for performance. Measurement ensures commitments are met. Governance requires monitoring against defined targets. Without tracking, deficiencies may remain unnoticed. Structured reporting enhances transparency. Continuous evaluation strengthens service management effectiveness.

Q536. Answer: C

Explanation: Change management policies ensure structured evaluation and approval of modifications. Allowing bypass without documentation weakens governance integrity. Executive exceptions without oversight create inconsistent practices. Accountability depends on equal application of controls. Undocumented changes increase operational and security risk. Strong governance requires adherence at all organizational levels.

Q537. Answer: A

Explanation: User acceptance testing validates that the system satisfies business needs. Without it, functional gaps may remain undiscovered. Governance standards require validation before production release. Inadequate testing increases likelihood of disruption. Stakeholder involvement ensures alignment with requirements. Proper testing strengthens operational effectiveness.

Q538. Answer: B
Explanation: Encryption protects data only when key access is tightly controlled. Broad administrator access undermines confidentiality safeguards. Governance frameworks emphasize least privilege for key management. Unrestricted access increases misuse potential. Segregation of duties strengthens protection. Structured controls ensure data confidentiality integrity.
Q539. Answer: C
Explanation: Identifying vulnerabilities without remediation leaves the organization exposed. Governance requires risk based prioritization and action. Budget limitations do not eliminate accountability for protection. Unresolved weaknesses may be exploited. Structured remediation planning reduces exposure. Effective risk management demands follow through.
Q540. Answer: C
Explanation: Redundancy ensures availability only if failover works properly. Testing confirms operational readiness. Governance standards require periodic validation of continuity mechanisms. Untested systems may fail when needed most. Structured testing identifies configuration issues. Reliable verification strengthens service resilience.
Q541. Answer: B
Explanation: Guidelines require supporting tools for consistent application. Without enforcement mechanisms, employees may apply classifications unevenly. Governance frameworks emphasize operationalization of policy. Inconsistent labeling weakens protective controls. Structured support enhances compliance. Effective implementation strengthens data governance maturity.
Q542. Answer: A
Explanation: Sole dependency creates concentration risk. If the supplier experiences issues, operations may halt. Governance requires evaluation of vendor risk and alternative arrangements. Diversification enhances resilience. Structured contingency planning supports continuity. Reduced dependency strengthens operational stability.
Q543. Answer: D
Explanation: Personal devices may lack enterprise level security controls. Without configuration standards, risks increase. Governance frameworks require defined baseline protections. Unmanaged endpoints expand attack surface. Structured policies enhance remote work security. Controlled configurations reduce vulnerability exposure.
Q544. Answer: A
Explanation: Severity levels guide allocation of resources. Without alignment, high priority incidents may not receive adequate attention. Governance requires coordinated planning. Structured prioritization improves response effectiveness. Misalignment delays containment. Proper resource mapping strengthens incident management capability.
Q545. Answer: D
Explanation: Internal networks may still be vulnerable to compromise. Encrypting only external transmissions leaves gaps. Governance promotes comprehensive data protection. Threat actors can exploit internal weaknesses. Structured encryption policies reduce interception risk. End to end protection strengthens confidentiality.
Q546. Answer: C
Explanation: Business units possess detailed knowledge of operational processes. Excluding them reduces insight into practical risks. Governance frameworks emphasize cross functional participation. Broader representation improves decision quality. Structured collaboration enhances risk management. Inclusive oversight strengthens enterprise resilience.
Q547. Answer: A
Explanation: Audit findings require communication to responsible parties. Without notification, corrective measures cannot occur. Governance standards require transparent reporting. Accountability

depends on awareness. Structured follow up ensures remediation. Effective communication strengthens internal control maturity.

Q548. Answer: C

Explanation: Retention schedules ensure records are kept according to legal requirements. Undefined timelines may violate regulatory mandates. Governance requires structured lifecycle management. Over retention increases privacy risk, while early disposal may breach compliance. Balanced retention strengthens legal defensibility. Defined schedules enhance accountability.

Q549. Answer: C

Explanation: Legacy systems often contain known weaknesses. Excluding them from updates leaves exploitable gaps. Governance requires compensating controls when patching is not feasible. Unaddressed vulnerabilities increase attack risk. Structured mitigation planning reduces exposure. Comprehensive management strengthens security posture.

Q550. Answer: D

Explanation: Dashboards depend on reliable data sources. Inaccurate inputs compromise decision making. Governance emphasizes data integrity. Without validation, management may misinterpret performance. Structured verification enhances reliability. Accurate reporting supports strategic planning.

Q551. Answer: B

Explanation: Code review identifies flaws before deployment. Without review, vulnerabilities may remain undetected. Governance standards require secure development practices. Early detection reduces remediation cost. Structured testing strengthens application security. Preventive measures enhance reliability.

Q552. Answer: B

Explanation: Public wireless networks may be insecure. Without secure connections, data can be intercepted. Governance frameworks emphasize protected remote access. Encryption safeguards confidentiality. Structured controls reduce transmission risk. Secure communication strengthens organizational protection.

Q553. Answer: B

Explanation: Temperature extremes can damage hardware and disrupt operations. Continuous monitoring detects anomalies early. Governance standards require environmental oversight. Lack of monitoring delays corrective action. Structured alerts enhance response. Proactive management preserves system availability.

Q554. Answer: A

Explanation: Key risk indicators highlight potential issues. Without reporting integration, management lacks timely awareness. Governance requires consistent communication of risk metrics. Structured reporting supports informed decisions. Visibility enables proactive mitigation. Effective integration strengthens oversight.

Q555. Answer: D

Explanation: Segregation of duties prevents individuals from concealing unauthorized activity. Combining processing and reconciliation increases fraud risk. Governance frameworks emphasize independent verification. Structured role separation enhances accountability. Conflicting duties weaken control environment. Proper segregation strengthens financial integrity.

Q556. Answer: D

Explanation: Maintaining legacy databases creates redundant access points. Attackers may exploit outdated systems. Governance requires removal of obsolete components. Consolidation enhances control consistency. Structured decommissioning reduces complexity. Eliminating duplicates strengthens security posture.

Q557. Answer: B

Explanation: Recovery objectives must be validated through testing. Without verification, assumptions may prove inaccurate. Governance standards require regular drills. Structured testing identifies performance gaps. Unverified targets weaken continuity planning. Practical validation strengthens resilience.

Q558. Answer: A

Explanation: Access controls must apply consistently to all personnel. Unrestricted contractor access increases theft or misuse risk. Governance requires uniform enforcement. Temporary status does not reduce exposure. Structured onboarding controls enhance accountability. Consistent policy application strengthens protection.

Q559. Answer: D

Explanation: Security strategy should support overall business goals. Misalignment may result in inefficient resource allocation. Governance requires strategic integration. Coordinated planning enhances value delivery. Structured alignment ensures relevance. Harmonized objectives strengthen enterprise performance.

Q560. Answer: A

Explanation: Regulations may change frequently. Waiting for annual review delays necessary adjustments. Governance frameworks require continuous monitoring of compliance obligations. Timely adaptation prevents violations. Structured tracking enhances responsiveness. Proactive management strengthens legal and operational stability.

Q561. Answer: B

Explanation: Automated decision systems must reflect current policies and regulations. Without periodic validation, algorithms may apply outdated rules. Governance frameworks require continuous alignment between business requirements and system logic. Failure to update criteria can result in noncompliant outcomes. Regulatory violations may lead to penalties and reputational harm. Ongoing review ensures responsible and accurate automated processing.

Q562. Answer: C

Explanation: Access restrictions are preventive controls, but monitoring provides detection capability. Without log review, suspicious behavior may go unnoticed. Governance standards require layered security mechanisms. Timely monitoring supports rapid response to incidents. Ignoring logs reduces accountability. Effective oversight strengthens protection of sensitive information.

Q563. Answer: C

Explanation: Policies must be supported by education to ensure consistent application. Without training, employees may misclassify data. Governance requires awareness programs to operationalize controls. Incorrect handling may expose sensitive information. Structured training promotes accountability. Proper understanding enhances overall data protection.

Q564. Answer: C

Explanation: Penetration testing identifies exploitable vulnerabilities. Delayed remediation leaves systems exposed. Governance requires timely corrective action based on severity. Known weaknesses present significant attack opportunities. Structured prioritization ensures risk reduction. Prompt resolution strengthens security posture.

Q565. Answer: D

Explanation: Segregation of duties prevents concentration of authority. Allowing administrators to both request and approve access removes independent oversight. Governance frameworks emphasize separation of responsibilities. Conflicting roles increase potential for abuse. Independent approval strengthens accountability. Proper segregation reduces fraud and error risk.

Q566. Answer: B

Explanation: Backup success does not guarantee restoration capability. Testing verifies that data can be recovered accurately. Governance standards require periodic recovery exercises. Untested procedures may fail under pressure. Structured validation ensures continuity readiness. Regular drills strengthen resilience.

Q567. Answer: D

Explanation: Excessively high thresholds reduce detection sensitivity. Fraudulent activities may fall below configured limits. Governance requires balanced risk tolerance and control calibration. Suppressing alerts for convenience weakens oversight. Proper configuration enhances detection accuracy. Effective monitoring protects financial assets.

Q568. Answer: D

Explanation: Privacy impact assessments evaluate risks to personal information. Migration may introduce new exposure points. Governance frameworks require evaluation before major changes. Failure to assess can result in regulatory noncompliance. Structured review identifies mitigation measures. Proactive analysis strengthens trust and legal compliance.

Q569. Answer: D

Explanation: Conflicting policies create ambiguity for employees. Inconsistent interpretation weakens enforcement. Governance requires clear and harmonized documentation. Ambiguity increases risk of noncompliance. Structured policy management ensures clarity. Consistent guidance strengthens organizational control culture.

Q570. Answer: B

Explanation: Service performance metrics establish measurable expectations. Without them, accountability is limited. Governance frameworks require clear contractual obligations. Lack of measurable criteria hinders dispute resolution. Structured agreements support oversight. Defined metrics strengthen third party management.

Q571. Answer: A

Explanation: Threat landscapes evolve rapidly. Training must reflect current risks. Governance standards emphasize continuous improvement. Outdated material reduces effectiveness. Structured updates enhance awareness. Relevant education strengthens defensive behavior.

Q572. Answer: D

Explanation: Longstanding reconciling items may indicate errors or fraud. Ignoring aged discrepancies undermines control effectiveness. Governance requires timely resolution. Structured follow up reduces financial misstatement risk. Unresolved differences weaken reporting integrity. Active management strengthens financial oversight.

Q573. Answer: D

Explanation: Unauthorized software may contain vulnerabilities or malicious code. Governance frameworks require controlled software installation. Unmanaged applications increase attack surface. Standardization enhances stability and security. Structured approval processes reduce risk. Proper control preserves system integrity.

Q574. Answer: B

Explanation: Defined roles ensure coordinated response efforts. Without clear assignments, confusion may delay action. Governance requires accountability and clarity. Structured role definition enhances efficiency. Ambiguity reduces effectiveness. Clear responsibility strengthens crisis management.

Q575. Answer: D

Explanation: Encryption strength depends on robust key management. Weak keys may be easily broken. Governance standards require adherence to strong cryptographic practices. Inadequate key strength undermines confidentiality. Structured key policies enhance protection. Strong implementation ensures data security.

Q576. Answer: D

Explanation: External data sources may contain errors or malicious input. Validation ensures integrity before processing. Governance frameworks require input controls. Unverified data may compromise financial accuracy. Structured validation reduces operational risk. Reliable processing strengthens trustworthiness.

Q577. Answer: C

Explanation: Senior management provides strategic direction and resource allocation. Excluding them limits enterprise level oversight. Governance standards require executive involvement. Risk decisions impact organizational priorities. Structured reporting enhances accountability. Active leadership strengthens risk management maturity.

Q578. Answer: B

Explanation: Threat definitions and detection mechanisms require frequent updates. Disabling updates weakens defense capability. Governance frameworks emphasize timely maintenance. Outdated protection increases vulnerability. Structured update policies strengthen resilience. Continuous refresh ensures effective threat mitigation.

Q579. Answer: D

Explanation: Backup power systems require maintenance and monitoring. Battery degradation may go unnoticed. Governance standards require preventive maintenance. Failure during outage disrupts operations. Structured oversight ensures reliability. Regular monitoring strengthens continuity assurance.

Q580. Answer: A

Explanation: Agreements outline responsibilities for data protection. Without monitoring, compliance cannot be confirmed. Governance frameworks emphasize oversight of shared data. Unverified compliance increases exposure. Structured audits enhance accountability. Ongoing review strengthens trust and protection.

Q581. Answer: A

Explanation: Documented rationale supports accountability and review. Without records, understanding control decisions becomes difficult. Governance standards require traceability. Transparency enhances auditability. Structured documentation facilitates improvement. Clear reasoning strengthens internal control integrity.

Q582. Answer: A

Explanation: Role changes may reduce necessity for certain privileges. Retaining access violates least privilege principle. Governance frameworks require periodic review and adjustment. Excessive rights increase misuse potential. Structured lifecycle management strengthens access governance. Proper revocation enhances security.

Q583. Answer: D

Explanation: Vendor circumstances may evolve over time. Initial assessment does not guarantee ongoing compliance. Governance requires periodic reassessment. Changing controls or financial conditions may introduce new risk. Structured monitoring enhances oversight. Continuous evaluation strengthens third party risk management.

Q584. Answer: D

Explanation: Coding standards require enforcement mechanisms. Without review, developers may not adhere consistently. Governance standards emphasize implementation verification. Structured oversight ensures compliance. Unenforced policies weaken security posture. Effective review strengthens application integrity.

Q585. Answer: A

Explanation: Accurate time synchronization is essential for event correlation. Inconsistent timestamps complicate forensic analysis. Governance frameworks require coordinated logging practices. Structured synchronization enhances reliability of audit trails. Clear chronology supports effective investigation. Proper alignment strengthens incident response capability.

Q586. Answer: A

Explanation: Many countries require certain categories of data to remain within national boundaries. Failure to implement residency controls may result in regulatory violations. Governance frameworks require alignment with local legal obligations. Centralization without jurisdictional awareness increases exposure. Noncompliance can lead to penalties and reputational harm. Structured oversight ensures lawful cross border data management.

Q587. Answer: D

Explanation: Privileged roles provide extensive system capabilities. Independent approval reduces risk of unauthorized elevation. Governance standards emphasize segregation of duties. Automated provisioning must include oversight mechanisms. Without independent validation, abuse risk increases. Structured approval strengthens access governance.

Q588. Answer: C

Explanation: Post implementation reviews assess whether systems meet objectives and comply with policies. Without review, weaknesses may persist undetected. Governance requires evaluation after major projects. Lessons learned support continuous improvement. Structured assessment ensures alignment with strategic goals. Effective review strengthens accountability.

Q589. Answer: C

Explanation: Logging changes ensures traceability and accountability. Direct modifications without records compromise integrity. Governance frameworks require monitoring of privileged activities. Untracked changes increase risk of fraud or error. Structured logging enhances transparency. Reliable audit trails support compliance and investigation.

Q590. Answer: B

Explanation: Recovery objectives define acceptable data loss thresholds. Without real time or near real time replication, gaps may occur. Governance standards require alignment between replication frequency and recovery point objectives. Delayed synchronization increases impact of disruptions. Structured configuration ensures continuity readiness. Proper replication safeguards critical information.

Q591. Answer: D

Explanation: Architecture standards ensure consistent and secure design. Deviations without risk assessment may introduce weaknesses. Governance frameworks require documented justification and approval. Uncontrolled variation increases complexity and exposure. Structured evaluation supports informed decisions. Consistent standards strengthen enterprise security posture.

Q592. Answer: C

Explanation: Monitoring effectiveness depends on skilled analysis. Untrained personnel may overlook critical indicators. Governance requires competency in control execution. Training ensures accurate interpretation of alerts. Without expertise, risks may remain unidentified. Structured capability development enhances oversight.

Q593. Answer: C

Explanation: Vendor offboarding must include access revocation. Failure to remove credentials leaves systems exposed. Governance standards emphasize lifecycle management. Persistent access increases misuse potential. Structured deprovisioning enhances accountability. Proper termination processes protect organizational assets.

Q594. Answer: D

Explanation: Portable devices are susceptible to loss and theft. Without encryption, stored data is easily accessible. Governance frameworks require safeguards for mobile storage. Encryption mitigates physical compromise risk. Unprotected devices threaten confidentiality. Structured controls strengthen data protection.

Q595. Answer: A

Explanation: Recovery objectives must be supported by adequate capacity. Insufficient resources hinder timely restoration. Governance requires feasibility validation. Misalignment creates unrealistic expectations. Structured planning ensures achievable targets. Proper allocation strengthens continuity assurance.

Q596. Answer: D

Explanation: Participation tracking provides assurance that training obligations are fulfilled. Without records, compliance cannot be demonstrated. Governance standards require accountability and documentation. Missing evidence increases regulatory risk. Structured monitoring strengthens oversight. Verified completion enhances compliance posture.

Q597. Answer: A

Explanation: Segmentation limits movement of threats between systems. Integration without separation increases exposure. Governance frameworks promote defense in depth. Compromised corporate systems may affect operational processes. Structured isolation enhances resilience. Controlled architecture reduces systemic risk.

Q598. Answer: A

Explanation: Risk based auditing aligns effort with exposure levels. Uniform frequency may overlook high risk areas. Governance standards require dynamic planning. Prioritization enhances effectiveness. Structured assessment supports optimal resource use. Adaptive scheduling strengthens assurance coverage.

Q599. Answer: C

Explanation: Administrator credentials provide extensive system control. Shared repositories increase exposure risk. Governance frameworks require secure credential management. Unrestricted access undermines accountability. Structured vaulting mechanisms enhance protection. Strong controls safeguard critical access rights.

Q600. Answer: D

Explanation: Independent assessments provide unbiased evaluation of controls. Without them, weaknesses may remain unnoticed. Governance standards emphasize objective assurance functions. External or independent review enhances credibility. Structured evaluation supports continuous improvement. Objective oversight strengthens overall governance maturity.

Question (601-700)

Q601. Which process ensures that all new systems meet security requirements before deployment?

A. Security incident response

B. Secure system configuration and hardening review

C. Business continuity testing

D. Physical security assessment

Q602. What is the main benefit of performing regular security audits?

A. Eliminates all security risks

B. Ensures compliance and identifies control weaknesses

C. Improves server performance

D. Reduces staff training requirements

Q603. Which control best prevents unauthorized access to sensitive mobile devices?

A. Device encryption and mobile device management (MDM)

B. Allowing users to disable device PINs

C. Using public Wi-Fi for updates

D. Storing credentials in text files

Q604. Which of the following is a detective control used in information security?

A. Firewalls

B. Intrusion Detection Systems (IDS)

C. Encryption

D. Multi-factor authentication

Q605. What is the main purpose of conducting penetration testing?

A. To verify system resilience against real-world attacks

B. To replace ongoing vulnerability assessments

C. To ensure compliance with HR policies

D. To monitor employee productivity

Q606. Which of the following actions is most appropriate when a security incident is confirmed?

A. Erase all logs immediately

B. Activate the incident response plan

C. Notify all employees simultaneously

D. Continue normal operations without change

Q607. What is the primary objective of implementing intrusion prevention systems (IPS)?

A. Block malicious activity in real time

B. Record network traffic for historical analysis

C. Encrypt sensitive network communications

D. Audit compliance with policy

Q608. Which of the following would best protect against social engineering?

A. Regular firewall updates

B. Network encryption protocols

C. Security awareness and training programs

D. Password rotation policies

Q609. What is the most critical consideration when collecting digital evidence?

A. Ensuring evidence integrity and chain of custody

B. Collecting as much data as possible, regardless of relevance

C. Editing files to simplify review

D. Copying only user-requested data

Q610. What control most directly supports accountability for data changes in financial systems?

A. Audit logging and change tracking
B. Redundant data storage
C. Database mirroring
D. Firewall segmentation

Q611. What is the main goal of using multi-factor authentication (MFA)?
A. To enhance password complexity
B. To verify identity through multiple independent factors
C. To eliminate password use entirely
D. To encrypt all user communications

Q612. What type of control is a policy requiring employees to report security incidents within one hour?
A. Administrative
B. Physical
C. Technical
D. Corrective

Q613. Which best mitigates risks from shadow IT (unauthorized IT solutions)?
A. Blocking all network ports
B. Implementing centralized software inventory and approval processes
C. Allowing all teams to install tools freely
D. Ignoring small unauthorized tools

Q614. What is the most effective method to ensure recovery readiness after a ransomware incident?
A. Maintaining offline, immutable backups
B. Paying ransom immediately
C. Restoring from online shared drives
D. Disabling all network connections permanently

Q615. Which control best helps detect unusual outbound traffic that may indicate data exfiltration?
A. Network monitoring and anomaly detection
B. Strong password policies
C. Data compression tools
D. Physical access restriction

Q616. Which control most effectively ensures the confidentiality of data stored on mobile devices?
A. Encrypting the device's storage using full-disk encryption
B. Disabling device password protection for convenience
C. Allowing unrestricted app installations
D. Using unsecured public Wi-Fi networks

Q617. What is the main advantage of network segmentation in enterprise security?
A. Improves network speed by reducing congestion
B. Limits lateral movement of attackers between network zones
C. Simplifies firewall configuration
D. Reduces the need for user authentication

Q618. Which of the following is a technical control for protecting information assets?
A. Security awareness training
B. Access control lists (ACLs) on file servers
C. Background checks on new employees
D. Clean desk policy enforcement

Q619. Which type of attack does encryption primarily defend against?
A. Data interception or eavesdropping
B. Denial-of-service attacks

C. Brute-force password guessing
D. Insider privilege abuse

Q620. What is the most appropriate reason to perform log reviews regularly?

A. To identify anomalies or unauthorized activities early
B. To reduce storage requirements
C. To delete outdated system files
D. To document normal operations only

Q621. What is the most effective control for preventing unauthorized software installation?

A. Application whitelisting
B. Strong password policies
C. Disabling user training
D. Firewall rules

Q622. Which of the following best describes data at rest?

A. Data actively moving between systems
B. Data temporarily stored in memory
C. Data stored on physical or digital media
D. Data currently being processed by applications

Q623. What is the primary purpose of using hashing algorithms in information security?

A. Encrypting data for confidentiality
B. Ensuring data integrity by detecting modifications
C. Accelerating network communication
D. Compressing large files

Q624. What is the main goal of access provisioning processes?

A. To grant users maximum privileges for efficiency
B. To ensure access rights align with job responsibilities
C. To prevent password expiration
D. To standardize device configurations

Q625. Which control is most appropriate to prevent unauthorized remote access?

A. Disabling VPN encryption
B. Implementing VPN with strong authentication
C. Allowing open ports on firewalls
D. Sharing remote desktop passwords

Q626. Which is the first step in responding to a detected malware outbreak?

A. Contain the affected systems to prevent spread
B. Notify law enforcement immediately
C. Conduct user awareness sessions
D. Delete all infected files

Q627. Which of the following represents a compensating control?

A. Enforcing the same control multiple times
B. Implementing additional monitoring where encryption isn't feasible
C. Ignoring a control due to cost
D. Applying unrelated operational measures

Q628. What is the main benefit of implementing data classification?

A. Reduces audit frequency
B. Enables appropriate security controls based on sensitivity
C. Simplifies data storage
D. Increases data redundancy

Q629. Which process best supports accountability in system administration?

A. Assigning unique user IDs for administrators
B. Using shared admin accounts
C. Disabling audit trails to save space
D. Granting full access to all users
Q630. Which activity is part of security incident recovery per NIST SP 800-61?
A. Restoring systems to operational status after threat removal
B. Identifying and logging new incidents
C. Conducting user training
D. Monitoring for initial attack indicators
Q631. What is the primary goal of implementing endpoint protection tools?
A. Enhance visibility into user productivity
B. Detect and block malicious software or activity on devices
C. Encrypt all internet traffic
D. Replace network firewalls
Q632. Which security measure best prevents unauthorized system configuration changes?
A. Implementing configuration management and change control processes
B. Allowing unrestricted administrative access
C. Disabling audit logs
D. Using open Wi-Fi networks
Q633. Which of the following best describes data in use?
A. Data stored on a hard drive
B. Data being transmitted over a network
C. Data being processed by applications in memory
D. Data backed up to offline storage
Q634. What is the primary objective of an incident post-mortem review?
A. Assign blame to responsible employees
B. Identify lessons learned and improve future response
C. Restore services immediately
D. Document the attack's financial impact only
Q635. Which measure best mitigates the risk of sensitive information disclosure through printed materials?
A. Secure shredding and document disposal processes
B. Keeping documents on desks overnight
C. Printing confidential data without labeling
D. Allowing guests to access printer trays
Q636. Which of the following best ensures secure disposal of electronic storage media?
A. Reformatting the media before disposal
B. Physically destroying or degaussing the media
C. Donating old drives to other departments
D. Overwriting only a few files with random data
Q637. What is the primary benefit of security baselines?
A. They define minimum acceptable configurations for systems
B. They replace patch management processes
C. They ensure network performance improvements
D. They eliminate all vulnerabilities automatically
Q638. Which of the following controls provides non-repudiation in electronic transactions?
A. Symmetric key encryption
B. Digital signatures using public key cryptography

C. Simple password authentication
D. File compression utilities
Q639. Which action is most effective in preventing unauthorized access after an employee termination?
A. Conducting exit interviews only
B. Immediately revoking all access rights and credentials
C. Waiting until payroll completes before revocation
D. Retaining access for potential rehiring
Q640. What is the main purpose of a data retention policy?
A. To define how long data must be stored before deletion
B. To determine encryption strength for data storage
C. To limit physical access to storage facilities
D. To establish internet browsing rules
Q641. Which security measure best reduces risks associated with lost or stolen laptops?
A. Encrypting the hard drive and enabling remote wipe
B. Keeping passwords written on sticky notes
C. Disabling device updates for consistency
D. Allowing auto-login for convenience
Q642. What is the primary advantage of using Public Key Infrastructure (PKI)?
A. Simplifies password sharing
B. Enables secure key management and digital trust
C. Eliminates the need for authentication
D. Reduces encryption overhead entirely
Q643. Which of the following is most critical to include in an information security policy?
A. Specific vendor product names
B. Roles, responsibilities, and enforcement mechanisms
C. Individual user passwords
D. Daily operational procedures
Q644. Which security control best protects against unauthorized modification of system configurations?
A. Change management with approval workflows
B. User awareness training
C. Regular password changes
D. Intrusion prevention systems
Q645. Which is the most effective way to protect backup media from environmental damage?
A. Storing backups near server racks
B. Using climate-controlled, off-site storage
C. Keeping tapes in unlocked drawers
D. Leaving media on desktops for convenience
Q646. Which of the following is a corrective control example?
A. Firewall rule enforcement
B. Antivirus quarantine and malware removal
C. Role-based access control
D. Security awareness training
Q647. What is the best method to prevent data leakage through email?
A. Implementing email-based DLP policies
B. Disabling antivirus software
C. Allowing unrestricted attachments

D. Ignoring outbound email scanning

Q648. Which of the following most effectively supports traceability in audit trails?

A. Sharing logins across users

B. Disabling time synchronization to save bandwidth

C. Synchronizing system clocks using NTP

D. Manually entering timestamps into logs

Q649. Which action should an organization take after eradicating a security incident?

A. Conduct a recovery process and restore services

B. Disconnect unaffected systems

C. Delete all logs for privacy

D. Stop all business operations indefinitely

Q650. What is the main purpose of user access recertification?

A. To periodically verify that user permissions remain appropriate

B. To provide users with higher privileges automatically

C. To increase system performance

D. To reduce password expiration frequency

Q651. Which security control is best suited to prevent brute-force password attacks?

A. File encryption

B. Account lockout policies after failed attempts

C. Firewall filtering

D. Access provisioning

Q652. What is the primary objective of security awareness training?

A. To educate users about threats and proper security behaviors

B. To replace technical controls entirely

C. To configure firewalls and IDS systems

D. To increase password reuse

Q653. Which of the following best protects against unauthorized wireless access?

A. Broadcasting SSIDs publicly

B. Implementing WPA3 and strong authentication

C. Disabling WPA3 encryption

D. Using default router passwords

Q654. What is the main benefit of conducting a vulnerability assessment?

A. Identifies security weaknesses before exploitation

B. Eliminates all risks automatically

C. Provides continuous intrusion detection

D. Guarantees compliance certification

Q655. Which control best ensures that encryption keys are changed periodically?

A. Implementing a key management policy

B. Storing keys in plaintext within software code

C. Sharing encryption keys between systems

D. Hardcoding keys for performance reasons

Q656. What is the primary purpose of implementing an access control policy?

A. To prevent audit trail creation

B. To provide administrative rights to all employees

C. To ensure users have only the permissions necessary for their role

D. To increase system speed by reducing authentication

Q657. Which control type provides real-time prevention of malicious activity?

A. Intrusion Prevention System (IPS)

B. Security Information and Event Management (SIEM)
C. Vulnerability scanning
D. Log archiving

Q658. Which best mitigates the risk of unauthorized use of personal devices for company work (BYOD)?

A. Implementing mobile device management (MDM) with compliance rules
B. Allowing unrestricted app installations
C. Removing password policies for convenience
D. Disabling all device monitoring

Q659. What is the main benefit of implementing audit logging?

A. Reduces system load by deleting old records
B. Enables tracking of user actions for accountability and investigations
C. Prevents all unauthorized activity automatically
D. Eliminates the need for authentication

Q660. Which security principle is reinforced by enforcing multi-factor authentication (MFA)?

A. Defense in depth
B. Least privilege
C. Confidentiality of access
D. Segregation of duties

Q661. Which of the following is a preventive control example?

A. User access provisioning with least privilege
B. Log review and alert generation
C. Root cause analysis after an incident
D. Post-incident forensic investigation

Q662. Which activity best ensures that sensitive information is properly handled by third-party vendors?

A. Ignoring third-party activities for efficiency
B. Assuming vendors have sufficient controls
C. Including security clauses in vendor contracts and performing due diligence
D. Allowing unrestricted data sharing

Q663. What is the primary goal of data masking?

A. To hide sensitive data values during non-production use
B. To encrypt data permanently
C. To delete redundant information
D. To compress stored data

Q664. Which of the following best prevents privilege escalation attacks?

A. Enforcing least privilege and role-based access controls
B. Allowing users to modify their own permissions
C. Using shared administrative accounts
D. Ignoring privilege audits

Q665. Which of the following is a logical access control?

A. Security guards verifying badges
B. Password authentication on systems
C. Encryption of server rooms
D. Fire suppression systems

Q666. What is the primary advantage of continuous security monitoring?

A. Detects potential incidents and anomalies in near real time
B. Guarantees that no incidents will occur

C. Reduces the need for an incident response plan
D. Eliminates audit requirements
Q667. Which best describes defense in depth?
A. Focusing on a single strong firewall
B. Using layered and complementary security controls
C. Relying only on employee awareness
D. Centralizing all assets in one data center
Q668. What should be the first step when creating an incident response plan?
A. Identify critical assets and potential threats
B. Conduct post-incident reviews
C. Notify regulators
D. Begin forensic data collection
Q669. Which control primarily detects policy violations and anomalies?
A. Security monitoring and alerting systems
B. Firewalls
C. Role-based access control
D. Patch management
Q670. Which of the following is a key objective of business continuity management?
A. Eliminate redundancy in infrastructure
B. Prevent all disasters entirely
C. Focus solely on IT security
D. Maintain critical operations during disruption
Q671. Which mechanism best ensures accountability for database changes?
A. Database audit logging and user traceability
B. Shared database credentials
C. Disabling logging to improve speed
D. Manual backups without logs
Q672. What is the most effective way to reduce human error in handling sensitive data?
A. Ignoring process standardization
B. Allowing unrestricted manual handling
C. Implementing automated processes and security awareness training
D. Reducing monitoring to avoid alert fatigue
Q673. Which measure ensures that security incidents are communicated effectively?
A. Defined communication protocols and escalation procedures
B. Disabling notifications to avoid confusion
C. Handling incidents individually without coordination
D. Allowing only end users to report to executives
Q674. Which control helps detect unusual data exfiltration over encrypted channels?
A. Network traffic analysis and behavioral monitoring
B. Simple firewall rules based on IP addresses
C. Periodic password resets
D. Manual inspection of print logs
Q675. What is the primary goal of conducting a tabletop exercise?
A. To replace technical security assessments
B. To physically shut down systems for recovery
C. To test the effectiveness of response plans in a simulated environment
D. To focus solely on compliance documentation

Q676. Which control best ensures that sensitive data stored in cloud environments remains confidential?
A. Encrypting data before uploading to the cloud
B. Relying solely on the cloud provider's internal policies
C. Storing unencrypted backups in shared folders
D. Using default public sharing permissions
Q677. Which of the following controls best addresses unauthorized USB device usage?
A. Disabling USB ports through group policy or endpoint management
B. Allowing unrestricted use of portable drives
C. Relying on employees to self-report usage
D. Using only antivirus software
Q678. What is the main benefit of performing regular user access reviews?
A. Enhancing network bandwidth
B. Increasing system uptime
C. Eliminating password requirements
D. Identifying and revoking unnecessary or outdated privileges
Q679. Which practice is most effective in protecting against phishing attacks?
A. Conducting periodic phishing simulations and user awareness training
B. Blocking all inbound emails
C. Using password rotation policies only
D. Ignoring suspicious messages to save time
Q680. Which control most directly protects against data interception during transmission?
A. Implementing TLS encryption on all communication channels
B. Using weak passwords
C. Disabling VPN access
D. Transmitting data via unencrypted HTTP
Q681. Which of the following best ensures that system patches are applied in a timely manner?
A. Ignoring low-severity patches indefinitely
B. Allowing users to install patches manually at their discretion
C. Establishing a formal patch management schedule and testing process
D. Applying patches without testing in production
Q682. Which of the following best describes tokenization?
A. Replacing sensitive data elements with randomly generated tokens
B. Encrypting data using symmetric keys
C. Deleting all sensitive records
D. Encoding data in binary format
Q683. What is the primary purpose of identity and access management (IAM)?
A. To ensure the right individuals access the right resources at the right times
B. To encrypt all network traffic
C. To manage hardware configurations
D. To replace security awareness programs
Q684. Which activity should be performed immediately after an incident is confirmed?
A. Conducting post-incident review
B. Containment to isolate affected systems
C. Recovery of all services
D. Legal reporting and closure
Q685. Which of the following controls best mitigates risks from unapproved software installations?
A. Implementing application whitelisting and restriction policies

B. Allowing all users to install any software
C. Removing antivirus software to boost speed
D. Ignoring license verification procedures

Q686. What is the primary purpose of log retention requirements?
A. To preserve records for audits, investigations, and compliance
B. To free disk space quickly
C. To reduce monitoring workloads
D. To hide evidence from review

Q687. Which control best reduces the likelihood of successful ransomware infections?
A. Allowing open RDP access without authentication
B. Disabling antivirus software
C. Regular system backups and user awareness
D. Ignoring patch management

Q688. What is the main goal of implementing role-based access control (RBAC)?
A. To assign permissions according to job responsibilities
B. To grant everyone full administrative access
C. To allow anonymous access to all resources
D. To simplify audit log deletion

Q689. Which of the following provides real-time alerting on security events?
A. SIEM (Security Information and Event Management) systems
B. Static policy documentation
C. Annual audit reviews
D. Manual Excel-based tracking

Q690. What is the primary function of a data breach notification policy?
A. To manage employee work schedules
B. To establish internal data labeling conventions
C. To define how and when affected parties are informed of data breaches
D. To set password complexity standards

Q691. Which security measure ensures that backups remain protected from ransomware?
A. Storing backups offline and verifying immutability
B. Keeping backups on the same online server
C. Allowing backup overwrite by users
D. Sharing backup credentials widely

Q692. Which of the following best describes security incident escalation?
A. Reporting incidents to higher management based on severity and impact
B. Disabling escalation paths to save time
C. Ignoring minor alerts to reduce workload
D. Handling all incidents individually without communication

Q693. What is the primary goal of endpoint detection and response (EDR) solutions?
A. Replace antivirus and firewalls entirely
B. Detect and respond to threats on individual devices in real time
C. Manage hardware inventory only
D. Disable incident reporting

Q694. Which control most effectively prevents privilege misuse by administrators?
A. Monitoring privileged activity and enforcing session recording
B. Allowing shared root accounts
C. Disabling audit logging for admins
D. Providing unrestricted access to all users

Q695. Which control is most appropriate for ensuring secure remote management of network devices?

A. Using encrypted protocols such as SSH instead of Telnet
B. Allowing unencrypted administrative access
C. Sharing root credentials among administrators
D. Using outdated remote management tools

Q696. Which of the following best ensures secure configuration of new servers?

A. Disabling operating system updates
B. Relying on default vendor settings
C. Applying hardened baseline images before deployment
D. Skipping security testing to save time

Q697. What is the main objective of implementing encryption key rotation?

A. To eliminate encryption altogether
B. To increase processing performance
C. To limit key exposure by changing them periodically
D. To reduce audit evidence requirements

Q698. Which activity best supports evidence integrity during an investigation?

A. Editing logs to remove sensitive data
B. Calculating and verifying file hash values before and after collection
C. Relying on unverified screenshots
D. Copying evidence using standard copy-and-paste functions

Q699. Which control helps detect unauthorized network connections?

A. Network intrusion detection systems (NIDS)
B. Data retention policies
C. Physical locks on server rooms
D. Employee onboarding training

Q700. What is the primary reason to use secure coding practices?

A. To improve hardware compatibility
B. To prevent vulnerabilities during development
C. To avoid documentation efforts
D. To enhance code readability only

Answer Key and Explanation (601-700)

Q601. Answer: B

Explanation: Secure configuration reviews verify systems are hardened, patched, and compliant with baseline security standards before production use. This prevents misconfigurations from becoming attack vectors. Option A responds after incidents occur. Option C and D address resilience and facilities, not system readiness.

Q602. Answer: B

Explanation: Regular audits validate control effectiveness, ensure compliance, and reveal deficiencies for corrective actions. They strengthen the overall security posture. Option A is unrealistic — risks can't be fully eliminated. Option C and D are indirect or unrelated benefits.

Q603. Answer: A

Explanation: Encryption and MDM enforce access controls, remote wipe, and policy compliance to protect data if devices are lost or stolen. They combine preventive and detective capabilities. Option B disables core security measures. Option C increases exposure to interception. Option D compromises credential security.

Q604. Answer: B

Explanation: IDS detects and alerts administrators of suspicious activity, enabling response actions. It identifies intrusions that preventive measures miss. Option A and D are preventive. Option C ensures confidentiality but not monitoring or detection.

Q605. Answer: A

Explanation: Penetration testing simulates real attacks to identify exploitable weaknesses before adversaries can exploit them. It provides assurance that controls are effective. Option B is incorrect — both are complementary. Option C and D are unrelated to security evaluation.

Q606. Answer: B

Explanation: Activating the incident response plan ensures coordinated containment, communication, and investigation steps. It limits damage and maintains process integrity. Option A destroys evidence. Option C may cause panic if uncontrolled. Option D neglects response entirely.

Q607. Answer: A

Explanation: IPS actively blocks malicious traffic based on signatures or behavior analysis, providing real-time prevention. It extends IDS capability into enforcement. Option B describes passive monitoring. Option C addresses confidentiality, and D focuses on oversight, not prevention.

Q608. Answer: C

Explanation: Awareness programs teach employees to recognize manipulation tactics, reducing susceptibility to social engineering. Training is the human element of defense. Option B secures data flow, not human behavior. Option A and D address technical aspects unrelated to deception.

Q609. Answer: A

Explanation: Maintaining integrity and proper documentation ensures evidence is admissible and credible in legal or investigative processes. It preserves accuracy throughout handling. Option B wastes resources and may violate privacy. Option C alters evidence, invalidating its use. Option D risks selective bias.

Q610. Answer: A

Explanation: Audit logs document user actions and data changes, ensuring traceability and accountability. They help detect fraud and unauthorized activity. Option B and C support availability, not accountability. Option D controls network flow but not data modification tracking.

Q611. Answer: B

Explanation: MFA strengthens authentication by requiring two or more independent verification factors—something known, possessed, or inherent. It greatly reduces credential-based attacks. Option A helps but doesn't verify identity. Option C is a long-term trend, not MFA's function. Option D deals with encryption, not identity proofing.

Q612. Answer: A

Explanation: Administrative controls include policies, procedures, and guidelines governing behavior and process compliance. They set expectations and ensure timely response. Option B protects physical assets. Option C implements technology-based safeguards. Option D restores functionality post-incident.

Q613. Answer: B

Explanation: Centralized inventory and approval enable IT to monitor and control application use, reducing hidden risks. It aligns with CIS Control 2 on software management. Option A hinders operations without precision. Option C and D invite unmanaged vulnerabilities.

Q614. Answer: A

Explanation: Offline, immutable backups prevent encryption by ransomware and allow reliable restoration. They ensure business continuity without compromise. Option B encourages attackers and doesn't guarantee recovery. Option C exposes backups to infection. Option D halts operations unnecessarily.

Q615. Answer: A

Explanation: Network monitoring and anomaly detection identify deviations in outbound data patterns, a key indicator of exfiltration. They support quick response to data theft attempts. Option B and D are unrelated to data flow. Option C aids transfer efficiency but not detection.

Q616. Answer: A

Explanation: Full-disk encryption ensures that data stored on mobile devices remains unreadable if the device is lost or stolen, maintaining confidentiality. It's a critical safeguard aligned with CIS Control 4. Option B weakens protection by removing access barriers. Option C increases risk through unverified apps. Option D exposes data to interception.

Q617. Answer: B

Explanation: Network segmentation confines attacks to specific areas, preventing adversaries from accessing critical systems laterally. It's a key part of defense in depth. Option A is a side effect but not the main benefit. Option C and D oversimplify network security at the expense of protection.

Q618. Answer: B

Explanation: ACLs define user permissions on systems, automatically enforcing access restrictions. They provide direct technical protection of data. Option A and C are administrative controls. Option D is procedural, not technical.

Q619. Answer: A

Explanation: Encryption ensures intercepted data remains unreadable, mitigating risks from eavesdropping during transmission. It's critical for securing communication channels. Option B targets availability, not confidentiality. Option C and D involve authentication and policy controls.

Q620. Answer: A

Explanation: Regular log reviews help detect suspicious behavior and policy violations promptly, enabling timely incident response. They are vital for compliance and audit purposes. Option B and C are maintenance tasks, not security objectives. Option D limits review effectiveness.

Q621. Answer: A

Explanation: Application whitelisting ensures only approved software can execute on systems, blocking unapproved installations. It aligns with CIS Control 2 and 4. Option B strengthens authentication, not application control. Option C weakens awareness. Option D filters network traffic but doesn't control installations.

Q622. Answer: C

Explanation: Data at rest resides on storage devices like hard drives or databases and requires encryption and access controls to remain protected. It's the most common data state. Option A refers to data in transit. Option B and D describe data in use.

Q623. Answer: B

Explanation: Hashing creates a unique digital fingerprint that changes if data is altered, verifying integrity. It's used in digital signatures and message verification. Option A involves reversible encryption, not hashing. Option C and D are unrelated to integrity assurance.

Q624. Answer: B

Explanation: Access provisioning ensures employees receive only the permissions necessary for their role, supporting least privilege and compliance. It minimizes unauthorized access risk. Option A contradicts this principle. Option C and D address password management and configuration, not provisioning.

Q625. Answer: B

Explanation: VPNs with strong authentication secure data in transit and verify user identity before granting access. They are essential for remote access protection. Option A exposes data to interception. Option C and D create major vulnerabilities.

Q626. Answer: A

Explanation: Containment prevents malware from spreading across systems, preserving forensic data for analysis. It's the top priority per NIST SP 800-61. Option B occurs later based on severity. Option C is preventive, not reactive. Option D risks losing critical evidence.

Q627. Answer: B

Explanation: A compensating control provides equivalent risk reduction when the preferred control cannot be implemented, such as monitoring replacing unavailable encryption. It maintains compliance and effectiveness. Option A adds redundancy. Option C and D provide no equivalent protection.

Q628. Answer: B

Explanation: Data classification identifies sensitivity levels, ensuring appropriate protection measures are applied according to risk. It improves control prioritization. Option A and C are administrative benefits, not primary goals. Option D adds storage overhead.

Q629. Answer: A

Explanation: Unique admin IDs ensure traceability of all administrative actions, enabling monitoring and accountability. They're key in audit and compliance programs. Option B removes accountability. Option C hinders forensic investigations. Option D violates least privilege.

Q630. Answer: A

Explanation: Recovery restores affected systems and services after eradication, ensuring safe resumption of operations. It validates that no remnants of the incident remain. Option B and D belong to detection. Option C is a preventive activity post-recovery.

Q631. Answer: B

Explanation: Endpoint protection detects, isolates, and prevents malware on individual devices, securing the last line of defense. It complements network-level controls. Option A is unrelated to security. Option C focuses on transmission security. Option D is a misalignment of layers.

Q632. Answer: A

Explanation: Configuration management ensures changes are authorized, tested, and documented, maintaining system integrity. It reduces configuration drift and risk. Option B violates policy control. Option C removes accountability. Option D increases exposure without relevance.

Q633. Answer: C

Explanation: Data in use refers to active data currently processed in memory by applications or systems. It requires runtime protections like memory encryption. Option A is data at rest. Option B is data in transit. Option D is archived data.

Q634. Answer: B
Explanation: The post-mortem review evaluates incident handling to enhance processes and reduce recurrence. It focuses on improvement, not punishment. Option A harms team collaboration. Option C and D address different response aspects but not learning.
Q635. Answer: A
Explanation: Secure shredding ensures printed confidential documents are destroyed beyond reconstruction, protecting against physical data leaks. It's an essential administrative and physical safeguard. Option B and D expose materials to unauthorized viewing. Option C increases mismanagement risk.
Q636. Answer: B
Explanation: Physical destruction or degaussing guarantees that sensitive data cannot be recovered from decommissioned storage devices. It's the most reliable method to maintain confidentiality after media use. Option A leaves remnants recoverable with forensic tools. Option C introduces data leakage risk. Option D provides incomplete sanitization.
Q637. Answer: A
Explanation: Security baselines establish the minimum required configurations for systems, ensuring consistency and compliance across environments. They serve as reference points for audits and hardening. Option B is a separate maintenance process. Option C is unrelated to security settings. Option D is unrealistic as no baseline can remove all risks.
Q638. Answer: B
Explanation: Digital signatures validate the sender's identity and confirm that the message wasn't altered, providing non-repudiation through asymmetric encryption. They ensure accountability in communications. Option A provides confidentiality but lacks sender verification. Option C offers weak authentication only. Option D is irrelevant to data authenticity.
Q639. Answer: B
Explanation: Promptly revoking credentials prevents former employees from accessing systems or data post-termination. It's a critical step in user lifecycle management. Option A gathers feedback but doesn't restrict access. Option C delays response, exposing systems. Option D violates security policy and accountability.
Q640. Answer: A
Explanation: A data retention policy specifies how long data is retained to meet regulatory, legal, and business needs before secure disposal. It ensures both compliance and storage efficiency. Option B is part of data protection, not retention. Option C handles physical security. Option D is unrelated.
Q641. Answer: A
Explanation: Full-disk encryption combined with remote wipe ensures data remains secure even if the device is lost. It prevents unauthorized access and data breaches. Option B exposes credentials. Option C prevents patching, increasing vulnerability. Option D removes access control.
Q642. Answer: B
Explanation: PKI provides a framework for secure key generation, distribution, and management, supporting digital signatures and authentication. It establishes trust between communicating parties. Option A violates key security principles. Option C is false—PKI strengthens authentication. Option D misrepresents PKI's computational requirements.
Q643. Answer: B
Explanation: Security policies must clearly define roles, responsibilities, and enforcement expectations to establish accountability and governance. They provide the foundation for implementing controls. Option A adds unnecessary specificity. Option C should never be documented in policies. Option D belongs in standard operating procedures, not high-level policy.
Q644. Answer: A

Explanation: Change management ensures configuration changes are documented, reviewed, and approved before implementation, reducing the risk of unauthorized modifications. It maintains system integrity. Option B supports human behavior, not technical enforcement. Option C strengthens accounts but not configuration control. Option D monitors threats but doesn't validate internal changes.

Q645. Answer: B

Explanation: Off-site, climate-controlled facilities safeguard backups from fire, humidity, and temperature fluctuations, ensuring data availability. This aligns with CIS Control 11. Option A increases risk from shared exposure. Option C and D neglect both physical and environmental protection.

Q646. Answer: B

Explanation: Corrective controls restore systems to a normal state after a security event, such as malware removal through antivirus quarantine. They focus on remediation. Option A and C are preventive. Option D is administrative and preventive, not corrective.

Q647. Answer: A

Explanation: DLP tools inspect outgoing emails and block or encrypt those containing sensitive data, preventing data leakage. They enforce compliance and confidentiality. Option B removes critical protection. Option C and D increase exfiltration risk.

Q648. Answer: C

Explanation: Time synchronization ensures consistent log timestamps across systems, improving correlation and forensic accuracy. It's vital for traceable audit trails. Option B disrupts accuracy. Option A removes accountability. Option D increases human error.

Q649. Answer: A

Explanation: Recovery restores affected systems and services following eradication to resume normal operations safely. It confirms systems are clean and functional. Option B wastes resources. Option C destroys valuable audit evidence. Option D halts productivity unnecessarily.

Q650. Answer: A

Explanation: Access recertification reviews and confirms that users maintain only necessary access, ensuring compliance and preventing privilege creep. It's part of governance and lifecycle management. Option B violates least privilege. Option C and D are unrelated to access control.

Q651. Answer: B

Explanation: Account lockout policies disable accounts after repeated failed login attempts, deterring brute-force attacks. They enforce authentication resilience. Option A secures data, not logins. Option C controls traffic, not credentials. Option D handles access assignment, not login protection.

Q652. Answer: A

Explanation: Awareness training empowers users to recognize threats like phishing, promoting secure practices and compliance. It's a fundamental preventive control. Option B misstates its role—it complements controls. Option C and D are unrelated or counterproductive.

Q653. Answer: C

Explanation: WPA3 uses advanced encryption and authentication mechanisms, securing wireless communications from unauthorized users. It ensures data confidentiality and access integrity. Option A and D weaken network defenses. Option B increases visibility without security benefits.

Q654. Answer: A

Explanation: Vulnerability assessments discover and prioritize system weaknesses, allowing remediation before attackers can exploit them. They improve security posture through proactive action. Option B is unrealistic—risk remains residual. Option C and D focus on detection and compliance, not discovery.

Q655. Answer: A

Explanation: A key management policy defines rotation schedules, storage standards, and access controls to ensure cryptographic key security. It aligns with NIST recommendations. Option B and D expose keys to compromise. Option C violates segregation and confidentiality principles.

Q656. Answer: C
Explanation: An access control policy defines authorization principles ensuring users only access resources required for their job, aligning with least privilege and accountability. It safeguards data integrity and confidentiality. Option B expands risk exposure. Option A removes accountability. Option D misunderstands security's purpose relative to performance.
Q657. Answer: A
Explanation: An IPS monitors traffic and actively blocks malicious packets in real time, preventing exploitation attempts. It's a preventive and dynamic control. Option B detects and correlates but doesn't block. Option C and D are periodic and reactive.
Q658. Answer: A
Explanation: MDM enforces policies like encryption, passcodes, and remote wipe to ensure personal devices comply with enterprise security. It protects organizational data in mixed-use environments. Option B increases attack surfaces. Option C weakens authentication. Option D eliminates oversight.
Q659. Answer: B
Explanation: Audit logs record user and system events, supporting accountability, forensics, and compliance verification. They are vital for post-incident analysis. Option A is maintenance, not purpose. Option C and D misrepresent audit capabilities.
Q660. Answer: C
Explanation: MFA enhances confidentiality by ensuring that only verified users can access sensitive systems, even if one authentication factor is compromised. It strengthens access assurance. Option A is a broader framework. Option B pertains to permissions. Option D governs task distribution, not authentication.
Q661. Answer: A
Explanation: Proper access provisioning limits exposure before incidents occur, embodying a preventive approach. It stops unauthorized access from happening initially. Option B is detective. Option C and D are corrective or investigative.
Q662. Answer: C
Explanation: Security clauses and due diligence verify vendor compliance and establish legal accountability for data protection. They enforce external governance and oversight. Option B creates blind trust. Option A and D increase risk exposure.
Q663. Answer: A
Explanation: Data masking substitutes sensitive information with fictional or scrambled values, allowing safe use in testing and analytics. It preserves data confidentiality outside production. Option B encrypts data but doesn't provide readable test sets. Option C and D are unrelated processes.
Q664. Answer: A
Explanation: RBAC with least privilege restricts users from gaining unauthorized higher-level access, reducing escalation opportunities. It enforces structured control hierarchies. Option B and C directly violate this principle. Option D neglects proactive oversight.
Q665. Answer: C
Explanation: Logical controls regulate digital access through authentication mechanisms like passwords and biometrics. They protect systems at the software level. Option A and D are physical. Option B is procedural and physical, not logical.
Q666. Answer: A
Explanation: Continuous monitoring identifies suspicious behavior as it happens, improving detection and response speed. It supports proactive defense. Option B is unrealistic. Option C and D ignore compliance and response requirements.
Q667. Answer: B

Explanation: Defense in depth combines multiple layers of controls—technical, administrative, and physical—to provide redundancy in protection. This mitigates failure in any one layer. Option A offers perimeter-only security. Option C and D ignore layered strategy principles.

Q668. Answer: A

Explanation: Defining assets and threats provides context for risk prioritization, ensuring the plan addresses what matters most. It sets the foundation for effective preparation. Option B occurs after incidents. Option C and D happen during or after response phases.

Q669. Answer: A

Explanation: Monitoring and alerting tools analyze logs and system behavior to identify deviations from policy in real time. They provide critical feedback for incident detection. Option B and C prevent unauthorized access, not detect misuse. Option D is preventive maintenance.

Q670. Answer: D

Explanation: Business continuity ensures that essential services and functions continue through disruptions, preserving organizational resilience. It integrates with disaster recovery planning. Option B is impossible. Option C and A narrow the scope improperly.

Q671. Answer: A

Explanation: Database audit logs record who made changes, when, and what was altered, ensuring full accountability and traceability. This supports forensic readiness. Option B erases accountability. Option C removes oversight. Option D provides no change tracking.

Q672. Answer: C

Explanation: Automation reduces reliance on manual input, while training reinforces correct handling behavior, minimizing errors. Together they improve reliability. Option B and A increase risks. Option D weakens detection capacity.

Q673. Answer: A

Explanation: Clear communication and escalation paths ensure timely notification, coordination, and accurate information flow during incidents. They prevent chaos and miscommunication. Option B delays response. Option C reduces efficiency. Option D bypasses structured communication channels.

Q674. Answer: A

Explanation: Behavioral monitoring tools detect anomalies in encrypted traffic patterns, identifying potential data exfiltration despite encryption. It leverages advanced analytics. Option B provides static filtering only. Option C and D are unrelated.

Q675. Answer: C

Explanation: Tabletop exercises simulate incident scenarios to evaluate communication, coordination, and procedural readiness without impacting operations. They enhance team preparedness. Option B is operational, not simulated. Option A and D miss the objective of readiness testing.

Q676. Answer: A

Explanation: Encrypting data before upload ensures confidentiality even if the cloud environment is compromised. Client-side encryption gives the organization direct control over keys and access. Option B places blind trust in the provider. Option C and D both expose unprotected data to potential breaches.

Q677. Answer: A

Explanation: Disabling or restricting USB ports through system policies prevents data theft and malware introduction via removable media. It enforces hardware-level access control. Option B undermines protection. Option C is unreliable and non-technical. Option D detects malware but doesn't block data transfer.

Q678. Answer: D

Explanation: Periodic access reviews ensure users retain only required privileges, reducing risk from privilege creep and insider misuse. It reinforces least privilege principles. Option B and A are operational goals. Option C compromises security entirely.

Q679. Answer: A
Explanation: Phishing simulations and awareness programs train users to identify and report malicious emails, significantly reducing compromise rates. It reinforces vigilance through education. Option B impedes communication. Option C doesn't address human deception. Option D encourages inaction.
Q680. Answer: A
Explanation: TLS encryption secures data in transit, preventing eavesdropping and tampering by unauthorized entities. It's a foundational network security control. Option B and D compromise security. Option C removes a secure channel altogether.
Q681. Answer: C
Explanation: A structured patch management process ensures updates are prioritized, tested, and applied consistently to reduce vulnerabilities. It aligns with CIS Control 7. Option B causes inconsistency. Option A leaves exploitable gaps. Option D introduces stability risks.
Q682. Answer: A
Explanation: Tokenization substitutes real data with non-sensitive placeholders, maintaining referential integrity while protecting the original values. It's widely used in payment systems. Option B describes encryption, not tokenization. Option C removes data entirely. Option D simply changes format.
Q683. Answer: A
Explanation: IAM systems control and verify access permissions across users and systems, enforcing least privilege and accountability. They centralize authentication and authorization. Option B and C deal with other security domains. Option D is unrelated to access governance.
Q684. Answer: B
Explanation: Containment stops the spread of damage, preserves evidence, and stabilizes the environment for investigation. It's the first operational step in NIST's incident response lifecycle. Option A occurs afterward. Option C and D follow eradication and documentation phases.
Q685. Answer: A
Explanation: Application whitelisting allows only pre-approved programs to run, reducing the risk of malware and unauthorized tools. It's key under CIS Control 2. Option B, C, and D directly weaken organizational control and compliance.
Q686. Answer: A
Explanation: Log retention ensures that records remain available for forensic analysis, audit trails, and legal compliance. It maintains traceability over time. Option B undermines compliance. Option C limits detection ability. Option D violates legal integrity principles.
Q687. Answer: C
Explanation: Backups and awareness training ensure resilience—data can be restored without paying ransom, and users recognize suspicious content. It combines prevention and recovery. Option A, B, and D all heighten exposure.
Q688. Answer: A
Explanation: RBAC assigns permissions based on organizational roles, ensuring users only perform actions relevant to their function. It enforces least privilege and simplifies administration. Option B, C, and D contradict governance and security principles.
Q689. Answer: A
Explanation: SIEM systems collect, correlate, and analyze logs to generate real-time alerts on threats, improving visibility and response speed. They centralize monitoring across platforms. Option B, C, and D lack automation and timeliness.
Q690. Answer: C
Explanation: A data breach notification policy ensures legal and timely communication to stakeholders, regulators, and customers after a breach. It maintains transparency and compliance. Option B relates to classification. Option A and D are irrelevant.

Q691. Answer: A
Explanation: Offline, immutable backups are isolated from the production network, preventing ransomware from encrypting or deleting them. They provide reliable recovery. Option B exposes backups. Option C and D undermine protection and accountability.
Q692. Answer: A
Explanation: Escalation ensures that incidents are communicated promptly to the appropriate authority level for decision-making. It enhances coordination and response efficiency. Option B, C, and D fragment response capabilities.
Q693. Answer: B
Explanation: EDR monitors endpoints for malicious behavior, enabling automated response and containment. It enhances visibility beyond traditional antivirus. Option A is incorrect—EDR complements other layers. Option C and D misrepresent its function.
Q694. Answer: A
Explanation: Privileged session monitoring records admin activities, deterring misuse and enabling forensic accountability. It's vital in sensitive environments. Option B and C remove traceability. Option D violates access governance.
Q695. Answer: A
Explanation: SSH encrypts administrative sessions, protecting credentials and commands from interception. It's the industry standard for secure remote management. Option B and D expose plaintext data. Option C eliminates accountability.
Q696. Answer: C
Explanation: Hardened baseline images contain preconfigured security settings, removing unnecessary services and applying patches before deployment, which reduces the system's attack surface. This control ensures uniform compliance and protection across environments. Option B is risky because vendor defaults often leave unnecessary ports or services open. Option A and D weaken integrity by disabling key updates and bypassing validation processes that are critical for secure implementation.
Q697. Answer: C
Explanation: Regular key rotation limits how long an encryption key is valid, minimizing the impact if one becomes compromised. It's a key element of cryptographic hygiene and aligns with NIST SP 800-57 recommendations. Option B and D are irrelevant to encryption lifecycle management. Option A undermines data confidentiality entirely, contradicting all best practices.
Q698. Answer: B
Explanation: Hash verification ensures that evidence remains identical from collection to analysis, preserving integrity for legal and audit purposes. Hashes like SHA-256 provide a tamper-evident record, making them indispensable in forensics. Option D and C lack validation, while Option A destroys original evidence and invalidates the chain of custody.
Q699. Answer: A
Explanation: NIDS continuously monitor network traffic for abnormal patterns, identifying unauthorized or suspicious connections. This detective control helps alert administrators early in an attack lifecycle. Option B and C serve compliance and physical security, not live detection. Option D improves awareness but doesn't provide monitoring capability.
Q700. Answer: B
Explanation: Secure coding prevents software vulnerabilities such as SQL injection, buffer overflow, or cross-site scripting from entering the codebase. It embeds security into development rather than relying solely on post-deployment testing. Option D focuses on aesthetics, not risk mitigation. Option A and C disregard secure design and accountability principles.

Question (701-750)

Q701. Which security measure helps ensure authenticity of downloaded software?
A. Installing software from unknown websites
B. Ignoring source verification
C. Disabling antivirus scans
D. Verifying digital signatures or checksums
Q702. What is the main advantage of network access control (NAC) systems?
A. They ensure only authorized and compliant devices can connect to the network
B. They disable encryption requirements
C. They allow unrestricted guest access
D. They replace firewalls entirely
Q703. Which of the following best prevents unauthorized data transfer via cloud storage services?
A. Implementing cloud access security broker (CASB) solutions
B. Disabling all internet access organization-wide
C. Allowing any cloud service for convenience
D. Ignoring data upload activity
Q704. What is the primary role of an information security awareness program?
A. To configure technical controls directly
B. To educate employees on secure behaviors and organizational policies
C. To reduce the need for management oversight
D. To replace access control systems
Q705. Which control best reduces exposure from insider threats?
A. Implementing monitoring of privileged user activity and behavior analytics
B. Disabling all logging to protect privacy
C. Removing all administrative accounts
D. Allowing unrestricted access to databases
Q706. Which of the following best supports confidentiality during data transmission?
A. Using open Wi-Fi without encryption
B. Encrypting data using strong cryptographic protocols
C. Sending sensitive files via plain text email
D. Disabling SSL/TLS verification
Q707. What is the most effective method for ensuring secure access to web applications?
A. Disabling session management controls
B. Allowing unrestricted HTTP access
C. Implementing web application firewalls (WAF)
D. Ignoring input validation
Q708. Which process best helps ensure that encryption algorithms remain effective over time?
A. Removing encryption to reduce processing time
B. Using the same algorithm indefinitely
C. Periodic review and upgrade of cryptographic algorithms
D. Ignoring industry standards
Q709. Which of the following best minimizes data exposure through printer misuse?
A. Leaving output trays unattended
B. Disabling print logs
C. Requiring user authentication before printing sensitive documents
D. Allowing unmonitored public printing
Q710. What is the main benefit of data loss prevention (DLP) tools?

A. They detect and prevent unauthorized transmission of sensitive data
B. They eliminate the need for user training
C. They increase system processing power
D. They replace encryption entirely

Q711. Which of the following controls helps ensure accountability during incident response?
A. Performing response actions anonymously
B. Allowing anyone to act without coordination
C. Clearly defined roles and documented responsibilities
D. Ignoring incident documentation

Q712. What is the most effective method for protecting sensitive data on portable USB drives?
A. Encrypting the drives and requiring password access
B. Using drives with no access controls
C. Sharing drives among multiple users
D. Disabling encryption for convenience

Q713. Which activity is most appropriate after an incident has been fully contained and eradicated?
A. Ignoring documentation to save time
B. Conducting a post-incident review to identify improvements
C. Restarting operations without evaluation
D. Immediately deleting all related evidence

Q714. Which control best mitigates risks of data exposure in public cloud services?
A. Using open credentials for convenience
B. Allowing unrestricted data sharing
C. Enforcing encryption and access controls for cloud data
D. Disabling activity logging

Q715. Which security testing activity identifies weaknesses in system configuration and patch levels?
A. Backup validation
B. Code review
C. Vulnerability scanning
D. Penetration testing only

Q716. Which control best ensures accountability for privileged administrative activities?
A. Disabling all administrator accounts
B. Monitoring and recording privileged sessions
C. Using shared administrator passwords
D. Allowing full access without oversight

Q717. What is the primary advantage of using multifactor authentication (MFA)?
A. It verifies identity through multiple independent factors
B. It eliminates the need for encryption
C. It reduces authentication time for all users
D. It replaces all forms of password management

Q718. Which of the following controls best mitigates data leakage risks via email?
A. Implementing DLP rules that scan outgoing email content
B. Allowing unencrypted attachments
C. Disabling email audit trails
D. Encouraging users to forward sensitive data externally

Q719. Which is the most appropriate way to protect against unauthorized wireless access?
A. Implementing WPA3 with strong authentication
B. Disabling encryption to improve speed
C. Using default router passwords

D. Broadcasting SSIDs publicly without restriction

Q720. Which control most effectively safeguards stored backup media?

A. Skipping encryption to reduce costs
B. Keeping all backups near production servers
C. Allowing user access to backup drives
D. Storing backups off-site in a climate-controlled and restricted facility

Q721. What is the main purpose of an incident response playbook?

A. To provide structured guidance for handling specific types of incidents
B. To replace forensic investigation procedures
C. To train only new employees
D. To eliminate the need for containment

Q722. Which of the following controls is designed to detect unauthorized configuration changes?

A. Configuration monitoring and change detection tools
B. Static documentation without review
C. Shared admin credentials
D. Removing version control systems

Q723. Which of the following best describes data in use?

A. Data stored in an archive
B. Data transmitted over a VPN
C. Data being processed in system memory by active applications
D. Data awaiting deletion in backup media

Q724. Which activity is part of security incident recovery?

A. Restoring affected systems after threat eradication
B. Performing threat containment
C. Identifying attack signatures
D. Initiating awareness training

Q725. What is the primary purpose of data classification?

A. To assign appropriate security controls based on data sensitivity
B. To simplify file naming conventions
C. To reduce data storage requirements
D. To improve data compression efficiency

Q726. Which of the following controls best supports forensic readiness?

A. Automatic deletion of old event logs
B. Comprehensive and centralized log management
C. Disabling security monitoring to save storage
D. Allowing manual evidence collection only

Q727. Which of the following represents a corrective control?

A. Antivirus software that removes detected malware
B. Firewalls filtering inbound traffic
C. Access approval workflows
D. Password complexity enforcement

Q728. Which of the following best mitigates the risk of unauthorized data sharing through collaboration tools?

A. Restricting sharing permissions and applying data access controls
B. Allowing unrestricted external sharing
C. Ignoring version control and audit logs
D. Using unverified third-party file services

Q729. Which process ensures that vulnerabilities are consistently identified and remediated?

A. Network capacity planning
B. Annual disaster recovery drills
C. Continuous vulnerability management
D. User awareness assessments

Q730. Which of the following best maintains the confidentiality of stored passwords?
A. Storing passwords using salted hash algorithms
B. Keeping passwords in plaintext for easy retrieval
C. Sharing passwords among users
D. Writing passwords on physical sticky notes

Q731. What is the primary goal of conducting post-incident analysis?
A. To punish responsible staff
B. To identify root causes and improve response processes
C. To avoid documentation requirements
D. To skip reporting for minor incidents

Q732. Which of the following helps ensure encryption keys are securely managed?
A. Using hardware security modules (HSMs) for key storage
B. Hardcoding keys into application source code
C. Sharing keys between multiple systems
D. Storing keys in plaintext files

Q733. Which of the following is the most critical step when evidence is first collected?
A. Documenting the chain of custody and securing evidence
B. Immediately modifying the data for readability
C. Storing evidence on public cloud drives
D. Sharing evidence with all employees

Q734. What is the best control for ensuring that only authorized devices connect to a corporate network?
A. Allowing connections based on MAC addresses alone
B. Using public guest Wi-Fi for all employees
C. Disabling device authentication
D. Implementing network access control (NAC) with authentication checks

Q735. Which activity is essential to maintain business operations during a security incident?
A. Activating business continuity and disaster recovery plans
B. Waiting until the threat is fully analyzed
C. Suspending all operations indefinitely
D. Deleting backups to prevent misuse

Q736. Which of the following is the most effective method for verifying the identity of remote users?
A. Multi-factor authentication combining passwords and tokens
B. Simple username and password only
C. Shared login credentials for teams
D. Anonymous remote access with IP filtering

Q737. Which control best ensures that data remains intact during transfer between systems?
A. Disabling integrity checks for speed
B. Relying on email delivery confirmation
C. Using checksums or cryptographic hash verification
D. Sending data without encryption or validation

Q738. Which of the following provides proactive detection of anomalies in network traffic?
A. Security Information and Event Management (SIEM) with behavioral analytics
B. Quarterly vulnerability scanning

C. Manual spreadsheet reviews
D. Static password audits

Q739. Which of the following best protects against social engineering attacks?
A. Implementing complex firewalls only
B. Regular employee awareness and simulated phishing campaigns
C. Ignoring suspicious email activity
D. Reducing training to save resources

Q740. What is the main purpose of incident classification during response?
A. To prioritize response efforts based on impact and severity
B. To delay response until full investigation
C. To assign incidents randomly
D. To close cases automatically

Q741. Which measure best protects cloud-based data against unauthorized administrative access?
A. Enabling role-based access control (RBAC) with least privilege
B. Using shared cloud admin credentials
C. Disabling audit logs
D. Allowing unrestricted API access

Q742. Which of the following is the primary goal of security incident documentation?
A. To delete all evidence post-resolution
B. To assign blame to individuals
C. To provide a record for analysis, lessons learned, and compliance evidence
D. To reduce the number of responders

Q743. What is the most effective way to protect an organization from spear-phishing attacks?
A. Conduct targeted awareness training and implement email filtering
B. Disable user awareness initiatives
C. Ignore suspicious sender domains
D. Allow users to disable spam filters

Q744. Which of the following best describes a compensating control in information security?
A. An alternative measure that provides equivalent protection to a required control
B. A duplicate control that increases redundancy unnecessarily
C. A control that is implemented after a breach occurs
D. A measure that violates compliance standards

Q745. Which measure best ensures confidentiality when transmitting sensitive email messages?
A. Sending via unencrypted SMTP
B. Using end-to-end encryption and secure email gateways
C. Allowing auto-forwarding to external accounts
D. Copying recipients publicly using CC fields

Q746. Which control best limits unauthorized privilege escalation?
A. Implementing strict separation of duties and access reviews
B. Granting blanket admin access
C. Allowing users to modify their roles
D. Ignoring privilege audit findings

Q747. Which is the primary objective of patch management?
A. To correct software vulnerabilities and maintain system security
B. To reduce server uptime for maintenance
C. To eliminate the need for antivirus software
D. To delay updates for testing indefinitely

Q748. Which of the following is the best indicator of an ongoing insider threat?

A. Decreased system alerts over time
B. Consistent adherence to security policy
C. Unusual access patterns to high-value data
D. Absence of log activity

Q749. What is the main benefit of encryption key escrow?

A. Ensures key recovery in case of loss or unavailability
B. Allows unauthorized access to encrypted data
C. Eliminates the need for encryption management
D. Replaces authentication systems entirely

Q750. Which of the following controls is most appropriate for preventing brute-force login attacks?

A. Implementing account lockout and CAPTCHA mechanisms
B. Allowing unlimited login attempts
C. Disabling password complexity rules
D. Logging in using default credentials

Answer Key and Explanation (701-750)

Q701. Answer: D

Explanation: Digital signatures confirm the publisher's identity and integrity of the downloaded file, ensuring it hasn't been tampered with. Checksums further validate that the binary matches the original release. Option A and B expose systems to malware from untrusted sources. Option C disables essential protection that could detect altered files.

Q702. Answer: A

Explanation: NAC verifies device security posture—patch levels, antivirus, configuration—before granting network access, enforcing policy compliance. This minimizes infection spread and unauthorized device usage. Option D overstates NAC's function; it complements, not replaces, firewalls. Option B and C directly contradict NAC's intent by reducing control and verification.

Q703. Answer: A

Explanation: CASBs monitor and control data moving between on-premise users and cloud services, enforcing encryption, access policies, and anomaly detection. They're essential for shadow IT and data leak prevention. Option B harms productivity. Option C and D eliminate visibility, allowing uncontrolled data exfiltration.

Q704. Answer: B

Explanation: Security awareness programs cultivate a culture of responsibility, teaching staff how to recognize threats like phishing, social engineering, and data misuse. They strengthen human defenses where technology cannot. Option A and D misplace technical responsibility. Option C falsely assumes awareness can replace governance.

Q705. Answer: A

Explanation: Monitoring privileged actions and analyzing user behavior detects misuse patterns early, balancing trust with verification. These systems deter malicious insiders and enforce accountability. Option B and D remove oversight and directly invite abuse. Option C is infeasible in any operational environment.

Q706. Answer: B

Explanation: Strong encryption (e.g., TLS 1.3 or VPN tunneling) ensures transmitted data cannot be read by eavesdroppers, maintaining confidentiality and integrity. It is foundational for securing communications. Option C and D expose credentials and content, while Option A leaves transmissions fully vulnerable to interception.

Q707. Answer: C

Explanation: A WAF inspects HTTP traffic, blocking malicious payloads such as cross-site scripting and SQL injections, providing a protective barrier between users and applications. It adds an active defense layer. Option A, B, and D each dismantle core protections, creating exploitable gaps.

Q708. Answer: C

Explanation: Regular algorithm reviews account for emerging vulnerabilities and advances in computing, ensuring encryption remains strong. This keeps systems compliant with standards like NIST SP 800-57. Option B and D lead to obsolescence. Option A removes security entirely in favor of convenience.

Q709. Answer: C

Explanation: Secure printing requires users to authenticate before releasing jobs, ensuring only authorized personnel access confidential documents. This reduces physical data leaks. Option A, B, and D all introduce vulnerabilities by removing accountability and access control.

Q710. Answer: A

Explanation: DLP solutions monitor data in motion, at rest, and in use, blocking or encrypting sensitive content that violates policy. They ensure regulatory compliance and protect intellectual property. Option D and B misrepresent scope, while Option C is unrelated to security function.

Q711. Answer: C

Explanation: Assigning and documenting specific response roles ensures traceability and effective coordination under pressure. It prevents duplication and confusion during incidents. Option A, B, and D reduce accountability and hinder proper escalation.

Q712. Answer: A

Explanation: Full-drive encryption ensures data remains unreadable if a USB device is lost or stolen, and password protection prevents unauthorized use. This control meets data protection and privacy standards. Options B through D completely undermine data confidentiality.

Q713. Answer: B

Explanation: Post-incident reviews identify lessons learned, allowing organizations to enhance controls, training, and procedures. They transform incidents into learning opportunities. Option A and C miss critical analysis steps, while Option D destroys essential evidence for accountability.

Q714. Answer: C

Explanation: Combining encryption with robust access control ensures cloud data confidentiality and restricts exposure to authorized users only. It also supports compliance with data protection laws. Options A, B, and D introduce visibility and access gaps.

Q715. Answer: C

Explanation: Vulnerability scans systematically detect unpatched systems, misconfigurations, and common exposures, allowing proactive remediation. They complement penetration tests by providing continuous insight. Option B and D serve narrower purposes, while Option A verifies recovery, not security.

Q716. Answer: B

Explanation: Monitoring and recording privileged sessions create a verifiable trail of administrative actions, enabling forensic review and deterring misuse. This practice reinforces accountability and aligns with least-privilege principles. Option A halts necessary functions, while Option C removes traceability. Option D violates both compliance and audit requirements.

Q717. Answer: A

Explanation: MFA combines factors such as knowledge (password), possession (token), and inherence (biometric) to provide layered identity assurance. Even if one factor is compromised, unauthorized access is still prevented. Option B and D are inaccurate—MFA complements, not replaces, these controls. Option C is false; MFA can increase, not decrease, authentication time.

Q718. Answer: A

Explanation: DLP systems analyze outgoing messages for policy violations and block or encrypt sensitive data, minimizing accidental or malicious leakage. This control is essential for compliance with privacy laws. Option B and D actively create exposure risk. Option C removes oversight and hinders detection of violations.

Q719. Answer: A

Explanation: WPA3 provides robust encryption and authentication, protecting Wi-Fi networks from eavesdropping and brute-force attacks. It is a modern standard for wireless confidentiality. Option B and C are severe vulnerabilities. Option D adds visibility without protection, inviting intrusion attempts.

Q720. Answer: D

Explanation: Off-site, controlled storage prevents environmental damage and unauthorized access, ensuring backup data remains secure and available during disasters. It aligns with business continuity best practices. Option B creates correlated risk. Option C introduces data breaches, while Option A compromises confidentiality.

Q721. Answer: A

Explanation: An incident response playbook outlines predefined steps for responding to different incident categories, ensuring consistency, speed, and coordination. It supports readiness and aligns with

NIST 800-61. Option B focuses on evidence analysis, not response flow. Option C and D reduce preparedness and reactive control.

Q722. Answer: A

Explanation: Change detection systems continuously monitor for configuration alterations, alerting administrators to unapproved or suspicious modifications. They maintain system integrity and accountability. Option B and D eliminate active oversight, while Option C destroys user-level traceability.

Q723. Answer: C

Explanation: Data in use refers to information currently being processed or manipulated by active systems, often residing in volatile memory. It requires runtime protections such as memory encryption. Option B represents data in transit. Option A and D describe inactive or archived data.

Q724. Answer: A

Explanation: Recovery focuses on safely restoring operations post-eradication, ensuring that systems are verified clean and stable. It's the final technical phase of NIST's incident response lifecycle. Option B and C occur earlier in the response process. Option D is preventive, not reactive.

Q725. Answer: A

Explanation: Data classification identifies the sensitivity level of information and aligns it with proper controls like encryption, access restriction, or audit requirements. This ensures proportional protection. Options B–D deal with organization and performance but not confidentiality.

Q726. Answer: B

Explanation: Centralized logging aggregates and protects system events for analysis, ensuring evidence is available when needed. This supports quick investigation and chain-of-custody maintenance. Option A and C erase critical data. Option D limits reliability and scalability.

Q727. Answer: A

Explanation: Corrective controls act after an event to restore systems to normal operations—malware removal is a classic example. It complements preventive defenses. Option B and D prevent issues, and Option C governs access rather than correction.

Q728. Answer: A

Explanation: Restricting sharing rights and applying access controls ensures sensitive data isn't exposed through cloud collaboration platforms. It enforces least privilege and accountability. Option B–D all bypass governance and create uncontrolled exposure.

Q729. Answer: C

Explanation: Continuous vulnerability management automates scanning, prioritization, and remediation, reducing window-of-exposure across systems. It aligns with CIS Control 7. Option B and C deal with continuity and performance, while Option D addresses human behavior.

Q730. Answer: A

Explanation: Salted hashing makes password databases resilient against rainbow table and brute-force attacks. It's an essential safeguard for authentication data. Option B, C, and D expose credentials directly, violating confidentiality and compliance standards.

Q731. Answer: B

Explanation: Post-incident analysis evaluates technical and procedural weaknesses to strengthen future detection and response. It converts incidents into learning opportunities. Option A is counterproductive, while Option C and D breach audit and compliance principles.

Q732. Answer: A

Explanation: HSMs safeguard cryptographic keys within tamper-resistant environments, isolating them from general systems. They enforce strong access control and lifecycle management. Option B, C, and D compromise keys through poor storage practices.

Q733. Answer: A

Explanation: Recording chain-of-custody details preserves the evidence's integrity and legal admissibility by documenting who handled it and when. It's foundational in forensic processes. Option B–D all risk contamination, loss, or exposure.

Q734. Answer: D

Explanation: NAC enforces device identity verification and compliance validation before granting access, ensuring unapproved hardware is denied. It reduces shadow IT risks. Option A-C lack strong authentication or can be easily spoofed.

Q735. Answer: A

Explanation: Activating BCP/DR ensures critical functions continue with minimal disruption, fulfilling availability objectives under duress. It integrates with incident response plans for resilience. Option B delays recovery, while C and D cause further operational damage.

Q736. Answer: A

Explanation: Multi-factor authentication combining passwords and tokens provides layered identity verification, significantly reducing the risk of unauthorized remote access. It ensures even if one factor is compromised, access is still protected. Option B is vulnerable to credential theft, Option C eliminates accountability, and Option D offers no real identity proof.

Q737. Answer: C

Explanation: Using checksums or cryptographic hash verification detects any alteration during transfer, ensuring data integrity. It is essential for reliable system-to-system communication. Option B confirms receipt but not accuracy, while Option A and D leave data vulnerable to tampering.

Q738. Answer: A

Explanation: Security Information and Event Management (SIEM) with behavioral analytics continuously monitors traffic for deviations from normal patterns, enabling early threat detection. Option B is periodic, Option C is inefficient, and Option D addresses identity, not network anomalies.

Q739. Answer: B

Explanation: Regular employee awareness and simulated phishing campaigns train users to recognize and avoid social engineering tactics, addressing the human element directly. Option A defends infrastructure but not users, while Option C and D increase vulnerability.

Q740. Answer: A

Explanation: To prioritize response efforts based on impact and severity ensures resources are allocated efficiently and critical incidents are addressed first. Option B delays action unnecessarily, Option C lacks structure, and Option D risks premature closure.

Q741. Answer: A

Explanation: Enabling role-based access control (RBAC) with least privilege restricts administrative actions to only what is necessary, preventing unauthorized access. Option B reduces accountability, Option C eliminates traceability, and Option D exposes systems broadly.

Q742. Answer: C

Explanation: To provide a record for analysis, lessons learned, and compliance evidence supports improvement, accountability, and regulatory requirements. Option B creates division, Option A destroys value, and Option D limits effectiveness.

Q743. Answer: A

Explanation: Conduct targeted awareness training and implement email filtering combines user education with technical controls to block and recognize spear-phishing. Option B removes prevention, Option C ignores threats, and Option D bypasses protection.

Q744. Answer: A

Explanation: An alternative measure that provides equivalent protection to a required control allows flexibility when standard controls are impractical. Option B adds inefficiency, Option C is reactive, and Option D undermines security.

Q745. Answer: B
Explanation: Using end-to-end encryption and secure email gateways ensures only intended recipients can read messages. Option A exposes content, Option C risks external leakage, and Option D reveals recipients unnecessarily.
Q746. Answer: A
Explanation: Implementing strict separation of duties and access reviews prevents users from elevating privileges without oversight. Option B grants excessive access, Option C enables self-escalation, and Option D ignores risks.
Q747. Answer: A
Explanation: To correct software vulnerabilities and maintain system security closes exploitable gaps before attackers can use them. Option B misstates purpose, Option C is false, and Option D increases exposure.
Q748. Answer: C
Explanation: Unusual access patterns to high-value data often indicate reconnaissance or exfiltration by insiders. Option B shows compliance, Option A may indicate evasion but is less direct, and Option D could be normal or failure.
Q749. Answer: A
Explanation: Ensures key recovery in case of loss or unavailability prevents permanent data lockout. Option B weakens security, Option C is incorrect, and Option D misrepresents function.
Q750. Answer: A
Explanation: Implementing account lockout and CAPTCHA mechanisms thwarts automated brute-force attempts while allowing legitimate users to proceed. Option B enables attacks, Option C weakens credentials, and Option D is a major vulnerability.

Made in the USA
Monee, IL
05 November 2026

67979971R00138